Fast Food, Fast Track

Fast Food, Fast Track

Immigrants, Big Business, and the American Dream

JENNIFER PARKER TALWAR

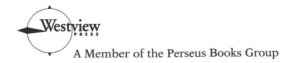

Westview
PRESS

A Member of the Perseus Books Group

Copyright © 2002 by Westview Press, A Member of the Perseus Books Group

Westview Press books are available at special discounts for bulk purchases in the United States by corporations, institutions, and other organizations. For more information, please contact the Special Markets Department at The Perseus Books Group, 11 Cambridge Center, Cambridge MA 02142, or call (617) 252–5298.

Published in 2002 in the United States of America by Westview Press, 5500 Central Avenue, Boulder, Colorado 80301–2877, and in the United Kingdom by Westview Press, 12 Hid's Copse Road, Cumnor Hill, Oxford OX2 9JJ

Find us on the World Wide Web at www.westviewpress.com

A CIP Catalog record for this book is available from the Library of Congress.
ISBN 0-8133-9828-2
The paper used in this publication meets the requirements of the American National Standard for Permanence of Paper for Printed Library Materials Z39.48–1984.

10   9   8   7   6   5   4   3   2   1

CONTENTS

ILLUSTRATIONS

Lists

Tables

Charts

Figures

Photographs

Fast Food,
Fast Track

1

Searching for
the American Dream

I never thought I could come into McDonald's. McDonald's is a big foreign corporation. My friend told me if I want to learn English you can try this. We are all from China but [speak] different languages. I speak Mandarin. They speak Cantonese. So we are always communicating with English.

—Tina, a fast food worker from Shanghai
working in Chinatown

Tina, who is from Shanghai, never expected to work in a fast food restaurant when she arrived in the United States at the age of twenty-four. In Shanghai, Tina was a television repair technician and had no reason to believe that she would change her job; compared to her parents' factory jobs, hers was a good one. Tina had never expected to leave Shanghai until her parents arranged for her to meet Paul, a prospective husband. Paul had moved to New York in 1984, where he had been working, but now he was back in Shanghai to find a wife. After meeting Paul, Tina readily agreed to the arrangement, and they married right away. When Paul returned to New York, Tina stayed behind, spending the next two and a half years waiting for her immigration papers and wondering what life in the United States would be like.

1

Tina harbored few illusions about streets paved with gold or of life in a luxury suite on Park Avenue; she was too sensible to be taken in by media hype. Her husband was not a Wall Street investment banker. He did not even speak English. Rather, he was one among tens of thousands of Chinese immigrants living and working in the satellite Chinatowns of New York's outer boroughs. These immigrants usually live in arduous conditions and work for less than the minimum wage. The *New York Daily News* reported in 1995 that Chinese workers in New York's Chinatown are likely to work in slave-like conditions: grueling hours for pitiful wages and no benefits.[1] Paul worked as a chef in a Chinese restaurant owned and staffed by Chinese immigrants. With a brutal schedule of twelve to sixteen hours a day, six days a week, and compensation at far below the minimum wage, he had no time, energy, or resources to pursue another job, or even to take English-language classes.

Although Tina knew she would need to work in New York, she did not anticipate taking a job in a McDonald's restaurant. American fast food was not completely unfamiliar to Tina; after all, there was a Kentucky Fried Chicken (KFC) restaurant in Shanghai. But she had never considered working there because only the "poor" or "jobless" accepted such work. Once she had arrived in New York, however, Paul encouraged her to get out of what he called the "Chinese environment" and venture into the "foreign environment." The "Chinese environment," according to Paul, is the Chinese ethnic enclave in the United States consisting of Chinese-owned restaurants and garment factories that typically employ people off the books. The "foreign environment," by contrast, refers to mainstream and legal sectors outside the Chinese enclaves, such as McDonald's and KFC, that are usually thought of as "American" institutions. It is interesting that Paul and Tina view McDonald's as foreign when the general public has long viewed Chinatown as foreign. Paul thought that in the so-called American environment Tina could learn English and gain mainstream skills; a guaranteed paycheck; safer working conditions; and important benefits, including health insurance.

An acquaintance, also from Shanghai, told Tina about a job opening in a McDonald's in New York's largest and oldest Chinatown, which is in lower Manhattan. This acquaintance was working at the restaurant and encouraged Tina to apply. She said that McDonald's was a big company and that the job would help Tina learn English and possibly give her an opportunity to move into management. If she reached the upper-level management ranks she could earn an annual salary of more than $15,000 and receive health benefits for her family. Because Tina wanted to start a family, she placed great hope in these prospects; she expressed particular concern about her husband's health and the need to have health insurance when having a baby:

> So many of the places [in the ethnic enclave] don't have benefits. Just now you ask me the most important thing and I say the benefits is very important. It is very useful for the whole family. When a newborn baby go to the maternity ward . . . I want to get benefits. My husband now does not have any benefits. Two months ago he was sick. The doctor told us he needs to operate. Now he has no benefits. He is applying for Medicaid. But I know it is very hard to apply because so many people apply for it. I told him now I want to have a job that covers the whole family, the benefits.

She also expressed the importance of providing a stable home for her children so that their education and future mobility would be secure. This goal included knowing the English language.

> It is very hard for my whole family when we have a baby and it grows up and goes to the school to speak English with other children [if the parents do not speak English]. When he or she goes home they maybe cannot communicate with the parent and we want to take care of that. . . . He [my husband] doesn't understand English, that is why he asked me to study and learn English.

Tina traveled one-and-a-half-hours (each way) by subway from her home in Flushing, Queens, to Chinatown in lower Manhattan to apply for the job at McDonald's. She was hired immediately by a Taiwanese general manager, despite her lack of fluency in English. Her only option, she said, was to join the thousands of other Chinese women working as sewing machine operators in Chinatown's garment factories.

Tina would seem to defy stereotypes of the typical McDonald's employee: an American-born high school student working for pocket change after school on his or her way to college, or at least to a better job. But thousands of new immigrants are finding jobs in the city's American fast food restaurants, and these workers now make up the majority of New York City's fast food employees. Whereas many immigrants, such as Tina's husband, continue to rely on traditional immigrant work sectors and niches in "ethnic" restaurants and factories or as maids and nannies in upper-middle-class homes, others are joining the mainstream consumer world: They serve cappuccino, take movie tickets, and flip burgers.

Since the new immigration policy began in 1965, the proportion of foreign-born residents in the United States has tripled, reaching its highest point in seventy years. New immigration policy changed restrictions on the national origins of immigrants; this means that people from all over the world, including millions of Third World immigrants who had been previously excluded, can now live and work in the United States.[2] Today, one in ten Americans are foreign-born.[3] Immigrants come to New York, one of the largest immigrant-receiving cities in the United States, from countries all over the world; they find homes and jobs in immigrant neighborhoods from Little Odessa, on the far reaches of South Brooklyn, to Little India in Queens and Little Dominican Republic on the northern tip of Manhattan.

It makes sense for these new immigrants to seek jobs at fast food restaurants; they are one of the fastest expanding industries in the low-wage economy, and immigrants have always filled bottom-rung jobs in the United States. Thousands of fast food franchise restaurants have sprouted throughout the city: in business districts, at tourist attractions, and in old and new immigrant neighborhoods. They provide a quick bite to eat for employees on their lunch breaks and for sightseers heading to the Statue of Liberty or the Metropolitan Museum of Art. But in the immigrant neighborhood, these restaurants are places where new immigrants find work, invest in ownership, and introduce their children to a piece of American culture and cuisine.

Fast Food Restaurants and Immigrant Neighborhoods

Immigrant neighborhoods having strong cash flows and a workforce eager to "Americanize" are ideal targets for the fast food industry. The in-

PHOTOGRAPH 1.1   A Dominican Family at McDonald's. (Photo courtesy of Samantha Rosemellia, reprinted with permission)

dustry's expansion into the immigrant neighborhood supports a common notion that fast food restaurants contribute to the homogenization of culture around the world. In his book *The McDonaldization of Society,* George Ritzer pessimistically envisioned a "McDonaldized" world culture in which Western-type corporate institutions devoured local cultures and institutions. To some extent, the fast food restaurant in the immigrant neighborhood does indeed upset local cultural tradition.[4]

A young family from the Dominican Republic, for example, may visit a McDonald's to celebrate a child's birthday rather than going to a public park for a cookout with their neighbors (see Photograph 1.1). Or, while their young children play at a safe indoor playground, parents are more likely to chat and sip "American" coffee from Colombia than to drink café con leche at a nearby Dominican restaurant. Or Chinese children, influenced by television commercials or their most recent school outing to a McDonald's, talk their parents into taking them to the local restaurant where they munch on Happy Meals while the parents drink tea.

It is surprising that contemporary studies of ethnic neighborhoods in the American city, particularly those that focus on immigrants' jobs and entrepreneurial efforts, have steered us into thinking almost exclusively about immigrants' segregation and isolation from mainstream society.[5] Consequently, we know a great deal about immigrants and the labor market in "ethnic economies"—where employers and employees share the same or similar ethnicity, and in "ethnic enclaves"—where ethnic economies are geographically concentrated in immigrant neighborhoods.[6] But we know surprisingly little about how immigrants fare in mainstream businesses, such as fast food, which often flourish in the same neighborhoods as ethnic enterprises.

Immigrant neighborhoods such as Chinatown and Little Italy have long helped us understand how immigrants adapt to working in the United States; these neighborhoods give immigrants an initial foothold in American society, their first step toward making the United States home. The immigrant neighborhood has been conceptualized as a geographically concentrated area where immigrants preserve their cultural traditions—language, religious customs, and family practices—from the old country. In Flushing's Chinatown, for instance, Tina and Paul live among other Chinese immigrants, attend religious services held in their native language, and shop for the Chinese spices and rice noodles that are not ordinarily found in mainstream grocery stores.

The cultural needs of the immigrant community often depend on small businesses and entrepreneurial enterprises that create jobs for immigrants. Chinese restaurants, food markets, and garment factories in New York's Chinatowns and Latino-run garment factories in New York's Little Dominican Republic are good examples; here, many immigrants, particularly those least qualified for good mainstream jobs, find work and entrepreneurial opportunity through neighborhood and ethnic networks. Jobs in the mainstream or general economy are largely unavailable to many of these immigrants because they lack legal work status, mainstream skills, social connections, fluency in English, and education.[7] But living and working in the same neighborhood is also convenient. The Chinese restaurant where Paul works, for instance, is a few minutes' walk from where they live. Meanwhile, Paul and others like him provide a stable and continuous source of employees for Chinese restaurant owners.[8]

Now we must wonder why and how immigrants are turning to fast food restaurants in these same neighborhoods. Is the industry drawing on the same people who work in these traditional ethnic sectors? Or is it drawing on different groups altogether? Are immigrants carving out an occupational niche in American fast food restaurants, an industry long perceived as the quintessential employer of American teenagers? Are immigrants using jobs that the American public considers dead-end and last-resort as a stepping-stone into the American mainstream culture and economy? Do fast food restaurants in the immigrant neighborhood provide the same opportunities as traditional ethnic enterprises or different ones? Or are fast food jobs in the immigrant neighborhood simply dead-end opportunities that reflect the already polarizing forces of the American city and the economy at large? And in the long run, does the fast food restaurant help reinforce or break down the ethnic community in the immigrant neighborhood?

Corporate Capital and Ethnic Enterprise: New Partners in the Global Economy?

Answering these questions requires us to move beyond the "Mc-Donaldization of Society" argument as well as the image of immigrant communities as homogenous and immigrants as socially isolated. James Watson, in his work on the global expansion of American-style fast food restaurants in East Asia, argues that the spread of global cultural institutions is not a unilateral process, as George Ritzer believes; nor are immigrant communities immune from these processes, as the ethnic enclave literature would suggest. Rather, it is a two-way street and it operates through "multilocalism." Local peoples and the state play significant roles in shaping the way global institutions such as Mc-Donald's operate, including the social uses and meanings associated with them.[9]

American fast food restaurants, and the corporate capital they represent, are woven into the local dynamics of the American city. Their foray into ethnic communities complicates the immigrant neighborhood's role in helping immigrants adapt to American society, more so than the ethnic-economies theory accounts for. They also complicate the "McDonaldization" thesis by allowing local actors to shape corporate-level processes. This new linking of the global with the local in ethnic neighborhoods is what this book is about.

On the one hand, fast food restaurants are similar to the traditional ethnic eatery. They are small and labor intensive, and they offer low-wage, non-union, and contingent jobs. They operate in immigrant neighborhoods and they target ethnic groups. Often, immigrants own them. Fast food restaurants hire cultural managers (who represent the neighborhood) and rely on ethnic networks to steer immigrant workers into the establishment. On the other hand, their links to giant corporate structures, what economists term *primary firms,* complicate the way they operate. This book examines these links and how they affect immigrant workers.

Unlike the independent immigrant restaurant, fast food restaurants are connected to outside organizations and hierarchies; these, in turn, link local restaurants to corporate headquarters. Although more immigrants are buying fast food restaurants, those still owned by large New York–based corporations enjoy large capital reserves. Because they are part of giant global corporations, their operations employ the economies of scale, advanced technologies, and global corporate marketing campaigns that provide advantages only dreamed of by independent immigrant owners.[10] In addition, trends in the corporate consumer economy at large demand that work processes emphasize image, personality, and flexibility.

Arlie Hochschild, in a study of flight attendants, identified a particular kind of service worker in modern corporate society—the "public contact" worker—whose main job is to interact with customers, perform "emotional labor," and comply with standards set by corporate-defined and publicly propagated criteria.[11] Immigrants, by selling their "smiles" behind the fast food counter, are the go-betweens linking impersonal mass institutions and new immigrant communities in the corporate quest for new ethnic markets. But as Robin Leidner points out, fast food work is temporary and contingent, and workers are unlikely to identify with their jobs and the companies they work for.[12] Is it any different among immigrants in the ethnic neighborhood?

Negotiating Work—American-Style

The varied experiences of immigrants as they bridge the mainstream and ethnic cultures of immigrant neighborhoods reflect the complexity of

PHOTOGRAPH 1.2   A Chinese McDonald's. (Photo courtesy of Atul Talwar, reprinted with permission)

new workplace arrangements. As Tina suggests at the beginning of this chapter, the fast food restaurant is a place where she, from Shanghai, can learn to speak English, become accustomed to mainstream workplace customs, and build what sociologists call *social capital,* or what the mainstream refers to as networking: developing relationships with people who are able to guide one to better opportunities. All this happens while Tina works alongside people having similar cultural origins and in a neighborhood that, in many respects, reflects her cultural past.

Tina works at a McDonald's restaurant in one of the largest immigrant communities in New York City—Manhattan's Chinatown. With its Chinese-theme décor, including Chinese lettering on the golden arches, and its diverse staff of immigrants from China and other countries, the restaurant markets itself as a "Chinese" McDonald's and caters to tourists as well as to local Chinese customers (see Photograph 1.2). Tina is poised between two cultural representations. In her day-to-day experiences and relations with Chinese customers and workers (and what managers fondly call a "United Nations" staff from around the world), she negotiates a new life and future in her adopted society.

Meanwhile, she familiarizes herself with American culture and learns how to succeed in the American workplace.

But what Tina negotiates cannot be called, in any sense of the terms, either "American" or "Chinese." Rather, globalizing forces bring her into a multiethnic workplace representing more than a dozen national origins, including other Chinese workers, many of whom do not share a common language or dialect with her. She also negotiates work values that may not coincide with the values of her personal life, her cultural past, and her ethnic community. The values embedded in the fast food organization are premised on the structural terms of fast food work. The part-time, temporary, and flexible demands of fast food jobs emphasize the contingency of commitment, short-term gain, and depersonalized relations with coworkers. Although workplace diversity may broaden the boundaries that define "ethnic community," the structural terms of fast food work challenge the core values that ethnic community is built upon.[13]

I'm most concerned with what the fast food restaurant in the immigrant neighborhood represents. Does it represent a kind of "postindustrial" immigrant factory, where various ethnic cultures from around the world come together and reshape a mainstream institution? Does it represent a cultural pluralism shaped at the bottom of a polarizing economy and characterized by ethnic distinctiveness, divisions of labor, social inequalities, and even cultural conflicts? Does ethnic diversity in the American fast food restaurant reflect melting-pot tendencies driven by corporate consumer culture? Or does it represent a postmodern global order signifying the new cultural parameters of dead-end work?

How This Book Came to Be

This book is based on interviews and on-the-ground fieldwork in various fast food restaurants in New York City.[14] But it did not start out as a study of immigrants. It began when my coworker, Roy, an American citizen many generations removed from his predominantly African ancestry, convinced me of the importance of writing about working in fast food restaurant chains in New York City. Roy and I worked together in the "back" (food prep area) of a Burger King restaurant in Brooklyn, where I took a job and became a participant observer for three months to study workplace culture as part of a course assignment in graduate school. Roy, who lacked a high school degree, was thirty years old, married, and the father of an infant child who was in the hospital and had no health insurance. His wife, Tanya, also worked at the restaurant. As my "crew trainer," Roy spent many hours with me during my first days on the job. His warm sensibilities and strong work ethic won my affection immediately; and as he trained me to make specialty sandwiches, he generously shared his work experiences in the minimum-wage economy. "You have to work at least two jobs just to survive today," he said, his eyes tired and bloodshot. He had previously worked at a McDonald's restaurant for seven years and had been promoted to assistant manager. When the restaurant was taken over by another owner, he lost his job; he started over again at minimum wage when he was hired at this Burger King restaurant.

I was impressed by Roy's immense knowledge of the technical workings of the fast food establishment. Roy was not a manager, but he tended to assume the role of overseer; in so doing, he made the daily routine of preparing food much simpler. The process required workers who had vastly different levels of experience and skill to prepare over thirty items, often at extremely rapid rates. This complex activity contradicted the highly simplified picture Americans have of fast food work and that may have contributed to the social and monetary devaluation of fast food jobs. It was difficult for me to imagine how the food could be properly prepared without the experience and expertise of the workers. At the same time, I was startled by Roy's complacency on the job. As much as he had developed valuable expertise over nearly a decade, he did not understand the workings of ownership, nor did he know who held the reins to his work history and conditions. When I questioned him about this, Roy flashed me a smile and answered, "It is just the way it is."

As I reflect on my first fast food job as a teenager in 1981 in the predominately white suburbs of Syracuse, New York, I can appreciate the way workers diligently pumped out fries and burgers from 400-degree oil vats, an ambiguous corporate mask watching over them. I briefly worked for McDonald's. After mopping the floor and cleaning the bathrooms for several days while my schoolmate customers taunted me, I quit. I got a "better" job as a supermarket cashier, where I won popularity for selling beer to my under-aged classmates. Few people in suburbia worked at a fast food restaurant for more than a few months in the early 1980s.

Had something changed over the years, or were conditions in the inner city just different? Why was it that hard-working people who had families were earning minimum wage after years of experience in jobs that we have long thought were for teenagers on their way to college, or at least to better jobs? These were my original questions, but during my on-the-job research, I realized that these urban workers did not fit neat categories. Rather, the workforce was diverse and changeable; it reflected the demographic shifts in the New York labor supply caused by immigration and labor-market restructuring.

Roy and I worked alongside immigrants from Latin America, South Asia, and the Caribbean. Many were similar to Roy. Arturo, from Panama, was also in his thirties and supported a family. He would come bustling into the restaurant filled with anxious energy and on the edge of exhaustion after working a day shift as a baggage handler. Maria, from Puerto Rico, was a single mother who lived with her mother. She usually worked on the "frontline" (as a cashier) during the day alongside other women the managers considered pretty enough to attract customers. But Roy seemed to have fewer opportunities than his immigrant coworkers. Two teenage cousins from Guyana planned to earn vocational degrees in the medical profession. Leo, a twenty-four-year-old from Honduras, was a part-time, public university student who did not have a family to support. And the managers, three of whom were from South Asia, had professional backgrounds and graduate degrees but had "fallen" into the fast food industry because they lacked opportunity elsewhere.

Although age, gender, nationality, and education seemed to reinforce ethnic diversity in this restaurant, they also helped determine divisions of labor in the larger New York labor market. Still, the extent of such diversity seemed to signify a growing dependence on minimum-wage industries by the New York City workforce. I thought it was important to learn more about this industry because its employment practices in the urban economy seemed to nullify our traditional stereotypes of the fast food worker.

In addition, my job at the fast food restaurant offered me a way to understand how different ethnic groups relate to each other in their attempt to survive but also improve their circumstances at the bottom of the American urban economy. Although Roy and people like him represented the downward spiral of many New Yorkers, especially native-born racial minorities, many immigrants seemed to be using the fast food industry as a way to assimilate into the American economy. Still, it was not at all clear that fast food work experience, even for immigrants, was a real stepping-stone to a better life in mainstream America. Such intriguing contradictions led me to expand my research into this book in an attempt to understand the immigrant experience in this industry.

I spoke with over one hundred fast food restaurant employees in Queens, Brooklyn, and Manhattan before deciding to focus on seven restaurants in three neighborhoods. Two of these neighborhoods comprise the largest immigrant enclaves in New York City: Chinatown and Little Dominican Republic. The third is downtown Brooklyn: an area historically shaped by people of African descent beginning with the great black migration from the South in the 1940s and 1950s and continuing today with the influx of immigrants from the West Indies. I focused on two of the biggest hamburger chains: McDonald's and Burger King. This book includes observations and in-depth interviews with restaurant workers at all levels of the fast food hierarchy—from corporate level staff and owners to managers and crewmembers.[15]

Persuading people to talk to me was a task full of twists and turns. As I discovered during my participant observation, employees found it hard to believe that someone could be interested in studying fast food work and they were, at best, wary of my intentions. If they hadn't already internalized the social stigma surrounding fast food work, they were at least deeply aware that it existed. Why, they thought, would someone want to study something of such little value and interest? I got a job at the Burger King by walking into the restaurant and asking for a job. I was fortunate; the restaurant had opened just the day before and I was hired immediately.

Before I went to work, I contemplated whether I should reveal my "true" identity as a social science researcher. I decided to tell the truth, and as a manager gave me my initiation tour on my first day at work I told him of my intentions. In a sarcastic tone that conveyed disbelief he re-

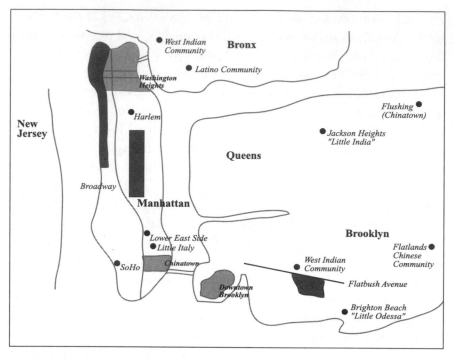

FIGURE 1.1   Map of the Five Boroughs

sponded, "Yeah right. Why don't you get a job at Macy's, that would be more interesting." I later learned that most fast food employees assert what sociologists refer to as a "primary status" (the particular role one prefers to be identified with)—whether it be father, student, or basketball player—to downplay one's status as a fast food worker. Roy, for instance, constantly talked about his baby as a reminder to everyone of his status as a father. Leo was always talking about his university classmates to demonstrate his membership in a higher-ranking social group. My assertion of being a graduate student and sociologist, I came to learn, was interpreted in the same way; I was giving myself a higher-status position in a low-status environment to downplay my desperation at taking a fast food job. Several employees, including Roy, treated me as someone who was new to the growing minimum-wage world and needed their guidance.

    The dynamics were different in the latter stage of my research because when I conducted formal interviews with restaurant workers my status as a social researcher was unquestioned. By visiting each restaurant and telling the managers about the study, I obtained their permission to interview the employees. I approached the restaurant managers by first becoming a customer. I would walk into a restaurant and order a coffee or coke, and maybe something to eat. This way I was taking advantage of the "customer is always right" policy. I thought that my being a customer would encourage managers to be more receptive to my request; they would at least feel obliged to hear what I had to say.

Although a few were openly enthusiastic about contributing to such a study, many were hesitant and even slightly annoyed, and gave in only after a great deal of persistence on my part. For example, in an extreme case, I spent three months trying to get an interview with one particular manager. I called him from two to four times every week, but each time he told me, with annoyance in his voice, that he was "too busy" and to "try again another day." When he finally made time, he was unexpectedly gracious, open, and helpful during the interview.

Managers hesitated mostly because the stressful demands of fast food work make taking time off, and giving workers time off, extremely difficult. Despite this, and even though they didn't immediately understand why I wanted to interview them, managers and workers appeared intrigued to think that someone was interested in their experiences. Employees were surprisingly candid in their responses. Because fast food workers are employed legally and usually temporarily, I posed little threat to the security of their jobs and identities, especially as I assured them of confidentiality. To protect their privacy, I have not used their real names, but I have presented their stories unaltered.

Although I do not believe that I was ever able to convince the workers that their stories were important, I hope this book will do it for me. Their stories are important because they offer a glimpse into fundamental changes in the American economy and how immigrants are faring in it. Immigrants come to America searching for a better life and they bring with them many different dreams. What does it mean to end up behind the fast food counter flipping burgers or taking orders? The bridging of corporate mainstream institutions and ethnic cultures not only implies a certain economic trend with the expansion of minimum-wage jobs into immigrant neighborhoods but also signals new cultural parameters of work in neighborhoods we have long considered relatively isolated from the practices of big business.

It's in the Neighborhood: Race, Place, and the Importance of Culture

If they speak French, German (or other foreign language), we hire them because it helps us translate to customers.

—Fast food manager from Malaysia,
working in Chinatown

Tina can be found behind the counter at McDonald's, where she greets customers, takes their orders, and entertains their children, sometimes in her native Mandarin. As a young Chinese woman with a vibrant personality and neat appearance, she fits into the restaurant's new consumer marketing strategy of targeting Chinese immigrants and international tourists. She was enthusiastic about being part of a big American corporation and playing a role in its drive for profit:

Sometimes we serve toys, apple pies, and the cookies for the kids. I know that in America, a lot of the babies like to eat this food, sometimes the parents say that it is up to the kids. When the kid like it then they always come [return] to McDonald's, especially on the weekends. So we serve them toys, cookies, and this increases sales.

The McDonald's restaurant where Tina works commands a powerful presence alongside the weathered Chinese restaurants and the rows of small open markets selling everything from fresh seafood to rice noodles. The restaurant's modern and bright multistory architectural design and neon-lit golden arches are visible for several blocks. To the international tourists and New Yorkers thronging the sidewalks, McDonald's lends coherence to an exotic order; a familiar American food place in a tourist and bargain-hunting niche. To the Chinese residents, McDonald's is the "exotic" order, a perception that helps frame the restaurant's marketing strategies for attracting new Chinese immigrants to American fast food.

This restaurant's multimillion-dollar renovation, which included building Chinese décor into the architectural design and creating new employment policies, was aimed at targeting local Chinese customers as well as international tourists to Chinatown. The restaurant's cultural marketing strategy, designed to portray an American and Chinese eatery in one, shapes the job standards and recruitment practices that help to explain why Tina was hired. As the quote at the beginning of this chapter implies, an emphasis on bilingualism in this restaurant led to the hiring of what managers refer to as a "United Nations team": a multilingual, multiethnic workforce. Most of the workers are Chinese, but many come from Russia, Africa, Latin America, and the West Indies.

Compared to the traditional ethnic restaurant, the fast food restaurant in the immigrant neighborhood approaches business from a different angle. The ethnic enterprise has traditionally catered to ethnic consumers who demand groceries from "back home." The Dominican coffee shop serving café con leche, the Chinese produce store specializing in soy products, the Indian grocery selling chutneys, basmati rice, and the Indian equivalent of the TV dinner—all serve a steady flow of customers seeking the foods they miss from home. The ethnic enterprise has also supplied nonperishable goods to outside markets, as in the case of Chinese and Dominican garment factories. The American fast food restaurant does not target existing ethnic or outside mainstream markets. Like the McDonald's restaurant in Chinatown, it brings to life *new* markets in immigrant neighborhoods by cultivating a taste for American fast food among local customers from new cultural groups, and by attracting tourists and shoppers from outside the vicinity. Language skills, ethnic affinities, and personality are job standards shaped in part by the way the local owner markets the restaurant in the neighborhood. It is important that job descriptions draw on immigrants' "cultural capital" (valued cultural features, which include language skills, ethnic affinities, and cultural knowledge). Cultural capital brings a new perspective to our typical view of these restaurants as reproducing "sameness."[1]

The fast food restaurant industry's demands for labor in New York City tend to be geographically and culturally dependent on local customers and the characteristics of the neighborhood, or what I refer to as geocultural processes; these consider not only the ethnicity of owners and managers but also the marketing strategies and neighborhood characteristics that define the locality. In general, fast food restaurants are a "public contact" industry. The managers I interviewed emphasized interactions between customers and employees, the image employees present to customers, and how people have adapted to their neighborhoods. Thus, fast food restaurants reflect the larger demographic changes in New York's populations and the constantly shifting ethnic and racial boundaries of the city's districts and neighborhoods. Cultural capital is an important asset for employees in an industry marketing to new immigrant groups. But the way local marketing strategies and customer relations determine hiring have not been the focus of previous books about employment in immigrant neighborhoods.[2]

Immigrants have long been natural workers for the low-wage jobs offered by traditional ethnic enterprises because they generally lack legal status, their English is poor, and they are ethnic minorities from impoverished backgrounds; these features make them malleable, cheap, and exploitable. But in American fast food restaurants, immigrants are desirable low-wage workers for different reasons: They possess valuable cultural capital, which includes foreign-language abilities; they are generally young and see their low-paying jobs as temporary measures because they plan to move into the mainstream; and not only are they legally eligible to work but they are unlikely to join a labor union. For all these reasons, they meet standards typical of the mainstream postindustrial economy, including a willingness to adopt flexible work schedules and the ability to present an appropriate image and attitude while representing diverse cultural backgrounds. Furthermore, these workers usually possess a strong work ethic; they are loyal, they work hard, and they are reliable. Tina was an ideal candidate for a McDonald's job in Chinatown. Not only did she fit into the restaurant's consumer marketing strategy but she possessed the job skills, the legal status, and the attitude required for postindustrial customer service jobs in big business.

The shaping of jobs in the fast food restaurant in New York City is often dependent on cultural reinvention, which is how a restaurant takes local ethnic culture and adapts it to the restaurant's décor, menu, and workers; and cultural matching, which aligns the ethnic composition of a neighborhood, including prospective customers, with the ethnic features of the workforce. Sometimes, job standards respond to cultural changes in a neighborhood, the ethnic composition of current employees, and the social and cultural backgrounds of job seekers.

Chinatown

Chinatown nestles at the southern end of Manhattan between the Broadway shopping corridor, City Hall, and other cultural tourist destinations such as Little Italy and the SoHo art galleries. Chinatown also borders the Lower East Side, where a population of Spanish-speaking immigrants from Latin America has steadily grown since 1965. Manhattan's Chinatown is New York City's oldest Chinese enclave and has existed since the beginning of the twentieth century.[3] Satellite Chinatowns have grown in the outer boroughs of New York City since the post-1965 immigration wave. But the old Chinatown thrives, and Chinese immigrants from all over the world come here to find homes, get work, establish businesses, and become entrepreneurs.

Chinatown contains a large residential district for Chinese immigrants and their children. Since 1965, its population has more than quadrupled to nearly a quarter of a million Chinese.[4] Its public schools and parks are filled with Chinese. On my way to early morning interviews in Chinatown's fast food restaurants, I saw groups of Chinese children on their way to school and elderly Chinese doing Tai Chi in a Chinatown park. In these early morning hours before the shops opened and the tourists arrived, it was easy to imagine that I was walking in a city on the Chinese mainland.

PHOTOGRAPH 2.1   Intertwining Chinese and Italian Culture and Cuisine. (Photo courtesy of Jennifer Parker Talwar, reprinted with permission)

The continuing flow of Chinese immigrants and enterprises has pushed Chinatown beyond its historic borders; as it overflows, it becomes acquainted with neighboring regions. Chinese businesses, including restaurants, extend south into SoHo, west of Broadway, and north to Little Italy. A sign I spotted in one Chinese restaurant window symbolizes the shifting and porous border between the Italian and Chinese cultures; it read: "We Serve Italian Macaroni" (see Photograph 2.1).

Millions of people each year visit Chinatown. Its constant bustle of activity hosts cultural tourism, shopping, and exotic cuisine. A Chinatown restaurant serving dim sum was a favorite meeting place for my graduate-school colleagues; we could sample plates of steamed vegetable dumplings and shrimp rolls, all at low prices—just one example of Chinatown's many attractions. It thrives, too, as a hub for business and banking. Street-vending carts, where I bought fried rice and scallion pancakes for only fifty cents; fish markets, produce stands, gift shops, and dozens of Chinese restaurants—all these stand out among the sights and sounds of Chinatown. Pastry shops and cafes, as well as drug stores, optical centers, and banks offering twenty-four hour ATM service, add to the heavy commercial flavor of Chinatown. They join the jewelry, leather, souvenir, watch, and perfume shops that were once owned by Jewish shopkeepers when the area was renowned as a Jewish market in the early part of the twentieth century. These shops are now owned by immigrants from Vietnam, Korea, Russia, and South Asia. South Asian-owned perfume shops, for example, are popular among people reluctant to buy the newest brands at retail prices. Rather than paying $60 for a six-ounce bottle of brand-name perfume, for instance, I usually make a trip to Chinatown and buy what appears to be exactly the same thing for $25.

Tourists from all over the world, including France, Germany, Japan, and Eastern Europe, are attracted to the bargains here as well as to Chinatown's other cultural attractions and cuisine. While walking a few blocks through Chinatown in the middle of the day, I would sometimes hear a dozen different languages. Chinatown also attracts low-wage job seekers from all over New York, especially young people interested in working in a dynamic neighborhood well connected to public transportation and such chic areas as SoHo and Greenwich Village.

Although Chinatown is so famous for its shopping and cuisine, it is also sometimes criticized for running sweatshops, exploiting labor,[5] and harboring conflict between ethnic groups. The social dynamics of the area do affect the way local businesses operate, including the fast food restaurant franchises. One fast food owner paid "protection money" to Vietnamese gangs; a manager at another fast food restaurant bought a bullet-proof vest because he was once shot at in the restaurant.

Building Chinese Taste for American Burgers: A Strategy

The McDonald's restaurant in Chinatown used cultural reinvention to target local Chinese immigrant customers—especially its second generation—as well as Chinatown's international tourists. Owned by a large corporation, it was able to invest nearly $3 million in cultural renovations, capital outlay typical of so-called primary firms but quite out of the reach of traditional ethnic enterprises. Job standards are reflected in its marketing strategy and architectural renovations. The McDonald's sign is in Chinese (see Photograph 2.2), and inside is a two-story

PHOTOGRAPH 2.2   A McDonald's Sign in Chinese. (Photo courtesy of Atul Talwar, reprinted with permission)

Chinese arch painted red for good luck. While dining on the second and third floors in the back half of the restaurant, visitors look across a three-story open space to the front wall displaying the four Chinese characters that symbolize long life, happy marriage, lots of children, and lucky money. Customers also look onto the street and its constant bustle of vendors, shoppers, and sightseers.

I often observed a common scene here: a first-generation Chinese couple and their young children. The parents would sip tea while their children munched Happy Meals of hamburgers and french fries. Sometimes, a McDonald's hostess entertained the children. The relatively new position of host and hostess is employed in some renovated McDonald's restaurants as part of the company's innovative "Customer Care Program." Hostesses, who are usually Chinese and female in Chinatown's restaurant, do not prepare food or take orders; rather, they greet customers at the front door, wish them farewell, introduce them to the menu, refill their coffee cups, escort them to their tables, help with their trays, translate for them, and chat with those eating alone.

In describing a host's duties, one manager reinforced the words Tina spoke at the beginning of this chapter:

PHOTOGRAPH 2.3   American Fast Food in Chinatown. (Photo courtesy of Atul Talwar, reprinted with permission)

Because the McDonald's restaurant is a fast food restaurant, it is an American that eats the breakfast. Those people who came in new immigration [as new immigrants], they don't know how to order it. But their kids want it. They come in because their kids want it. They don't know anything about the breakfast. [But] they will try it and we will treat the kid like a friend and they will come back.

As part of its marketing strategy, this McDonald's restaurant has hired "neighborhood marketers," employees who hand out McDonald's coupons to Chinese workers at factory gates and go from door to door with the McDonald's menu (printed in Chinese). As one manager said, "Every month we went out to the neighborhood schools. . . . There are a lot of factories around here, Chinese factories, so we go there with coupons, like one dollar off." Neighborhood marketers also maintain the McDonald's logos plastered onto garbage cans throughout Chinatown. This McDonald's restaurant also delivers orders (they must be $10 or more) by foot or bicycle to homes and businesses throughout most of Manhattan (100th Street and below).[6]

The general manager, Charles, came to the United States from Taiwan to earn a master's degree in engineering. He later abandoned his plans and went into the restaurant industry, eventually becoming the owner of an award-winning Chinese restaurant. He was drawn to the fast food franchise industry to pursue corporate-level opportunities; with his higher education and Chinese restaurant experience, Charles was ideally suited to become the general manager of a McDonald's restaurant targeting the Chinese neighborhood. He sits on community and school boards and gives donations to community functions, activities that have made him a kind of local politician in the community. And because McDonald's has extensive involvement with the schools in Chinatown, Charles promotes and arranges restaurant tours for school classes and birthday parties for children. "We are tied into the school system with the elementary schools. I know all the principals, all the school teachers—not all of them but most of them," he told me. Charles hands out McDonald's "certificates of achievement" to those who contribute to the community and to children who earn good grades. McDonald's and its employees are involved with various community organizations, and local newspapers catering to the Chinese community—*Sing Tao Daily,* the *China Press,* and the *United Journal*—often report on these activities.[7] The general manager of this McDonald's sits on the advisory boards of the Chinatown Manpower Project and the local office of the U.S. Post Office.

Community involvement is part of a corporate strategy to rally support and provide McDonald's with the image of a good neighbor.[8] The ultimate goal of good community relations is to increase sales. As Charles explained, "All these relationships are built up. Good relationships. You are bound to have stronger foundations because people get to know you and you have better chances for them to come and spend their money here." McDonald's managers are rewarded for their community involvement with acknowledgements, pay raises, and promotions.[9]

According to Charles, the Chinese in New York have not historically patronized fast food restaurants. This McDonald's restaurant has made an explicit attempt to attract Chinese customers—beginning with the children—by cultivating a taste for American fast food and acclimatizing the Chinese to the fast food restaurant. One manager said that before the cultural renovations, most customers were non-Chinese. Another manager said that the Chinese market had increased from 10 to 25 percent in eighteen months, and sales saw a 40 percent increase.[10] The greatest increase in Chinese business comes on weekends, according to this manager, when from 60 to 70 percent of customers are Chinese.

The renovations in McDonald's represent a deliberate cultural marketing strategy and include workers that ethnically reflect the restaurant's targeted customers. The company hired Charles, who then hired a hundred-member staff, 60 percent of whom are Chinese immigrants from Taiwan, Malaysia, Hong Kong, and China. Their diversity encompasses national origin, language, and socioeconomic background. Unlike Tina, who comes from a working-class background, many McDonald's employees come from professional backgrounds.

Alison, for instance, is a college student in New York City who emigrated from Malaysia in the early 1990s. Her parents own a highly profitable international business and were against her working, not only because it would detract from her studies, but also because of the independence it would foster. Unlike Tina, who works because she must, Alison works to fit into an American youth culture that stresses independence and consumption. She eventually became an assistant manager at McDonald's and believes her job is an ideal complement to her business studies. In respect to her socioeconomic background, educational status, and chances for success, Alison represents the upper demographic extreme of the fast food workforce as a whole. Because it draws on a diversity of socioeconomic backgrounds, the McDonald's restaurant is assured of building a workforce enjoying a range of career aims and chances rather than settling for a collective class condition.

Depending on their origins, the Chinese workers speak various languages, including Malay and Chinese dialects such as Cantonese, Mandarin, and Taiwanese.[11] These employees often begin working soon after arriving in New York, before they have learned English; but when they do speak English, it becomes the only common language among them. Tina explained how it was with her: "I remember the first day I go to work, I went to the lobby, the second floor, I try to communicate with a customer. I don't understand. I am very shy. And I am afraid I lost my job. But the manager says, 'It is nothing. If you go day by day you can make progress.'"

Employees' native languages are valued in the restaurant for communicating with Chinese-speaking customers. When Tina stands and smiles at the front entrance of the McDonald's restaurant, she helps produce a particular cultural ambiance. She welcomes local Chinese customers who have traditionally patronized the local Chinese restaurants, not the "American" ones. She also welcomes international tourists who sample familiar food as well as symbolic aspects of the Chinese culture.

The non-Chinese workers at McDonald's are globally, ethnically, and racially diverse. They are also hired for their cultural capital, particularly their language skills, which allow them to communicate with international tourists and to fit the restaurant's image as a multicultural gathering place. They include Brusso, a Russian immigrant who commutes ninety minutes each way from Little Russia (or Little Odessa) in Brighton Beach, the southernmost point in Brooklyn.[12] Working in a fast food restaurant is unusual for Brusso and young Russian immigrants like him. He said that his "male friends think it is strange. Others work in car service, taxis. Something like that." But Brusso was interested in cuisine and couldn't find a job in any other restaurant. When he applied at a McDonald's near his home in Brooklyn, he was called for an interview at a restaurant under the same ownership, but in Chinatown. Because this restaurant was looking for people who spoke foreign-languages, Brusso was hired immediately. Although he says he has spoken Russian only twice on the job, he operates a cash register that is identified with a Russian flag. Like Tina, Brusso finds his job helpful in developing his English, and at the same time he is learning some Chinese. Brusso is joined by workers from other parts of the world: a French speaker from Togo, Africa, and Spanish speakers of various national origins.

The "United Nations" workforce has, according to Alison, replaced a once largely American minority workforce. On the payroll are ninety-one crewmembers and other nonsalaried staff and eight salaried managers. She said that before the renovations most employees "were black, Spanish, or American . . . not many Chinese." African Americans make up a small minority at this restaurant. (See List 1.1 in Appendix A for the cultural features of my respondents among this workforce.)

The employment of a majority Chinese workforce and management team resembles the traditional ethnic enterprise in the way it brings together a majority of workers of similar national and cultural origin. But it is different because the Chinese in this case are not hired on the strength of their vulnerable and co-ethnic minority status; rather, they are hired to attract local Chinese and international tourists to American fast food. They are not ethnically similar: They are cross-national and cross-cultural, speak various dialects, and come from different socioeconomic backgrounds. This workforce might be better labeled "pan-ethnic," or "global," rather than "co-ethnic."

A Latino Workforce in a Chinese Neighborhood

Like every American fast food restaurant, the McDonald's restaurant in Chinatown has a unique association with the surrounding neighborhood, which is reflected in its marketing approach. A Burger King restaurant close-by is both similar to and different from the McDonald's restaurant. It is similar in its employment of a globally and ethnically diverse workforce, although the majority is Latino rather than Chinese. In some ways, though, it is closer to the traditional ethnic enterprises nearby. The Burger King is owned by a Vietnamese entrepreneur, not a corporation, as is the McDonald's. The owner is one of the many new Vietnamese shopkeepers and restaurateurs moving into the fringes of Chinatown. As an independent entrepreneur, he can ill afford the kind of capital investments and marketing strategies employed by the corporate-owned McDonald's restaurant. Therefore, like other immigrant-owned ethnic enterprises in the area, the Burger King restaurant is not equipped with the latest technology and does not employ a deliberate and aggressive marketing strategy intended to target particular cultural groups.

Even so, the Burger King is still very different from the traditional ethnic enterprise. The owner does not employ a co-ethnic workforce as many other independent and immigrant-owned firms in the neighborhood do, and for several reasons. First, a low-wage Vietnamese workforce is not abundant in New York City; second, Vietnamese is not a dominant language in Chinatown among fast food customers; and third, there are few Vietnamese tourists. Therefore, Vietnamese cultural features are not valued in fast food restaurants in Chinatown. The Vietnamese owner's own language limitations (he does not speak English or Chinese) and the demands of operating a mainstream customer-service enterprise in a Chinese neighborhood that hosts international tourists forces him to rely on Pedro, his general manager, to take care of daily operations.

Pedro is from Colombia and speaks Spanish and English. He joined the industry when he took a fast food job in a Latino neighborhood in Queens in 1990. The Italian American who owned that restaurant later bought the Burger King in Chinatown and promoted Pedro to a manager there. A few years later, the owner asked a Vietnamese entrepreneur who owned a small "Gucci" shop in Chinatown (now the current owner) to become his partner. But when profits declined for several months, the Italian American partner pulled out, leaving the Vietnamese partner with sole ownership.

The other Burger King managers are Jamaican, Chinese, and Puerto Rican; in general, the workers are ethnically diverse and speak English. This Burger King also reflects the diversity of job seekers and the cultural changes occurring in this area. But although McDonald's strategies can be viewed as overt or deliberate in the way it both responds to the community and attempts to alter tastes and patterns of consumption, Burger King simply reflects the neighborhood's dynamics while absorbing some of its changes.

The Burger King restaurant is smaller than the McDonald's and does not command as great a visual presence. It consists of a floor at ground level, and is tucked between small Vietnamese-owned shops. With only one window at the front, the restaurant seems gloomy unlike the McDonald's, where a tri-level glass exterior lets sunlight pour in throughout the day. Burger King did undergo renovations recently, but at a much more modest level; it spent approximately $30,000 and, as Pedro expressed it, "hired some Mickey Mouse construction guy to do it." The Vietnamese owner's Gucci shop, according to Pedro, is more lucrative than the Burger King restaurant and its profits helped finance the Burger King renovations. Burger King has fewer than thirty people on its payroll. Wages, salaries, and opportunity structures reflect the small company ownership and the heavy competition from McDonald's.

Since the McDonald's new opening (after the renovations), Pedro said, Burger King's business has declined. McDonald's is winning out simply because it has more money for marketing and renovations.

McDonald's heavy outreach to the Chinese community has affected Burger King by drawing Chinese customers not only to McDonald's but to American fast food in general; thus, while the proportion of Chinese clientele at Burger King has increased, its overall business has decreased. The Burger King's owner has cut costs by taking away managers' health insurance benefits and giving workers fewer wage increases. Some of the upper-level assistant managers earn wages rather than salaries. (While it is usual for lower-level managers to earn hourly wages, it is less common among upper-level managers.) As a smaller, more independent and less profitable company, the Burger King offers less in wages, benefits, social activities, and opportunities for advancement than the McDonald's gives its crewmembers and managers. The difference in size, company resources and support, local marketing strategies, and sales and profits between Burger King and McDonald's in Chinatown affect the restaurant's ambiance, the nature of the work, and, ultimately, job characteristics.

Workers are ethnically and globally diverse, which partly reflects the diversity of job seekers in Chinatown. The workforce represents a shift from several years ago when workers were "all black," according to the general manager. But Chinese immigrants make up a only small percentage of the staff at Burger King. Most of the Burger King employees are Latino immigrants from various countries, including the Dominican Republic, Puerto Rico, Venezuela, and Central America. Many come from nearby Latino neighborhoods, such as the Lower East Side. Alongside the Chinese, South Asians from Bangladesh and India also make up a small minority of the workforce. American-born minorities also work here but are vastly outnumbered by immigrants. (See List 1.2 in Appendix A for the cultural features of my respondents among this workforce.)

A majority Latino staff at Burger King reflects various factors. First, the general manager is Latino and admitted to favoring Latino workers over others when hiring. Second, Burger King attracts a workforce that is more socioeconomically disadvantaged than the McDonald's staff, and Latinos represent the most socioeconomically disadvantaged immigrant groups in the city. From the perspective of an employee, Burger King and McDonald's are different in regard to their working environments (McDonald's is bigger, brighter, and uses the newest technologies); their hierarchical pay-scales (although they both pay minimum wage to entry-level workers, raises are more frequent and managers are paid substantially more at McDonald's); and the opportunity to become a manager (McDonald's offers more opportunity mainly because it's larger).[13]

Jesus, seventeen years old and the son of Puerto Rican and Dominican parents, typifies Burger King employees in ethnicity and class. He lives with his cousin on the Lower East Side because his mother, also a fast food employee at a smaller chain (at Burger Boy), cannot support him and his sisters. As he says, "My mom, she can't deal with me and my sisters and all that . . . so I be needing more money for books, and clothing and all that." His biological father lives in the Dominican Republic, and his stepfather works off and on, "off the books." Jesus got a job at Burger King through a cousin who was quitting her job at the same restaurant.

Nearly all employees in this restaurant, including Jesus, speak English, the only language required for employment.[14] This is unlike the McDonald's restaurant, whose employees speak several languages without, necessarily, having a common language. The lack of the newest technology in this Burger King affects how many languages are spoken. As I will discuss in Chapter 5, the most advanced communication technology (such as the computerized cash register, employed at the McDonald's restaurant) alters the way workers communicate and enables a multilingual staff to work together. Without this technology, workers must communicate in one language. Pedro explained the importance of speaking English in this restaurant and its effect on the kinds of immigrants eligible for employment:

> We had one Chinese girl who came in. She seemed very nice, very presentable. And when we talked to her we just thought she was shy. She would just nod her head and so forth. But then we started working with her and we noticed her English is not too good. First we thought she was just a bad worker. And then we found out she just doesn't understand us. We would tell her to do something and then we would find her like walking around.

Pedro's assistant, Julia, who is of Puerto Rican descent, added:

This neighborhood they speak Chinese. When I first got here a lot of our [Chinese] girls couldn't communicate with our English customers. Customers got really annoyed when they would order something and the girls would order something else. She didn't understand. That aggravated the Spanish people, the black people. The only ones who got on her line were the Orientals. We couldn't run a business like that. . . . I am not saying I don't like the Orientals. I am just saying you have to assimilate.

Still, Chinese workers are needed to enhance the restaurant's marketability. They are hired, according to the general manager, "to make the store look better. People come to Chinatown and tend to want to see Chinese people working in restaurants." But the few Chinese who are employed speak English. According to Pedro, one Chinese employee worked with the "all black" workforce several years ago. "But she was Americanized," he said. "She spoke just like the blacks. She had no sort of Chinese culture in her at all." The economic value of Chinese employees became apparent when, as Pedro said, the McDonald's restaurant across the street "stole them" from Burger King: "They actually took them all. They would come in and ask them if they wanted to work across the street and they would pay them more. They knew that if more Chinese people work there, then more Chinese people would come in to eat, to work, and it is better for them. They actually asked [the Chinese workers] right in front of me. They didn't even ask me."

The primarily Chinese multiethnic workforce at the McDonald's restaurant represents a deliberate cultural marketing strategy intended to target customers from particular cultural groups by reinforcing the area's ethnic and symbolic history. Its corporate ownership and heterogeneous staff make it different from the traditional ethnic enterprise. At the same time, its deliberate strategy of hiring Chinese workers implies that ethnicity is a tool for profit-making, a part of the service commodity.

Although the Burger King employs Chinese workers to enhance its marketability, it does not deliberately cultivate them. The multiethnic workforce at Burger King simply reflects the way the restaurant has absorbed Chinatown's cultural complexity. The Burger King may appear to be embedded in the Vietnamese ethnic enclave through its owner and his links to the Vietnamese business community, but its link to corporate America means that it must uphold uniform policies, including placing a premium on customer service. Given this, the owner must operate the Burger King in ways different from those he uses for his "Gucci" knock-off shop in the same neighborhood.

Little Dominican Republic

The northern part of Washington Heights (commonly referred to as "Little Dominican Republic"), located above Harlem between 170th Street and the tip of Manhattan at 218th Street, has received a steady stream of immigrants since 1965, mainly from the Dominican Republic. Dominicans are one of the largest immigrant groups in New York City, and this community in Little Dominican Republic is home to the largest group of Dominicans outside the Dominican Republic.[15] Dominicans have largely replaced German Jewish and Irish immigrants, who moved into the area at the beginning of the twentieth century, and Cubans, who gained a strong presence in the 1950s.[16] The relatively mixed community is composed of Dominicans, a minority of other Spanish-speaking immigrants, and a small but growing population of white, Asian, and black professionals who have been "priced-out" of other Manhattan neighborhoods.[17]

Unlike Chinatown, this area attracts few visitors because it lacks popular cultural attractions and is so far from the center of Manhattan. In addition, the northern area of Manhattan from Harlem up is known as a drug-ridden and violent area. When I talk about my research to New Yorkers, for instance, everyone seems familiar with Chinatown, but many are not even aware that Little Dominican Republic exists. Unless you live or do business there, or are a part of the community, it is not a place one ordinarily visits or hears much about. Most business enterprises, including restaurants, cater to locals. As with most New York neighborhoods, its borders are socially and ethnically defined, though "old" remnants of the past still remain in the "new" neighborhood. An eastern border marks the divide between an old German Jewish residential area, commonly called the "Jewish Alps," and the Dominican population. Greek-owned pizza joints and diners, Irish pubs, and Jewish bakeries that mix with Dominican restaurants and

bodegas are reminders to the new Dominican residents of their prede-
cessors, the "white ethnics" who built the neighborhood.[18]

Little Dominican Republic covers fifty blocks. All three of the restaurants I visited are located on streets filled with vendors, newspaper
stands, restaurants, retail stores, and fast food chains, the busiest streets
in the neighborhood. Little Dominican Republic is significantly different from Chinatown. Not being a tourist area, it is less commercially
ethnic because local businesses do not market themselves as "Dominican." There are no souvenir shops, as there are in Chinatown. (Until it
closed in 1999, an Irish gift and souvenir shop operated as a kind of
replica of the neighborhood's ethnic past).

Despite the absence of tourist attractions, Dominican culture is alive
in the Spanish conversation of passers-by, in the street vendors who yell
prices in pesos, and in the lively Latino music playing loudly from the
shops. As in Chinatown, the street food—chimichurris, slices of Dominican cake—reflects the neighborhood's cultural origins, and large
vending trucks that sell various Dominican snacks are also a common
sight in this neighborhood (see Photograph 2.4). As in Chinatown, local
businesses are owned by an ethnically mixed group, many of its members being new to the business community: Arabs own electronics
stores, South Asians sell clothing, Mexicans operate an American-style
coffee shop, and Chinese run a Mexican take-out restaurant. Corporate
franchise stores are springing up, too, including Dunkin' Donuts, Pay-
less Shoes, and the Children's Place (see Photograph 2.5). But Dominican entrepreneurs command a large presence as the owners of corner
bodegas, Dominican restaurants, and, as Photograph 2.6 illustrates,
American food franchises.

The cultural strategy in Little Dominican Republic matches employees with customers. I saw few cultural symbols in the décor of the fast
food restaurants I visited because marketing strategies do not, by and
large, include ethnic symbols. Nothing in Little Dominican Republic is
equivalent to Chinatown's McDonald's restaurant, where ethnic symbols such as the Chinese arch are built into the architectural design.
The fast food restaurant's ambiance focuses on providing a leisurely
place to dine, an establishment where families and young children can
enjoy a piece of American culture. Weekends, as in Chinatown, are the
busiest times. One Saturday afternoon, I stood in line at McDonald's

PHOTOGRAPH 2.4   Street Truck and Dominican Food. (Photo courtesy of Jennifer Parker Talwar, reprinted with permission)

PHOTOGRAPH 2.5   American Fast Food in Little Dominican Republic. (Photo courtesy of Jennifer Parker Talwar, reprinted with permission)

PHOTOGRAPH 2.6   McDonald's in Spanish. (Photo courtesy of Atul Talwar, reprinted with permission)

for twenty minutes to order a chicken fajita and a coke, and then waited another ten minutes for a table. (This is *fast* food?!) I had come to take photographs of families eating at McDonald's, but before doing so I wanted to blend in as a customer to make what I was doing less obvious. The restaurant overflowed with families, and the small children romped merrily in the indoor playground. In general, the neighborhood restaurants cater primarily to the local working poor, many of whom speak only Spanish.

Patterns of ethnic hiring are spatially rooted in Little Dominican Republic. Language ability largely determines where one works in this community. Although the three restaurants I visited were in Little Dominican Republic, the closer they were to cultural borders within the ethnic neighborhood the more diverse I found the language, race, and ethnicity of the workers. In other words, the ethnic diversity of the customers roughly matches the ethnic diversity of the employees. In a predominately Spanish-speaking and Dominican residential population, the majority of the fast food employees are Spanish-speaking Dominicans and others representing various Latino groups. Hiring practices, then, vary according to a restaurant's location within Little Dominican Republic.

One manager described how hiring has to represent the neighborhood: "You try to represent the neighborhood as far as you hire. You try to make it as easy as possible for people to come in. You represent the neighborhood the best way you can and you try to have as many people as you can who are willing to work and willing to deal with whatever the clientele is. And in this case, it is basically Hispanic." Job seekers in this area are mainly Latino and Spanish-speaking, and most do not live in the neighborhood. They are from the Dominican Republic, Puerto Rico, Cuba, and several countries in Central America. One major exception is a network of immigrants from Antigua who work in a restaurant that emphasizes English rather than Spanish and has been in business for at least ten years.

"Only English Spoken Here": Matching Ethnic Borders in a Latino Neighborhood

The first restaurant I looked at, a McDonald's, is on one of the busiest streets in the area. It is close to an ethnic divide within Little Dominican Republic between an area of low-income Latinos and a more affluent section of aging German Jewish residents and several new middle-class groups, including young white, Asian, and black professionals. It also borders a small community of orthodox Jews who do not patronize fast food restaurants. More than the other two sites that I examined in the neighborhood, this McDonald's caters to a diverse group of customers who speak mainly English and Spanish and reside throughout the area, as well as local non-Latino business people. This diversity affects the composition of the workforce, which in turn is diverse, consisting as it does of first- and second-generation Dominicans and Puerto Ricans as well as a group of Antiguans and a handful of other West Indians (see List 1.3 in Appendix A for the cultural features of my respondents among this workforce.)

The general manager, Jose, is typical of those who work in fast food in this neighborhood. He was born in New York, spent most of his childhood and teenage years in the Dominican Republic, and is bilingual. He started at McDonald's as a crewmember in 1985 while he was a high school student after two cousins at the restaurant encouraged him to apply. Although he resisted the idea at first, he said, "I didn't want to make my cousins look bad or anything so I came and I was like, I'll be here a week or two." But Jose is different from most who wind up in the industry because he has stayed the course for nine years and moved up the ranks. He has also earned a college degree. Jose plans to stay with McDonald's and eventually become a store supervisor.

In this restaurant, half the managers are Latino and, like Jose, are bilingual in Spanish and English; the other half are from Antigua and speak only English. Laurie, Jose's assistant manager, immigrated to New York City from Antigua when she was sixteen. Her lifelong dream was to become a teacher, but she gave that up when she could not find the means to complete a college degree. She had never heard of American fast food restaurants until she arrived in New York City. Now in her late twenties, she is a fast food manager, and, like Jose, she started as a crewmember and worked her way up the job ladder. Unlike Jose, who aspires to a lifelong fast food career in the United States, Laurie plans to return to Antigua someday.

All the employees in this restaurant speak English, and about half are bilingual in English and Spanish. Many, including the Antiguans, who speak only English when they start working, learn Spanish on the job. Jose explained: "Right now we have many black kids (Antiguan), and especially on my management team who only spoke English at the time I was here four years ago. Now, 1994, basically all of them can speak Spanish a little bit and they can basically understand. They can defend themselves." "Defend," a commonly used word in Little Dominican Republic, describes workers' ability to counter customers' "defamations," requests for special favors, and other actions that are considered abusive or threatening to a worker's reputation. Although talking back to customers is generally forbidden, managers do tend to encourage their employees to respond tactfully to insults.

Like some of the traditional ethnic enterprises in the area, this restaurant is owned by immigrants, these particular owners being relatives from Cuba who also own several other McDonald's restaurants. But this restaurant is different because it does not employ a strictly co-ethnic workforce.[19] (Co-ethnic refers to the sharing of a common ethnic origin. No Cubans were employed at this restaurant at the time of the study, and half the employees do not even speak Spanish.) As in the restaurants in Chinatown, the workforce is ethnically diverse.

Say "Permiso," Not "Excuse Me": Catering to
Spanish-Speaking Customers

A few blocks away from McDonald's and away from this ethnic border is a Burger King. Although it is in a predominantly Latino area of Little Dominican Republic and the majority of its customers are Dominican, other Spanish-speaking groups patronize the restaurant as well. The majority of employees here are first-generation Dominican, Puerto Rican, Cuban, or Central American, bilingual in Spanish and English. One employee is Jamaican. Some employees speak only Spanish, but, save for the Jamaican employee, no employees speak only English. The dominant language spoken in the restaurant is Spanish (see List 1.4 in Appendix A for the cultural features of my respondents among this workforce.)

The employees have been instructed to say "permiso" on the floor, rather than "excuse me." According to Gitu, the general manager, "The whole neighborhood is Dominican. If I start having people in my front line dealing with customers who do not know Spanish I am not going to be making a lot of money because most of my customers do not know English." Communication is important because the interaction between employees and customers does not end with ordering food. Gitu explained that if customers are not familiar with the items on the menu and cannot read, they may, for example, describe a hamburger to the cashier rather than name it. Or they may order in Spanish. As Gitu said, "They don't ask for a Whopper, you don't know what they are asking for. . . . They would say a 'big burger' or 'big hamburger' in their language and it is difficult to understand. If they are asking for fries, they call it something else in Spanish. Soda, something else in Spanish. It is not the same thing. That is where we have problems."

Gitu is from India (Mumbai), and speaks Hindi, Malay, and English, but not Spanish. Like the Vietnamese owner of the Burger King restaurant in Chinatown, Gitu relies on his subordinates to manage the restaurant. Two of three assistant managers are Puerto Rican, the third is Panamanian, and all are bilingual in Spanish and English. An Indian manager who oversees a Latino workforce reflects, to some degree, the larger global and ethnic hierarchy among immigrants in New York; but it also shows that Indians in New York have secured a *particular* occupational niche in the fast food industry that crosses the boundaries of geocultural contexts. Indian immigrants make up one of the most highly educated immigrant groups in New York; Latinos and Dominican immigrants are among the least educated.[20]

Indian immigrants like Gitu, usually male, are increasingly found in managerial positions of franchise restaurants no matter where they are located. Typically, they start out on the management rungs. Many immigrants from India come to the industry possessing high levels of human capital (in education, professional work experience, and job training), and even possess graduate degrees; they are aided by Burger King and other such companies that do not have a hard-and-fast "promote from the ranks" policy. From an industry perspective, Asian Indians are ideal managers. They are highly educated, and because they come from a former British colony, they speak English as a native tongue. They are also perceived as possessing a strong work ethic.[21]

This Burger King restaurant is very different from the Spanish bodegas and other ethnic enterprises surrounding it. Like the McDonald's restaurant in Chinatown, and unlike the other two fast food restaurants in Little Dominican Republic, it is owned by one of the largest restaurant corporations in New York City. This corporation owns twenty-six other Burger Kings, twelve of which are in New York. Although the ownership makes this restaurant different from the traditional ethnic enterprise, its similarity is found in its workers, most of whom are Latinos from Spanish speaking-countries. A pan-ethnic workforce of Spanish-speaking Latinos is constructed around language and other cultural job standards at this restaurant and reflects the cultural features of its location.

No Spanish/No Service:
Only Spanish-Speaking Employees, Please.

About a mile away and even further from the cultural divide in Little Dominican Republic is the second McDonald's. This restaurant lies in the heart of Little Dominican Republic, a predominantly Spanish-speaking area with few non-Latinos living, shopping, or working in the neighborhood. The restaurant is owned by the same Cuban immigrant relatives who own the first McDonald's restaurant. Nearly all the employees are immigrants from a Spanish-speaking region or country in Latin America and consist of Dominicans, Puerto Ricans, Salvadorans, Ecuadorans, and Cubans. They all speak Spanish, but only some speak English. This was the only restaurant I visited where my order was taken in Spanish and where I interviewed employees in Spanish. With a few exceptions, most of the employees come from poor and working-class origins (see List 1.5 in Appendix A for the cultural features of my respondents among this workforce.)

This restaurant employs fifty-eight crewmembers and five managers. All the managers are from the Dominican Republic, Puerto Rico, or elsewhere in Latin America. Two of the managers speak only Spanish. Unlike the other two restaurants in Little Dominican Republic, Spanish is not only the dominant language spoken in this restaurant but also the only language required for employment. As one of the managers, Fabiola, who is from the Dominican Republic, said:

> Some of them only speak Spanish. Our whole morning crew. The whole grill team only speaks Spanish. The front counter, I won't say they know perfect English but they can defend themselves. [Note that the manager of the first McDonald's in this neighborhood said that they can defend themselves with the *Spanish* they know.] Our night crew, some of them speak English and some don't. They try. They can defend themselves. They are not going to defend themselves that well. But good enough to get by for McDonald's. I have a lot of people who speak English who don't want to apply because they feel like they will never be hired because they don't speak any Spanish.

This manager did hire someone who didn't speak Spanish, proving the exception to the rule. Fabiola explained:

> I have a guy who doesn't speak one drop of Spanish. It is very interesting because I thought he wasn't going to last that long. But he has. His mother is Arab and his father is Cuban. But he doesn't live with his father. She doesn't speak any Spanish. Sometimes people talk to him in Spanish and he just acts like he really understands. He tackles everything. I told him the other day, "Wow I didn't think you were going to stay here that long." But he has been here for more than five months.

At this restaurant, most of the customers speak Spanish and the employees speak to them in Spanish.[22] As far as language is concerned, this restaurant is the reverse of the first McDonald's in Little Dominican Republic because it is a Spanish-language fast food franchise in an American city. This restaurant, more than any other in this study, most closely resembles the traditional ethnic enterprise because it is immigrant-and Latino-owned, it employs pan-ethnic Latino workers, and it presents itself as wholly ethnic in its verbal dealings with customers.

In Little Dominican Republic, we see that Latinos differ from the Chinese in Chinatown in that many do not learn English on the job and are not necessarily required to do so. This restricts their mobility outside the immigrant neighborhood and works to maintain their identities as "Latino" rather than "American." The retention of Spanish is a product both of the area's peripheral location in New York City and its concentrated population of Latinos, as well as its economic impoverishment. Little Dominican Republic not only harbors enclaves that are majority Spanish-speaking but also fails to attract non-Spanish-speakers from other neighborhoods. Furthermore, according to Fabiola and the other managers I interviewed in Little Dominican Republic, this area lacks city programs that teach English-language skills, although the public schools in the neighborhood emphasize bilingual education. Another assistant manager noted that English classes in the area teach more Spanish than English. And unlike Chinatown, where English binds a pan-ethnic workforce of Chinese who also speak various Chinese dialects, all Latinos of Hispanic descent, regardless of national or regional origin, share a common spoken language (Spanish). These factors allow one of the restaurants to be a virtually Spanish-only McDonald's in New York.[23] A global workforce of native Spanish speakers not only helps to shape a pan-Latino identity rather than a particular national identity but it also helps to construct a cross-national Latino context in an American fast food workplace.

The necessity of speaking English in the other two restaurants, especially for managers, reflects the spatial contingency of job and promotion standards in an immigrant neighborhood; these standards depend on how close to ethnic borders the restaurant is and how much it attempts to attract various ethnic groups as customers. Language affects not only who is hired but also the ethnic composition of job seekers. Although the third restaurant employs a pan-Latino workforce as a result of its Spanish-only requirement, the first restaurant brings together an English-speaking West Indian and bilingual Latino workforce able to serve Latinos and non-Latinos—customers coming from both sides of the ethnic border. Whether in an exclusively Spanish-speaking restaurant or one that brings together a diverse group of Latinos and English-speaking West Indians, multiethnic workforces in this area are determined by the local market. The market in turn responds to the transforming geographies, borders, and cultures created by an influx of new immigrants. Ethnicity, in this case, becomes a market-based mechanism used to ensure a brisk business.

Downtown Brooklyn

Downtown Brooklyn is one of New York City's oldest commercial centers, and New Yorkers are very familiar with it. Located just across the Brooklyn Bridge and partially on the waterfront, it is only minutes away from downtown Manhattan by car or subway. Municipal buildings and court offices of nineteenth-century architecture cover several blocks and constitute the core structures around which this area has been built. Today, the municipal complex stands at the heart of an area becoming more and more diverse with workers, shoppers, and entrepreneurs from all over the world, especially the developing world.

Unlike Chinatown and Little Dominican Republic, downtown Brooklyn is not considered an ethnic neighborhood. Immigrants do not live here and most fast food patrons are workers, students, and shoppers. These customers are not looking for an ethnic ambiance, nor do they expect cashiers to speak anything but English. Yet downtown Brooklyn is similar to Chinatown and Little Dominican Republic in the way it has become a predominately immigrant area in its business activities. Its global character is being molded around what has always been a piece of traditional America: government buildings, court houses, public service employment, shopping, and workers socializing during the lunch-hour; indeed, these characteristics make downtown Brooklyn unique. This piece of traditional America has been markedly shaped by and around American minorities, especially African Americans; since the 1970s, the public sector has been a major employment niche for

PHOTOGRAPH 2.7   African American Teenagers at McDonald's. (Photo courtesy of Samantha Rosemellia, reprinted with permission)

minorities, offering as it does well-paying and unionized jobs that come with benefits. Although African Americans do not tend to own businesses in downtown Brooklyn, they do work, shop, and dine here (see Photograph 2.7), and the large corporate franchise stores cater to the cultural demands of their predominantly black customers. Woolworth's on Fulton Street, for example, carried sweet potato pie (before it closed down in 1996), and the owner of the McDonald's restaurant introduced fried chicken in downtown Brooklyn as a regional dish when it was developed in southern cities and towns. As he said,

> This fried chicken product that we are selling here was actually developed locally. But previously McDonald's wanted almost a generic menu across the country. But I think in the last several years they wised up because there are regional differences. So we are going to be able to increase our market share by catering to the regional differences that are there. The fried chicken product that we are selling is in the New York region (including New Jersey) at about fifty restaurants. Certain markets, like I think Raleigh, or Roanoke, Virginia, is on a market-wide. Everyone on their television market is on their product.

The basic laws of economies of scale coupled with the relative impoverishment of the black population in New York City enable these corporate chains to maintain a consumer market of black New Yorkers in demand of cheap goods.[24] There are many reasons for this. First, although immigrant entrepreneurs flourish through such immigrant mutual-aid networks as Koreans in the deli and nail salon businesses and South Asians in newspaper stands, cabs, gift shops, and Indian restaurants, black Americans enjoy no such industry-wide niche. Second, the immigrant enterprises that do flourish have developed market niches that have not been taken over by corporate America and that often cater to their own ethnic groups. These include the Nigerian gypsy cab[25] business in Brooklyn, the Spanish bodegas in Little Dominican Republic, and the rapidly growing Indian food manufacturers in New Jersey. Many immigrant enterprises succeed because they provide New Yorkers with a cheaper and more accessible version of some commodity—an example being the Korean-owned nail salons—or they provide a novelty commodity such as "exotic" and "ethnic" cuisine. In the case of Chinatown, for example, Chinese restaurants serve tourists looking for a different and exotic experience as much as they serve Chinese looking for affordable native food. These kinds of establishments are *particular* to immigrant groups.

Aside from certain types of ethnic food, inexpensive food is increasingly being taken over by corporate giants in the form of retail chains. This cheap cuisine is more evident in suburban America: We are all familiar with the ubiquitous corporate franchise boulevard strip that may include Pizza Hut, McDonald's, Burger King, Wendy's, Taco Bell, Bennigan's, Denny's, or a variation of these. It is the same strip that people travel on to reach the local shopping mall, which itself usually has a food court with some of the same restaurants alongside a few more sophisticated chains offering Cajun or Chinese food and cappuccino and espresso coffee. In New York, the franchise takeover is not as pervasive; this is partly because of the tremendous diversity of New York's population, which, in turn, is matched by a diversity of cuisine. Food demands differ according to class, culture, and ethnicity. But these demands are also shaped by the many types of cuisine available in New York—even at the low-cost level.

A mid-town American white, Asian, or black office worker who decides to go out for a cheap lunch is just as likely to pick up a chicken and rice dish for $2.50 from a Pakistani street vendor as she is to buy a slice of pizza or a McDonald's cheeseburger and fries for the same price. Among the city's middle class and white-collar class, regardless of race or ethnicity, American corporate franchise cuisine is a food of only occasional choice. Fast food joints stand alongside street vendors from the Third World, New York hot dog and knish stands, Jewish bagel shops, Greek diners, independent pizza shops run by Latinos, Korean delis offering hot and cold buffets for $3.99 per pound, low-priced ethnic eateries serving Mexican, Indonesian, or Chinese cuisine, mid-scale franchise restaurants such as Friday's and Houlihan's, upscale haute cuisine, Japanese sushi bars, and elite suit-and-tie restaurants overlooking midtown parks.

The range and extent of cuisine is also shaped by immigrant, ethnic, and corporate capital among entrepreneurs, local business people, local and global corporations, and fluctuations in the real estate market. In immigrant neighborhoods, such as Chinatown and Washington Heights, the persistent demand for ethnic food among residents and nonresidents alike ensures survival of Chinese and Dominican food and the existence of Chinese and Dominican restaurants. But in a highly competitive restaurant market for inexpensive food, corporate franchises enjoy a competitive edge, partly because of economies of scale. The strategy of, say, offering two Big Macs for ninety-nine cents is nearly impossible for an independent to reproduce unless he is able to capitalize on the advantages of low labor costs and a captive market in the ethnic enclave. Even when the independent ethnic restaurateur does survive, profit levels are much lower than the average profits made by a McDonald's restaurant.

For these reasons, entrepreneurs find it increasingly difficult to compete with corporate fast food, which has become not only a part of traditional American culture but also a food supply that Americans, especially the poor, depend upon. Rather than compete with corporations, more entrepreneurs—even immigrant entrepreneurs, who have access to large amounts of capital—have been opening corporate fast food franchises rather than independents. (The average tenure of a franchise restaurant is ten years as opposed to five years for an independently owned restaurant.)[26] Without a large entrepreneurial and ownership presence in downtown Brooklyn, we would not expect African Americans to maintain many businesses, even as employees, in the face of new immigrant capital and labor.

Several changes have been occurring in downtown Brooklyn that work to recast issues of race and employment and intensify the global character of this area. New York City's privatization efforts have emptied municipal office buildings of thousands of their workers, including African Americans who have relied on public sector employment as one of their only professional employment niches in New York. Commerce in the area has seen constant change. Upscale- or moderate-scale independent retail space has been converted to immigrant enterprises and corporate franchises. A new corporate plaza brought thousands of workers into the area from Manhattan, many of them middle class, who do not typically travel outside the plaza boundaries into the surrounding neighborhood. Significantly, Third World immigrants, especially people from the Caribbean Basin who are of African descent, are finding homes in the borough of Brooklyn and coming to downtown Brooklyn to work and shop.

A global workforce here sorts and structures itself around declining and growing industry sectors where the ethnic character of the area is undergoing change. In downtown Brooklyn, we can see in dramatic ways how the employment of an immigrant workforce is interrelated with what one fast food manager in Chinatown called the "fizzling out" of American-born workers, especially racial minorities. I looked at two restaurants here, a McDonald's and a Burger King. They stand side by side with other corporate franchises, downscale retailers, and immigrant enterprises. Government housing projects where mostly poor black and Latino Americans live are located within a mile of these restaurants. In the opposite direction, and within blocks of the restaurants, is a high-priced, mainly white residential area surrounded by private schools, upscale and moderate scale ethnic restaurants, and various commercial retail enterprises. These residential areas, as one manager put it, are either "too poor" or "too affluent" to provide a substantial supply of workers to the fast food restaurants; the local shortage of labor in turn helps to attract workers from the West Indian immigrant neighborhoods that are about thirty minutes away by subway.

Downtown Brooklyn's historical legacy as an area popular among African Americans, especially for low-wage work, significantly affects marketing practices and, consequently, current employment dynamics. With the new dishes they promote, fried chicken being one example, the fast food restaurants reflect, to a certain extent, the demographics of the area, although they give little or no emphasis to cultural themes. Fast food restaurants in downtown Brooklyn serve mainly a business crowd, lunch being their busiest time. They provide fast, convenient service, a brisk turnover of customers, and cheap food, as opposed to leisurely dining where one enjoys entertainment or samples a different culture and ambiance.

The owner of the McDonald's restaurant commented on how McDonald's uses a different emphasis in different locations:

> We are selling different things in different locations. This is a very mature market here. We have a lot of competition. This block here, I got here eight years ago. Now we have a Deli across the street. There is a new pizza place going next door. There is a full service restaurant there. There is the bagel place. There is the seafood place on the corner. So the competition is much greater than it was before, a few years ago. They are not going to line up outside our door, like they do in Moscow. We are not that much of a novelty. Then we have to sell a different commodity here than they do.

Although they show signs of catering to an African American clientele, they do not employ deliberate strategies of ethnic matching between workers and clientele.

Although there are no *explicit* cultural job standards, such as foreign-language matching or fitting into an ethnic décor, recruitment practices in downtown Brooklyn do respond to neighborhood cultural characteristics and changes. First, English is the defining language of the area and the language requirement for being hired. These restaurants, then, attract not only native English speakers, including African Americans, but also West Indian immigrants from the Caribbean and South America as well as immigrants from South Asia. But employers in the area have succumbed to the negative stereotyping that African Americans suffer and see them as poor workers; this discrimination affects hiring preferences in favor of the foreign-born (I will examine this subject in Chapter 7). A fast food workforce in downtown Brooklyn combines West Indian, South Asian, as well as a few second-generation Latinos, white Americans, and a declining proportion of African Americans.

Little Caribbean: West Indian Fast Food Workers in an English-Language Neighborhood

The McDonald's restaurant has two levels and a seating capacity of over a hundred. From the outside, its appearance is similar to Chinatown's McDonald's. It has a two-level glass exterior with a large McDonald's golden arch visible from several blocks away. From the second floor, one can look out onto a street congested with traffic. Dunkin Donuts and a food court that includes Nathan's, Pizza Hut, and Roy Rogers are nearby.[27] The McDonald's restaurant is owned and operated by two white American-born brothers of Jewish descent.[28] Although the ownership is typical of the traditional ethnic enterprise, the employees are not from the owners' ethnic group; yet they are composed primarily of one cultural group (West Indians), a similarity to the ethnic enterprise.

This McDonald's has about fifty employees, including Peggy, a Jamaican immigrant who speaks favorably about the ethnic environment fostered in the workplace. When she was six, Peggy and her parents left Jamaica and came to New York. Like most West Indians in New York, Peggy has not forgotten her social roots. She lives in a West Indian neighborhood where the sounds and sights of her native cuisine, music, and holiday festivities shape one of New York's most vibrant communities. Every few years, Peggy visits her homeland and a wide network of relatives who still live there (see List 1.6 in Appendix A for cultural features of my respondents among this workforce).

Fast food employment is not unusual for West Indians in New York and thousands have found jobs in fast food restaurants in Brooklyn during the past decade. The employment of a West Indian workforce points to the larger trends in downtown Brooklyn toward hiring immigrants from the English-speaking Caribbean and toward hiring immigrants over the American-born. Four out of five managers at this restaurant are West Indian, and the workforce consists largely of immigrants from Barbados, Jamaica, Trinidad, and Guyana. According to

Julio, one of my manager respondents whose parents are from Puerto Rico, the proportion of foreign-born workers at the downtown Brooklyn McDonald's has increased from about 15 to 20 percent nine years ago (when he started) to well over 50 percent at the time of my interview. The rest of the workforce consists of Americans from racial minorities and a few white employees. A majority workforce of West Indians reflects patterns of ethnic hiring by co-ethnic managers, similar to those in the traditional ethnic enterprise.

Just So Long As They Are Foreign: Tapping English-Speaking Foreigners At the Burger King

The Burger King is a short walk away from McDonald's and is also located on a major shopping street. The restaurant has a bilevel glass exterior and a seating capacity of over a hundred; its Burger King logo looms large, visible from several blocks away. An armed security guard stands at its doors after the lunch hour, and surveillance cameras monitor every part of the interior—frontline, dining room, kitchen, basement, and stairwell—except the restrooms. Television screens at the frontline and in the manager's office behind the kitchen provide an ongoing record of what the cameras are filming.

The workers, including all five managers, are more ethnically diverse than those at the nearby McDonald's restaurant. But similarly, most are immigrants and speak English, either as a first or second language. They come from countries in Latin America, South Asia, and the Caribbean, the fastest-growing group coming from the English-speaking Caribbean. The restaurant is owned by a large company that owns nine other Burger King restaurants. According to one of the managers, this restaurant serves 1,700 to 1,800 people every day and, based on an average sale of $5 per person, brings in about $9,000 per day. This amounts to over $3 million in sales every year, the same range as the Chinatown McDonald's. This Burger King has even given managers such incentives as profit sharing beyond sales and profit quotas. At the end of one month, the managers, the production leaders, and selected crewmembers were awarded $16,000 to share among themselves. Managers here claim to make considerably more than nearby McDonald's managers, enough to save for future investment in their own less prestigious and more inexpensive fast food franchises. Because the McDonald's is not owned by a big corporation, it cannot offer profit-sharing schemes.

Like the Burger King restaurant in Little Dominican Republic and a food court in downtown Brooklyn, this large restaurant corporation employs Asian Indian immigrants as managers. Three out of five managers at this Burger King are from India, including Sandeep, who once owned a profitable tourism business in India but joined Burger King after losing all his money in the United States (see List 1.7 in Appendix A for the cultural features of my respondents among this workforce). The non-Indian managers in this restaurant are African Americans and white Americans from working-class backgrounds.

An available labor supply made up of native English speakers from South Asia, but especially from the Caribbean Islands, helps account for a changing workforce in downtown Brooklyn and the so-called fizzling out of American racial minorities from the low-wage workplace. English-language skills and quick, friendly service imply the employment eligibility for any English speaker. But the absorption of negative stereotypes surrounding American youth, particularly racial minorities, has led to a preference for foreign-born workers. Thus, a globally diverse workforce is attracted because, even though downtown Brooklyn's cultural legacy is African American and English speaking, employers currently prefer foreign-born workers; these include South Asians and Latinos, but primarily pan-ethnic workers from various West Indian countries.

American Fast Food and the Ethnic Community

Although American fast food restaurants are exemplars of standardization, they adapt to their local environments. Like the contemporary ethnic enterprises we are familiar with, they respond to and help shape New York's changing geographies, demographics, and patterns of consumption. New York City may be an unusual place in this regard because of the many mom-and-pop stores and restaurants that set expectations for this sort of behavior. But their role in the immigrant neighborhood is different because they aim to alter, not reinforce, existing cultural patterns by developing a taste for American fast food among new cultural groups. They are also different in the way market-ing strategies correspond with job standards and where the ethnic fea-tures of immigrant employees, rather than co-ethnic employer-em-ployee relations, become the more important part of the profit equation.

Fast food marketing strategies help shape jobs through a demand for locally determined cultural capital such as language skills and cultural knowledge. The need for particular cultural capital, alongside typical job requirements in the postindustrial economy (including flexibility, a good attitude, and communication skills) usually brings together a di-versity of workers who represent different class backgrounds, national origins, and chances for success. Such diversity helps broaden and re-construct the ties that bind immigrant neighborhoods and ethnic labor markets.

Where cultural matching is the predominate marketing principle—and Little Dominican Republic is an example—diversity preserves a sense of ethnic community in the immigrant neighborhood by recon-structing it within a pan-ethnic framework of Spanish-speaking immi-grants having many national origins. At the Chinatown McDonald's, di-versity may diffuse a sense of ethnic community through the use of several languages, yet emphasize English as the only common language of communication. Chinese workers at this restaurant, for instance, are required to display their ethnicity and speak "ethnically" while per-forming mainstream duties that include improving their English-lan-guage skills. In downtown Brooklyn, on the other hand, diversity has transformed the cultural character of the neighborhood. Employers' preference for the foreign-born has altered the ethnic composition of the staff's African ancestry from African American to West Indian; it also attracts English speakers from South Asia and Latin America. The next chapter examines how immigrants find jobs in these restaurants.

3

Word of Mouth and Getting Your Foot in the Door: Qualifications, Recruitment, and the Path to a Fast Food Job

I would start out with them [current employees]. I would say "Do you know someone who can work in the evenings?" "Yah, my cousin is really looking for a job." "Bring him in." That is pretty much how it works.

—Fast food manager of Puerto Rican descent working in Brooklyn

In Chapter 1, I introduced Tina, who, as we know, obtained a job at a Chinatown McDonald's the way many other immigrants find work in immigrant neighborhoods: She used her social capital and found her job through a Chinese friend who was already working at the restaurant. We know that Tina had recently arrived in the United States and was barely able to say a word in English, but she got on a subway by herself and ninety minutes later arrived at Manhattan's Chinatown to meet her friend and fill out a job application.

We would not expect anything different given what we know about the way ethnic networks operate. We have assumed that ethnic employers rely on informal recruitment methods such as hiring through referrals from current employees and tapping community and family networks, all of which bypass advertising, employment agencies, and formal applications. As Roger Waldinger or Portes and Bach would remind us, immigrants have always navigated the labor market through people they know.[1] Sociologists call this "network recruitment."

Although the literature concerning immigrant employment holds that networks distinguish ethnic enterprises from firms in the general economy, other literature shows that networking is common, even among mainstream employers.[2] Still, the general public sees flipping burgers or taking orders at the fast food counter as entry-level positions available to anyone who shows minimal motivation, ambition, ability, and initiative; the job seeker has only to inquire about job openings, fill out an application form, and prove worthy of employment during an interview. Ritzer's McDonaldization theory reinforces this view by ignoring the role that certain communities and people play in counteracting the rationalizing forces of corporate institutions.[3] According to my respondents, the recruitment methods used by fast food establishments in immigrant neighborhoods are indeed more like those of traditional ethnic employers than what the public expects of corporate mainstream employers.

Word of Mouth and Employee Referrals

Fast food managers generally agree that they tend not to use formal methods when they hire workers. They accept applications, but do not depend on them to find employees. And even though they usually conduct on-site interviews with prospective employees, those who are hired have typically been referred by another employee or manager. The interview primarily ensures that the applicant possesses the appropriate social skills, personality, and appearance necessary for postindustrial customer service jobs.

Employers, then, tend to rely foremost on word of mouth and employee referrals when recruiting fast food workers. As Table 3.1 shows, more than two-thirds of my respondents used their social capital and found their jobs through someone they knew; most named siblings, cousins, or friends who were already employees or managers. Brenda, an employee from Antigua working in a McDonald's in Little Dominican Republic, for instance, was typical of my respondents. She found her job through Antiguan friends working at the restaurant: "My two friends' boss was from Antigua. One talked to him and I filled out an application and that is how I got the job."

Employers were explicit about asking current employees to recommend friends and relatives when there are job openings. As one explained:

> I have never worked in a store where we had to go out and get people. If I put a NOW HIRING sign I would run out of applications. . . . Our main source of hiring comes from the rest of the people here. "Hey fellows, listen, I need someone in the afternoons." You ask your best people or the people that you really like to be with. Their judgment can't be as bad as what you are getting from the street. You don't know what comes from the street. I would start out with them. I would say "Do you know someone who can work in the evenings?" "Yah, my cousin is really looking for a job." "Bring him in." Thirty percent of my staff have brothers or sisters or cousins working here. That is pretty much how it works.

Julio, the second-generation Puerto Rican manager in downtown Brooklyn, said, "Typically people who work in the restaurant will tell their friends. So if there are two or three Jamaicans in the restaurant we may find that their friends come down for interviews and so then you have five Jamaicans in the restaurant." Jose, the Dominican general manager in Little Dominican Republic, was more explicit: "We do referrals through the kids who work pretty well. Those are the ones we ask, 'Do you know anyone who would like to work at McDonald's?' We go about it different ways. It is rare that we advertise through a newspaper or anything like that. We just would rather keep it McDonald's—referrals and word of mouth."

Managers emphasized over and over the sense of reliability that comes through hiring a friend or relative of an existing employee. Fabiola, the Dominican assistant manager of the Spanish-language McDonald's restaurant in Little Dominican Republic, explained it this way: "I tell them to come to see me because . . . my crew's friends, I feel like . . . if your friend is like you, then I don't mind hiring them. I interview them and keep them on hold and when there is an opening I usually tell their friends first. So sometimes I don't even have to do interviews because I ask them 'Do you have a friend who can work these days'—things like that. So sometimes I don't do interviews." Jose elaborated on how "word of mouth" linkages among Dominican youth work to favor the fast food restaurants in the area even at the expense of traditional "ethnic" employers.

> Well, you see the kids talk. For example, especially nowadays the kids that you wouldn't see working in McDonald's [a few years ago] are working in McDonald's. It is because they talk amongst themselves. Like, I'm quoting here the cool guy playing basketball in the street or playing baseball. At one time [he] wouldn't be caught dead working in McDonald's. But it is changing. They realize that McDonald's is not that way. I guess a put-down job or whatever.

Tina said that some of her Chinese friends are interested in working at McDonald's because of what she tells them about her experiences. "When I go home and I have time I call my friend and I say today I learned something else [at McDonald's]. I tell her I learned a lot of things. She admires me. She says that she wishes to have the time to apply for this job. I think maybe it is a good start." Some managers even offer financial incentives for their workers to recruit their friends and relatives. As Julia, the Puerto Rican manager in Chinatown, said, "We used to give them $50 if you brought in a person you recommended to work and they lasted more than six months."

Only about a quarter of my respondents filled out an application without knowing someone who worked at the restaurant. A few got their jobs only after excessive persistence, repeated visits, and/or calls to the store pleading for a job. A Honduran teen's explanation of how she got a job at the Chinatown McDonald's illustrates the way managers discount formal applications but occasionally give in to persistent job seekers. Lila said, "I always come down here to shop, for my jewelry and stuff. I always come in here [the McDonald's restaurant] every time I come down here. I applied for a job. They said they would get back to me and they never did. So I kept calling and calling to show them I was really interested. So they sent me in for an interview the next day and I got it."

TABLE 3.1   How Respondents Got Their Jobs

Social Capital ("Who You Know")		Formal Process of Inquiry (Filling Out an Application)		Excessive Persistence	
Number	Percentage	Number	Percentage	Number	Percentage
38	68	15	27	3	5

SOURCE: Interviews.

Roger Waldinger might refer to this practice as an exclusionary bias that brings certain groups together and excludes others.[4] But the way networks operate in fast food restaurants is more complicated than the way they function in traditional ethnic enterprises in three distinct ways. First, various immigrant linkages are often present in the same restaurant. Second, these linkages are usually cross-national. Third, network recruitment is employed, in part, as a means to recruit employees who live outside the neighborhood where the restaurant is located. Traditional ethnic enterprises, in other words, tend to rely on monopoly chains of co-ethnic networks. But fast food restaurants complicate this process by relying on "multiple-ethnic chains" and "pan-ethnic networks" when searching for nonlocal workers.

Chains of Ethnicity

The traditional ethnic enterprise typically features long-term employment and extensive work hours; it helps sustain monopoly niches for long periods, often throughout a generation. According to Roger Waldinger, monopoly niches break down when ethnic groups no longer replace themselves in the same sector. This usually happens when the next generation becomes upwardly mobile and moves on to better jobs.[5] Employment in fast food restaurants works differently: Indicative of jobs in the postindustrial labor market, the fast food workforce is constantly changing because the work is temporary and contingent. As a result of the industry's capital intensive nature, the rationalized labor process, and the limited training requirements, fast food employers can quickly fire and hire, depending on, according to one manager, "who does and does not work out."

Firing employees, as I quickly learned while working at Burger King, is not usually a direct action. Normally, managers severely reduce the hours an employee works on the following week's schedule, or schedule them to work undesirable hours. I well remember employees who complained about having to "close" several nights in a row (when they were hired to work mornings); or they might get only one four-hour shift in the week, which meant they would gross little more than $20 for the week. Such employees are eventually forced to quit on their own, and the employer escapes having to pay unemployment insurance.

The constant turnover of employees helps promote the coexistence of different immigrant chains and groups in the same fast food restaurants. These include Antiguans, Dominicans, and other Latino groups in a restaurant in Little Dominican Republic, the "United Nations" team in Chinatown, and the mix of West Indians, Latinos, and South Asians in a restaurant in downtown Brooklyn. Employers, who claim to prefer workforce diversity, encourage various immigrant niches and chains that work well together. This ploy supports the highly visible and universal marketing and advertising campaigns that promote the multi-ethnic and multiracial teams now commonplace among giant corporate retailers, including Benetton, Banana Republic, the Gap, and fast food chains. Loren, an African American assistant manager at Burger King in downtown Brooklyn, discussed how the industry's advertising campaigns affect their hiring practices:

> My boss likes to see that diversity and that just comes naturally. We don't look and say, "Okay fellows, we need a little more white in this corner and a few more black people just for the nighttime." We don't do that. It just happened to be that way. Studies are going on all the time, Burger King, McDonald's, everywhere. If you see an application nowadays, they are hiring on TV. Four different nationalities will be represented coming to Burger King and being hired.

Carla, a nineteen-year-old cashier from Guyana, was hired by Loren in this restaurant and is a good example of how ethnic chains work:

> I go to school and I just wanted some money, so my father suggested one of these fast food places. I came and put in an application and they called

me and they gave me a part time job. My cousin [who was working at the restaurant] told me about the job. I have told my other cousin about a job. She is from Canada and is having a hard time to get a worker's permit. She came here to go to school. But they say as soon as she gets all that straightened out they will see if they need anyone.

Only a handful of employees at this restaurant are from Guyana, and only a few come from Puerto Rico. As Carlos commented, a Puerto Rican teenager who also obtained his job at this restaurant through a relative, "My cousin used to work here. He told them about me and they hired me." He has since assisted another cousin and a friend in getting jobs at the same restaurant.

And Jose, the Dominican manager in Little Dominican Republic, started out as a crewmember after his cousins coaxed him into applying for the job:

I got into McDonald's when I was in high school. I was a sophomore in a Bronx high school. My cousins worked here. They started working a year before. My cousin asked me if I wanted to work, they were hiring. And I said "No, I wouldn't work at McDonald's." That was my initial reaction. She said, "Well, fill out an application, you never know." And then about two months later, I think May or August, I don't remember, they called me. I didn't want to make my cousins look bad or anything so I came and I was like, I'll be here a week or two and ended up being here for nine years. I moved up the ranks.

As both a crewmember and a manager, Jose claims to have assisted Dominican friends and relatives in getting jobs at the same restaurant. But while Dominicans outnumber every other immigrant group in the restaurant, they are accompanied by various other national and ethnic groups, including Antiguans, Puerto Ricans, and Ecuadorians.

Ethnic linkages may also exist at the professional level; these aid members of certain immigrant groups entering positions in management across the fast food industry at large rather than within a particular restaurant. Gitu, the Asian Indian general manager in Little Dominican Republic, is a good example of the way professional immigrants from India have come to dominate manager positions in some of the biggest fast food chains in New York City. "I have a college degree [in physics] from India. I came over here and I had somebody [from my home country] who was working in Burger King and they got me hired. I landed in this country and someone who knew me got me the job and then once I was in the line, I just stayed in the line."

But Gitu works alongside managers from the Dominican Republic and other countries in Latin America. Managers, in general, draw on the friends and relatives of their employees, but selectively, depending on the restaurant's needs, their tendency to favor certain national or ethnic groups over others, and the pressure they feel to diversify their staffs. Fabiola, a manager in another restaurant in Little Dominican Republic, explained what happened in her restaurant when these multiple factors interacted.

> Basically this is a Dominican area. We are trying to get more Puerto Rican and blacks [African Americans] to come into McDonald's to work. So we can teach them how it is to work with different races. But this is a Spanish area. So I guess these jobs tend to be filled with Spanish workers. Half of the managers are black [Latino]. We just need more different races. We used to have a Chinese girl who worked here. That was fun because we never believed that someone Chinese would come into this neighborhood to work here. And I think that was nice.

Pedro, the Colombian manager in Chinatown, was more explicit. "We do ask. Especially with the Chinese people. We ask do you have any friends? We usually don't ask the Spanish people or the blacks if they have any friends. We usually have enough of them coming in. You don't get a lot of Chinese people coming in to apply off the bat."

The functioning of multiple ethnic chains in a fast food restaurant may also reflect, to a certain degree, co-ethnic hiring practices on the managers' part, when management staffs are already diverse. Managers sometimes promote managers from their own ethnic groups who then have the power to further "hire and promote their own." As Pedro explained,

> I think what happens is that people tend to hire within their own races. I think I tend to hire more Spanish. The black manager, he tends to hire

more blacks. I know the Spanish people seem to come to you because they feel there is more camaraderie. They won't go to the Chinese manager. They will always come to me or the other girl who is Puerto Rican. And the black people won't go to the Chinese guy. They will go to the black guy. If you go across the street, there are mostly Chinese because the managers are mainly Chinese.

The Antiguan chain that commutes from the Bronx to a McDonald's restaurant in Little Dominican Republic, for example, has coexisted with Latino chains in this restaurant since 1985. During this time, at least one Antiguan has always been a manager. At Burger King in Chinatown, Pedro's assistants—a Puerto Rican, a Chinese, and a Jamaican—do reflect the composition of the workforce. Even at the Chinatown McDonald's, a West Indian and Latino join three Chinese managers. In this way, management teams are often ethnically concentrated and ethnically diverse. They perpetuate diversity by reproducing themselves. On the other hand, managers may feel constrained in hiring "their own." Gitu, for instance, needs to hire Latinos to function in a Spanish-speaking neighborhood. And Loren, the African American manager in Brooklyn, prefers foreign-born workers because he has internalized the negative stereotypes that plague African American workers.

Many Local Colors: Behind the Fast Food Counter

Any particular ethnic chain in a fast food restaurant rarely represents one national group; rather, the chains are usually cross-national, or what I refer to as "pan-ethnic," especially when several national groups are concentrated in residential neighborhoods. For instance, West Indian immigrants who reside in a Caribbean neighborhood in Brooklyn hail from various countries, including Jamaica, Haiti, Barbados, Trinidad, and Guyana.[6] As a group, they represent one pan-ethnic chain that has secured an occupational niche in downtown Brooklyn.

Peggy, the Jamaican cashier at McDonald's, has always relied on her friends and relatives, who come from various West Indian countries, to get entry-level jobs, including her current position. Peggy and her cousin, who is also eighteen years old, got their first fast food jobs through Peggy's sister, who was a crewmember in a fast food restaurant in the West Indian neighborhood where they live. Peggy's sister eventually became a manager at this restaurant. But Peggy and her cousin left that establishment because of neighborhood peer pressure and the intrigue that accompanied working in a new and different location. They found their current jobs, thirty minutes away by train, through a friend from Trinidad. As Peggy explained, "A friend of mine was here a month or two ahead of me. She is from Trinidad. She was here like four or five months. She said they were hiring here so we just came, filled out an application, and they said they would contact us if we could work. Then they called me the next day and told me I had gotten the job. . . . Now two of my cousins are working here."

Peggy often refers her West Indian friends and neighbors to the hiring managers at the restaurant where she works. Peggy said she would leave her fast food position if she found a higher-paying job, but she also expressed her fondness for the close-knit social and ethnic environment in her workplace. Most of her West Indian coworkers and managers (who are from many different islands) live in her neighborhood, and she "hangs out" with them in her spare time. Laurie, the Antiguan assistant manager in Little Dominican Republic, also found her job through a pan-ethnic contact. As she explained, "There was this guy who worked here. We all came from the Islands. He was from another island and he was a friend of my aunt. My aunt talked to him and that is how I got the job."

Spanish-speaking Latinos from the Dominican Republic, El Salvador, Colombia, Ecuador, Cuba, Venezuela, as well as Puerto Rico, often live in the same neighborhoods and share information about jobs. Ria, a swing manager and second-generation Puerto Rican, for instance, travels from the Bronx to work at a McDonald's in Little Dominican Republic so that she can work with friends who are from the Dominican Republic and Ecuador. She said, "Basically all my friends were working here. I had two or three friends working here from my school. They are basically Hispanic, one Dominican, and another from Ecuador."

When I interviewed Ria, she had been working at McDonald's for three years; during that time, she has helped her two younger brothers get jobs at the same restaurant. Julia, the Puerto Rican manager, had been working in fast food restaurants for more than five years at the time of my interviews. She got her fast food jobs, including promotions, through Pedro, the Colombian manager whom she became friends with when they were both working at another Burger King restaurant in their neighborhood in Queens:

> We met in Sunnyside Queens. Then we both went somewhere else in Queens. Then we went to Canal Street, to Delancy, and then here. I quit when I was in high school and got another job at an advertising company. I would always come by and see him. And he would always say why don't you come back and eventually I came back. And then I left when I got married and I stayed close to his family because we had a friendship. Every time I left, he would offer me another job.

David, also Puerto Rican, got his fast food job in Little Dominican Republic through a cousin and has since referred friends of various ethnic and national origins to the hiring manager. "I had a cousin who was working here and he had called me and told me that the manager had me get people. So I came and spoke to the manager and he gave me the okay and hired me. . . . Now my girlfriend works here. She is Dominican. Her brother works here also."

Miriam, a young woman from Cuba, got her job at a McDonald's restaurant in Little Dominican Republic through a Dominican friend. As she said, "A friend of mine helped me get the job. She is Dominican and we met in school." Chinese immigrants from Taiwan, China, Hong Kong, and Malaysia also settle together in Chinatown and its offshoots, and their shared networks have boosted their finding employment in the Manhattan Chinatown's fast food restaurants.[7] Alison, the Malaysian assistant manager in Chinatown, got her job through a friend who is from the Chinese mainland. As she said, "I was in high school. I have a girlfriend from China [the mainland]. Her name is Jenni and she was my classmate. She asked me, 'Are you interested in working at McDonald's for part-time and only work weekends?' And I said, 'OK.'"

The Distancing of Home and Work: Taking the "7" Train

Multiple ethnic chains and their pan-ethnic character are aided by employers' tendencies to hire people who do not live in the immediate

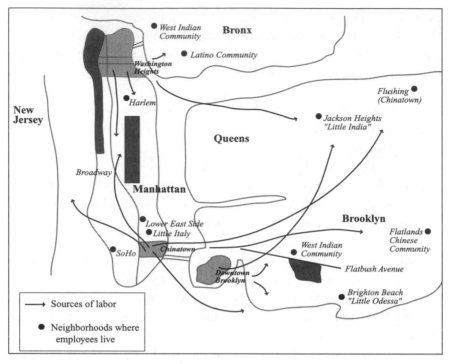

FIGURE 3.1   Map of Restaurants and Geographical Source of Labor

vicinity of the restaurant. Social networks, then, do not operate primarily on a neighborhood level as is often the case in the traditional ethnic enterprise. Even though fast food workforces tend to reflect the characteristics of the neighborhood and marketing strategies of the restaurants where they work, the staff usually lives somewhere else (see Figure 3.1).

Fabiola described where her largely Latino staff lives: "A lot of them live in the Bronx. A lot of them live in Manhattan, but either they live in lower Manhattan or upper Manhattan. We have some who live in the neighborhood. . . . They are close but not so close." Fast food employees often commute more than an hour to work each way, nearly double the average commuting time of thirty-four minutes (each way) among New Yorkers.[8]

The distancing of home and work occurs for several reasons: fast food establishments prefer to hire employees who live outside the neighborhood; employers do not prefer locals and don't rely on the neighborhood to provide a workforce; as other fast food studies have shown, employers "worry that locals will bring problems—for example, friends who badger them for free eats."[9] My employer's respondents said that frontline employees, especially cashiers, tend to give in to peer pressure to give away food. Ethnic networks enable restaurants to find employees from outside the immediate vicinity; and no matter where fast food restaurants are located, they attract job seekers. Fast food restaurants in America are symbols of easy job opportunities, and it is no different in immigrant neighborhoods. Such restaurants, then, receive more applicants and a greater variety of them than other immigrant enterprises; this, in turn, sets into motion a constant source of new ethnic groups and networks to draw from.

Still, potential workers are also selective. Most fast food employees do not live where they work, and many commute long distances, bypassing other fast food restaurants along the way. The employees I spoke to provided two reasons for this: First, they prefer to commute out of their own neighborhoods to avoid managers' distrust and the threat of losing their jobs. "You be like, 'Go away, you're gonna get me fired,'" said one cashier about how she responds to her friends when they stand in her line. A McDonald's worker expressed a typical sentiment. "I wouldn't want to work at McDonald's around my block because then a lot of my friends would know and they would be like, 'Hook me up, hook me up, give me free this, free that.' If they [managers] see that they'd be thinking I'm giving away free food. So I wouldn't. I would rather work far away."

The Stigma of the Burger Flipper

Employees also want to avoid the ridicule and harassment rooted in the social stigma surrounding fast food work. They feel devalued by peers, customers, and employers, who, they claim, degrade them because they are fast food workers. Employees and their managers commonly describe the ill treatment of workers, especially frontline workers, by customers. Customers are often perceived by crewmembers to embody the stigma associated with the low status of fast food workers. Linked to this low status is the idea that those who work in fast food restaurants simply cannot find a better job and therefore are at fault. Fast food crewmembers claim that customers often humiliate them and treat them as losers. One Burger King employee expressed a general feeling among workers: "I was at a party and a friend of mine works at another Burger King. They began to make fun of him. . . . They act like they are the customers and the guy who needs to get their food is like their slave."

One day as I walked in Greenwich Village, I struck up a conversation with a teenager who was making a McDonald's home delivery. She told me that she didn't like making deliveries because people "make fun of me all the time." Because of the stigma, many employees refuse to wear their uniforms to and from work. I, too, was affected by the fast food stigma, and I never wore my uniform to or from work! When I saw a young doctor in his scrubs as I went home on the subway one night, I thought about this. Uniforms indicate status, and I knew that, if this young doctor were a Burger King employee, he would not be wearing his uniform away from the job.

When I asked Elizabeth, a fast food cashier from Guyana, whether she thought some young people might not want to work here, her response reflected her experiences with customers and how she thought the customers perceived her status as an employee. She said, "When the customer come in, if they have to wait on their food they be nasty to you and then they say, 'You better be glad you have this job because I think it is the only job you can get.' So I guess, people like them, I guess they wouldn't come and work here because that is the way they treat us." Elizabeth does not seem to internalize the perception customers hold, for she added, "It is someone's choice whether or not to work in fast food," implying that the customer is simply wrong. She has lived in New York City for only two years, but those who have been here for all or most of their lives may be more vulnerable to peer pressure and to customers' defamations because they share the dominant values of society regarding fast food jobs; this would support what managers commonly refer to as an internalization of the social stigma of fast food work by those who have grown up in New York City.

Some employees have even reported being physically harassed by customers. As one employee explained,

Some of the customers be getting frustrated with us. I remember one time I was working on the express line when the head manager and this one customer came in and had a $100 bill. But we have on the register that we don't take nothing over fifty. We was like, "We don't take $100 bills, do you have something smaller?" He said, "No." We was like, "We cannot serve you because we don't take bills over fifty." So he started getting real hyper. He was getting an attitude and he was startin' to steal everything. He tried to snatch up the food that we had brought out for him. So my manager was like, "Put back the food because you didn't pay for it." He tried to leave the store with the food and the manager tried to stop him and he punched out the manager.

Another employee told how customers get out of hand with cashiers. "There was one who put his hands on my face and everything but there was a manager there so they moved me away and he handled it." Thus, working outside one's own neighborhood is thought to reduce the risk of humiliation from friends and relatives and to help in coping with harassment from customers.

In general, fast food restaurants' spatial strategies of labor recruitment combined with job seekers' preferences to work outside their own neighborhoods reinforce and shape the way network recruitment operates. For instance, while maintaining an emphasis on the cultural features of employees in Little Dominican Republic—such as speaking Spanish—a diverse pan-Latino workforce comes together to represent various ethnic groups as well as neighborhoods from Spanish Harlem and the Bronx to the Lower East Side. Only a few employees live close by.

Chinatown's restaurants also bring together a diverse group of Chinese workers who speak various dialects, come from a multitude of national origins, and live in satellite Chinatowns in Queens and Brooklyn. Many Chinatown workers representing other cultural groups, such as the Latinos from the Lower East Side, live closer to Chinatown than the Chinese employees who commute from the outer boroughs. Alison, for instance, lives in a Chinese neighborhood in Brooklyn and Tina lives in a Chinese enclave in Queens. They each commute more than one hour to and from work. Others, such as Brusso, the Russian immigrant from Brooklyn, commute just as far as the Chinese employees and some of the South Asian immigrants from Indian neighborhoods in New Jersey and Queens. The restaurants in downtown Brooklyn draw on workers who are largely from the West Indian community in Brooklyn,

Indian neighborhoods in New Jersey, and various other parts of Brooklyn. The fast food restaurant in the immigrant neighborhood, then, depends on multiple ethnic networks simultaneously, often drawing on various immigrant pools from several places.

In summary, we have seen how multiple and diverse ethnic chains with their nonlocal workers point to weakened geographical roots linking the workplace and the larger ethnic community in the immigrant neighborhood, a condition very different from the monopolizing co-ethnic chain that characterizes the traditional ethnic workplace.

4

Day Off, Nothing!
The Work's Got to Be Done:
Flexibility and Work Time

We hire those who are willing to work any hours. If they make themselves completely available.

—Fast food manager from Colombia,
working in Chinatown

Tina plans her private life around her job because the hours she works are constantly changing. She is a part-time temporary employee, and she is given a new schedule every week. From day to day, she never knows when she will be asked to "clock out" and go home earlier than scheduled; and sometimes she is called at home and asked to work on a day off. Tina's fluctuating schedule and paycheck mean that she and her family are usually in the middle of a balancing act. With such terms of employment, Tina joins millions of other Americans at the bottom of the postindustrial economy as the nation's new cadre of flexible workers.

These terms differ from those found in traditional ethnic enclaves, such as Chinatown, where work is more consistent and people work long hours every day. Tina's husband, for instance, rises at 5:00 A.M. six mornings a week to go to work in Chinatown, and he arrives home every evening at around 8:00 P.M. Tina's irregular schedule affects not only how she structures her time and the amount of money she makes but also the kinds of people she works with and the relationships she develops. Unlike her husband, for instance, who has been working with many of the same people every day for the past eleven years, Tina rarely works with the same people each day, and this affects her chances to form close relationships with coworkers.

Cheap Help and Available Workers

"Flexibility" has become a buzzword used by economists today to describe virtually any feature of the modern corporation that deviates from the rigidity of the mass manufacturing system prevalent before the 1980s.[1] In fast food, I view flexibility as integral to the organization's emphasis on keeping the costs of production at a minimum. This is closely related to the temping phenomenon where temporary workers are hired out by an agency for specific tasks or for certain lengths of time.[2] Fast food restaurants are concerned with creating a labor supply that is always ready for work while keeping labor costs at a minimum. Employees must be available according to the restaurant's changing demand for labor and be flexible in the assignment of work tasks. The demand for labor is directly associated with how many customers patronize a restaurant; although the number of customers cannot be predicted, mealtimes are generally the busiest times. Even so, one cannot predict a sudden speed-up with the visit of a school group on a field trip, or a weather-induced slow-down.

Like any labor-intensive industry, fast food restaurants place a premium on minimizing labor costs, which is nothing new to the retail industry in itself. As Edward Kirkland noted about a letter F. W. Woolworth wrote to his store managers in 1892, more than a century ago: "We must have cheap help or we cannot sell cheap goods."[3] A more recent development is how fast food technologies and automation are used to maintain human labor at the lowest cost, which includes the ability to use labor *only* according to immediate need.[4] The intensity with which the fast food organization is able to do this is new; it includes automated food preparation, computers for clocking in and out, and labor costs controlled so closely that management is concerned with unproductive *minutes* on the clock.

Most fast food restaurants maintain a payroll that far exceeds how many employees are required to operate the restaurant because a large reserve of employees ensures that the restaurant will always be adequately staffed. One manager explained why he needs to hire people who are willing to work at any time: "A lot of people come in and they can only work a few hours at certain times. They are the ones we can't really use because then when they come here, they give you a hard time with the schedule. Availability really. [We need] people who can work any hours, who can work later, or come earlier."

Managers spend considerable amounts of time strategically controlling and limiting how many employees, as well as who, are on the clock according to need. As Karl Marx appropriately wrote a century-and-a-half ago: "The value of labor is completely destroyed if it is not sold every instant."[5] Strategies for controlling workers' paid time range from making a weekly schedule for all employees based on weekly sales projections to pulling crew members on and off the clock during their scheduled shifts according to fluctuations in consumer demand. Employees may be asked to take an extended break or to go home early if business slows down; or they may be asked to stay beyond their shifts or skip a break if business unexpectedly picks up. Workers may even be asked not to start their scheduled shifts if the restaurant appears slow, or called at home to come in when not originally scheduled if the restaurant becomes unexpectedly busy. Such practice has no legal restrictions.

While working at Burger King, for instance, I was told several times to clock out for an indefinite time because business had slowed down and fewer workers were required to handle customer orders. (After clocking out, one is no longer being paid.) Once, after waiting in the dining room for half an hour to clock back in, I was told that I could go home because business had not picked up, a common occurrence with employees at this restaurant. Sometimes employees would come to work and then be told to go home before clocking in because business was too slow.

Employees dislike managers' interfering with their weekly schedules, especially the extension of a shift. Managers justify their actions by referring to the kinds of people who work in fast food restaurants. In New York City, managers say, many workers are high school or college students attending classes (whose hours are also legally restricted if under the age of eighteen), the working poor who hold other jobs, or single mothers balancing childcare with working. They are people with other schedules, restrictions, or responsibilities that fast food managers must work around. In other words, managers try to make it seem that they are doing their employees a favor by accommodating their busy schedules. Indeed, when managers work around an employee's individual schedule or particular restrictions, the worker usually considers it a job benefit. On the other hand, employers do prefer to hire those who are willing to bend their schedules in the interests of restaurant business.

This kind of practice is also nothing new to restaurant work. The unpredictable nature of the restaurant business has always resulted in employers' attempts to make employees bend their schedules according to the restaurant's need. George Orwell vividly portrayed his own experiences when he worked in a hotel restaurant in Paris in the 1930s:

> At half-past five I was suddenly awakened. A night watchman, sent from the hotel, was standing at my bedside. He stripped the clothes back and shook me roughly. "Get up!" he said. *"Tu t'es bien saoulé la gueule, eh?* [You have gotten drunk (with vulgar emphasis)] Well, never mind that, the hotel's a man short. You've got to work to-day." "Why should I work?" I protested. "This is my day off." "Day off, nothing! The work's got to be done. Get up!"[6]

Of course, today we can hardly imagine that a McDonald's or Burger King manager would stand at the bedside of a crewmember—or can we? Because what sometimes happens today isn't too far off. Phoning employees provides a much more efficient way for managers to round up a crew when needed. As Julia, the Puerto Rican manager at a Chinatown restaurant, said, "I have to call the employees up and make sure they are coming in. They can't hide from me. If they don't show up, I am going to be on them. If they have to be here at 8:00, I am calling them at seven in the morning. I wake them up to make sure they are coming to work." Every manager has his or her own technique for controlling employees' adherence to work schedules, and not every manager indulges in the practice just described. Still, such a practice is not limited to the fast food restaurant but could occur in any low-wage industry.

On a more general level, managers' meeting memos are usually explicit about controlling labor time. One such memo stated: "Managers *must* control. If the sales are lower than projected, managers must control accordingly. Managers who use more hours than projected must justify that with *sales* only. No overtime will be allowed." Such control is based on the legal relationship between the employee and employer. Upon being hired, employees do not enter into a contractual relationship with the employer; rather, they are at the employer's mercy and command. Employers are bound only by the few legal codes established by the state that refer to the regular payment of at least minimum wage for working forty hours or less in a week, overtime pay for more than forty hours, hourly restrictions on minors, and workplace safety. Employees have no legal recourse to contest issues involving irregular hours or schedule changes. And managers often work around these legal codes to avoid complications with the law while ensuring the lowest labor costs.

For example, managers enforce flexibility among employees by making a schedule according to employees' performances during the past week; this strategy enables managers to decide who works, when, and for how many hours. One manager, noting that many of his employees wanted to work forty hours per week—the maximum allowed—said that workers "are awarded that forty hours a week, provided their performance [is good], of course! That [performance] is a big issue." Managers avoid scheduling employees beyond forty hours to avoid paying overtime. Despite this, managers admit that more fast food applicants are looking for full-time work. According to managers, the percentage of full-time employees is currently about 50 percent, and in one restaurant, full-timers were 60 percent of the workforce. (Full-time in this industry refers to part-time status while working the maximum hours one is allowed.) Managers say that full-time employees have become more numerous since the economic slowdown of the early 1990s, adults' greater reliance on minimum wage jobs, and increasing barriers to higher education.

Managers also individually stagger employees' shifts to enforce flexible work time. Employees usually begin and end their shifts as individuals rather than as a group to help manage the precise amount of labor required at any given time. This practice also deters employees from any kind of social interaction that could affect their motivation to work. When I worked at Burger King, I usually changed into my uniform, clocked in, and left the restaurant unaccompanied.

The demand for a flexible labor supply affects job standards as well as the way managers perceive job seekers' ability to adapt to the organization. These perceptions are often structured according to job seekers' ages, socioeconomic backgrounds, and cultural heritages. Restaurants may avoid hiring minors, for example, because of legal restrictions on how many hours they can work, when they can work, and the jobs they can perform. According to one manager,

> We only have eighteen and up. Not because they don't apply. But because they can only work weekends. They only can work certain hours. On Fridays, they only can work until 10:00. Saturdays, they can only work eight full hours and only until 10:00. Sundays they can only work until 7:00. Sometimes when it gets extremely busy and we forget about them . . . we go over the limit [of eight full hours or past a certain time]. The last time we got a fine.

Nonetheless, managers claim that high school kids and teens are more flexible because they don't have family responsibilities. The balance between legal restrictions and the benefits of young people's greater flexibility translates into a nearly universal preference for those who are at least eighteen but not beyond their early twenties—those who are perceived to have no family obligations.

Age is mediated by financial status. Immigrants considered best able to adapt to a fluctuating demand for their work, particularly at the entry level, are those who do not depend on their fast food wages for their only income. Tina, for example, is married to the primary breadwinner in her household. (Even though Tina earns more per hour than her husband, her husband earns more per week because he works many more hours than Tina.) Fast food employees typically hold another job(s), live in multiple-earning households, or live with their parents or other relatives who are primarily responsible for supporting the household. The poorest immigrants and those who have the weakest household support structures are less likely to apply for and be hired into a fast food job. When they are hired, they usually have one or two other jobs. The most desirable fast food employees, from a manager's perspective, are the more economically stable who work for pocket change or provide marginal contributions to their households because they are less dependent on the fast food wage for survival. In this way, most fast food employees are subsidized by family members.

Many managers hold certain stereotypical views about various immigrant groups that affect how they perceive their overall availability. The Chinese are considered studious, their rigid schedules determined by the importance of education and home life in Chinese culture. Latino employees are regarded as less rigid with their schedules and more spontaneous because they enjoy a more relaxed home life. Managers held varying views on how these cultural differences affect ability to adapt to fast food work. Julia, for example, said,

> I don't know why the Oriental girls never volunteer for extra work. They don't want to come in early. They don't want to stay late. They never want to work on their day off. Like today we were short-handed. She came in [Latina] and two Oriental girls came in. She [Latina] was supposed to start at 3:00 and she started at 12:00. I told her I need you and she came in. The two Oriental girls sat down, had lunch on their day off and then they didn't want to work. They had lunch on the store. I don't think it is because of the nationality. But I see the difference in them. All of them are like that. Every single one of them. And they are constantly late. And they want to go home early. They don't want to work 'til it is dark outside because their parents want them at home. With the Spanish girls, they call their parents up and say, "Listen, I am working late and that is it."

Pedro, the manager from Colombia working in the same restaurant, viewed the Chinese employees differently. He said, "The Chinese are all study, study, study . . . but they are the hardest workers. Less complainers. They will do anything . . . anything at all . . . they are the nicest ones." Alison, the manager from Malaysia, reinforced Pedro's view of Chinese employees: "The Chinese people just work. They are quiet. They just work, and go home and punch out."

Managers perceive the relationship between workers' work roles and their external responsibilities both positively and negatively. The

Chinese, they say, rigidly adhere to a strict work ethic, at work, at home, and at school. This translates into a perception of the Chinese as the "model minority": reliable, hardworking, and diligent, but usually according to their inflexible external responsibilities and goals. Although Latinos are seen as less hardworking and motivated because of their loose archetype, managers also have more power to structure, and alter, their Latino employees' time on the clock.

The All-Around Worker

The flexible worker is also versatile. The universal aim of McDonald's and Burger King is for each employee to become proficient in every station and auxiliary task so that workers are interchangeable. The tendency is toward employee homogenization rather than specialization; to create the all-around worker rather than the specialist. In the traditional ethnic restaurant, by contrast, workers usually perform the same tasks every day.

The corporate giants create the all-around worker by maintaining a distinction between the technical division of labor (stations and jobs) and the social division of labor (employees' roles) to enhance productivity and reduce labor costs. The technical division of labor refers to the stations where one or more items are made and tasks are performed: the specialty sandwich station or the Whopper station. The social division of labor refers to what employees do; but what they do does not directly correspond with these stations because employees are encouraged not only to master several stations, and even shift from one station to another, but also to perform secondary tasks such as sweeping the floor, taking out the garbage, and unloading supplies from trucks. According to the manager of one restaurant where team work was especially stressed, "All crew persons are encouraged to step outside of their stations and view the restaurant as a whole . . . to see that each person is not a cog but a part of a much larger machine that is dependent on each other working as a team." All crewmembers, regardless of the work they do, wear the same uniform (although the uniform is adjusted according to gender in some restaurants). Managers emphasize aesthetics: how one works and how one looks while working. They also stress cleanliness and instruct employees to "sanitize" their hands regularly, maintain a clean station, and, when not busy, clean utensils or mop the floor. All employees—not just frontline workers—are required to be well-groomed and wear clean uniforms.

The more stations a worker is competent to handle, the greater value he or she adds to the organization. When the ideal is accomplished—when most employees are competent in several stations—the organization can be flexible when assigning stations; employees can also move to any other station, depending on the need, to replace or assist a coworker. If a customer orders thirty fish fillets to go, for instance, a highly competent employee should be able to move quickly from the specialty sandwich station to help out with fish fillets, yet still keep up with his or her own station. Roy, my crew trainer when I worked at Burger King, was so proficient that he was able to work two or three stations, including his own, during a rush. He was an impressive sight when he kept an eye on three or four monitors at once and darted from one station to another, his hands moving like a magician's. If our Burger King had been fortunate enough to find more employees like Roy, it would have needed fewer of them.

The goal is an interchangeability in which all employees can perform competently at other stations.[7] But even though fast food restaurants stress this goal, all-around workers, like Roy, are rare because the high turnover in fast food restaurants counters the organizational ideal for maximum employee interchangeability.[8] The workforce at fast food restaurants typically consists of employees with a range of experience and proficiency levels.[9]

Managers look for various characteristics in employees that will make them an especially interchangeable part of the team. Immigrants who appear to be versatile are those who smile, are attractive and poised, have good language skills, and are flexible with their schedules. Additionally, workers who exhibit high energy and enthusiasm are thought to have the motivation to keep up with the changing demands of production tasks. One manager claimed he detected such desirable traits through "a sense during the interview process." Imparting family history, involvement in extracurricular school activities (such as sports and gymnastics), and smiling during the interview reinforce this "sense."

McDonald's has developed various questions designed to measure motivational levels that managers should pose to prospective employees.

One manager cited them for me: "What would you do if it is in the middle of a rush and it is time for you to go home? Would you stay or would you want to go home?" "If it gets extremely busy and you haven't had a break, would you get in a bad mood?" He added, "We have a lot of people who say, 'That is OK. If you're busy, and you need me to stay, I will stay.'" This usually means that the candidates who are youthful, financially stable, and maintain a positive attitude will be the most successful. Although these features are not necessarily associated with any particular ethnic group, some groups are thought to lack these attributes, especially American-born racial minorities (I will discuss this further in Chapter 6).

These criteria, in general, are in tremendous contrast to what we know about the traditional ethnic workplace, where legal and economic vulnerability, rather than youth, enthusiasm, and a promising future, are regarded as more suitable to the restaurant's needs. Flexibility and work time in fast food generally refer to the way time and skills are adjusted to the organization's needs, not the way the organization adapts to suit the home and family lives of its employees, as is true of the traditional ethnic restaurant. Unlike immigrants such as Tina's husband, Paul, who work in the enclave's traditional sector, fast food employees are unlikely to forge long-term relationships with their coworkers. They are employed on a temporary and part-time basis and their schedules are constantly changing; this means that they do not necessarily work with the same people every day. In this way, fast food employees do not have the same opportunity to incorporate their work with their family and community lives while on the job.[10]

The fast food restaurant, then, may accommodate local culture, but on different terms, these according to market goals rather than community principles. Fast food employers in Chinatown, for example, may accommodate their Chinese workers' strict adherence to school and family life, but only as far as their cultural heritage is of value to the restaurant (as in the case of fulfilling particular language needs) and when these same features can be turned around and treated as organizational assets. Strict adherence to school and family life also imply hard working, committed, and diligent employees.

Family and ethnic traditions are not necessarily accommodated within the workplace, at least not on employees' terms. Employers, for instance, may organize such activities as "United Nation's potlucks" for staff during slow hours to promote organizational unity; they are less likely to provide employees their own space for celebrating a religious holiday or bringing their children to work. Family values are organized around market goals. Rather than allowing children to accompany their mothers to work, the restaurant provides a "child-friendly" ambiance to attract children and families as customers. Rather than honoring employees' ethnic traditions, employers reconstruct tradition as part of its marketing strategies in the form of décor, in menu choices, and in language.

Pop-o-matic Grills and Redefining Skill: Technologies and Divisions of Labor

To learn to work the grill, it takes about fifteen minutes. We used to cook on the grills, turning the meat, seasoning. . . . Now, we have "pop-o-matic" grills. You put the meat on, close the grill, and it opens in thirty-nine seconds. So everything is standardized. This job is a lot easier when it comes to a technical standpoint.

—Fast food manager from the Dominican Republic
working in Little Dominican Republic

Tina works on the frontline at the Chinatown McDonald's, where she operates a high-tech computerized cash register while taking orders in her native Mandarin from Chinese customers. When the register transmits the orders to Spanish-speaking workers preparing food in the back, the computer translates the orders into universal "techno" symbols and displays them on a monitor. The computerized cash register, then, enables Tina to work effectively alongside people who speak different languages. Fast food technology in this way contributes to the globalization of fast food workers. In contrast, a traditional ethnic restaurant normally uses the most basic technology—a cash register, a

81

bilingual menu, perhaps a credit card machine—and workers and managers speak the same language.

According to many managers I spoke with, technology in the fast food restaurant constantly changes and improves. Though technology has altered aspects of fast food work, this innovation is not necessarily a simple rationalizing process where workers lose jobs, tasks are simplified, and skills decline, as George Ritzer[1] describes it, or as Braverman[2] envisioned nearly thirty years ago. Rather, work in many restaurants in New York has been redefined and reshaped as different skills and social divisions have emerged.

Most important, fast food technology that speeds food preparation has resulted in more management emphasis on frontline service and has even created more jobs, including dining room hosts and neighborhood marketers. Job requirements for fast food workers now stress personal and subjective qualities even though the first step in finding a job still depends on social contacts. Flexibility, a good attitude, a neat appearance, and a bright personality are now more important than technical skills or work experience in many fast food restaurants.[3] In the immigrant neighborhood, as I discussed in Chapter 2, cultural capital—such as speaking the language of local targeted customers—is important.

Most of my respondents (79 percent) shared the same ethnic heritage of at least some of the targeted market. Eighty percent claimed to possess at least one personal attribute that was valuable to a customer-oriented workplace: a drive to do well, friendliness, attractiveness, and so forth. Only one respondent claimed that technical skills and experience had helped him get his job.[4] This shift away from technical knowledge has contributed to the feminization of frontline work, where Tina and female immigrants like her are credited with the interactive skills, personality, looks, and "sweet temperament" thought necessary to attract and best serve customers.

The increased emphasis on serving customers in the fast food restaurant can be partly explained by technological advances that have reshaped the relationship between service and food preparation. Fast food work is divided between what Robin Liedner calls "interactive service work" and food preparation. This distinction, according to social researchers who have examined fast food labor, is spatial and it divides the front and the back of the restaurant.[5] The front includes the service counter and dining room, where restaurant staff interact with customers; the back corresponds to the kitchen, where the food is prepared.

McDonald's and Burger King list about thirty items on the menu. There are generally between three and seven different back stations, each involving between one and six dishes. Back stations at Burger King, for instance, may include steamer/boiler, fries/onion rings, specialty, and sandwich prep. The sandwich prep station handles six kinds of sandwiches, each requiring different ingredients and designs. Maintaining a clean, well-stocked, and well-ordered station is part of a station assignment. Aside from the stations, back employees are responsible for various auxiliary tasks such as cleaning utensils; keeping the kitchen stocked with food and amenities; heavy work, such as unloading stock from trucks; and "breaking down" equipment during closing hours. Front stations usually handle beverages, counter service, dining room, and, in some restaurants, drive-through.

Grilling, "Swirling," and "Chuting": Technology and Preparing Food

The automation of preparing food redefines what cooks do and shifts on-site managers' emphasis from the back of the restaurant to the front. The most advanced french fry technology (the Arch Fry system developed by McDonald's) is a good example of the way automation has redefined the work employees do when preparing food. An employee simply puts the frozen fries in a basket-like container. Fries are automatically drawn from this container and slowly lowered into hot oil to fry at a steady rate. The fries are then automatically raised up out of the oil, dumped into a fry chute (a bin), and packaged. Working the grill at McDonald's has also been automated in some restaurants as the quote at the beginning of this chapter illustrates. Rather than grilling a burger manually (as is still done in traditional diners), an employee simply puts the burger into the "pop-o-matic" grill, which seasons it, grills both sides, and indicates when it is done.

The Burger King hamburger broiler is another good example of how labor has changed along with technology. Burgers are placed on a conveyer belt that transports them at a preset speed beneath the broiler and out at the other end, fully broiled. Deep-frying (of fish fillets and chicken nuggets) is simplified with computerized timers that buzz when the food is cooked. Braverman, in *Labor and Monopoly Capital,* cited a *New York Times* article a quarter of a century ago about a woman who applied for a job with the Stouffer's chain and was told that they didn't need any cooks, only "thawer-outers."[6] A common assumption in the labor studies field is that technology contributes to workers' losing their jobs,[7] but this is not the case in many American fast food restaurants; rather, the numerous tasks required of employees often have a different dynamic.

When it comes to preparing food, we must consider that the simplification of tasks caused by automation does not necessarily eliminate human labor; rather, it alters it. McDonald's and Burger King increases the speed and volume of production and sales while reconfiguring what workers do without displacing them. In the fast food restaurant, automation usually reduces steps in a station assignment. For example, working the grill (or broiler) is only part of step one in preparing a bacon double cheeseburger at Burger King. There are fifteen more. When I worked at Burger King, I put together the numerous ingredients in a precise order. These are the sixteen steps in preparing a bacon double cheeseburger at a Burger King:

1. Take burgers and bun out of storage bags and run through broiler.
2. Assemble the burgers and bun and put them in the steamer.
3. From above the counter, pull out the double cheeseburger wrapper and lay it flat on the counter. (Each item on the menu has its own wrapper.)
4. Pick a bun with two burgers inside from the steamer—called a "double."
5. Place the double on the wrapper—in the middle where the wrapper indicates.
6. Take the top bun off and place it top side down on the counter.
7. Place a slice of cheese between both burgers.
8. Place a slice of cheese on top of the two burgers.
9. Arrange three pieces of bacon horizontally on top of the cheese.
10. Put the top bun back on top.

11. Mark the sandwich wrapper with a crayon marker if the customer has requested something special (i.e., extra cheese, ketchup, etc.)
12. Mark the expiration time of the sandwich on the wrapper with a crayon.
13. Put the sandwich in the microwave and push the appropriate button for the number of sandwiches in there.
14. When the microwave timer indicates the sandwich is done (it will beep), take the sandwich out of the microwave.
15. "Chute it"—put it in the appropriate rack that slides the sandwich to the frontline.
16. Erase the order from the computer screen by pressing the appropriate keys under the screen.

My main point is that automating some steps does not necessarily reduce, or even simplify, work. Rather, it enables a worker to produce more meals in a given amount of time and/or perform other tasks in the restaurant simultaneously.

It takes nearly the same amount of time for an experienced crewmember to make one hamburger or two hamburgers. He is considered increasingly productive the more burgers he makes at the same time. And he is considered increasingly valuable the more menu items he is able to prepare. It may take two minutes to make one hamburger. In one minute, the beef patty is being automatically broiled and the bun is being automatically warmed. If the restaurant is receiving a constant flow of customers, beef patties are usually broiled at a constant pace—not according to customers' orders. The crewmember then assembles the hamburger by first placing the bottom part of the bun on the appropriate (hamburger) wrapper. Next, the crewmember sets the burger on the part of the bun that is on the wrapper. Then he picks up a plastic squeeze bottle and swirls ketchup on the patty; next, he picks up another squeeze bottle and swirls mustard on the patty. (He may be reprimanded, as I was a few times, if a manager catches the crewmember "blobbing" instead of "swirling" the ketchup or mustard.) He then picks up a slice of pickle and plops it on the center of the patty. Finally, the crewmember positions the top part of the bun on top and wraps the paper packaging around the hamburger in the required way.

It may take fifteen seconds longer to make another hamburger at the same time. Or it may take twenty-five seconds longer to make two more hamburgers at the same time, or twenty seconds longer to make three more hamburgers at the same time. It takes less and less time for each additional hamburger. In total, it may take two minutes to make one hamburger and two minutes and thirty seconds to make four hamburgers. The reason for this is that each new step—such as putting the beef patties in the broiler, picking up the ketchup container, then picking up the mustard container—when compared with the actual making and packaging of the burgers takes a smaller proportion of time in the overall process with increasing numbers of hamburgers. Thus, one aim behind simplifying each task is enabling employees to produce more burgers in the same amount of time and still be interchangeable.

Increased production is dependent upon increased demand for products. In a factory, food dishes are mass-produced in standardized fashion. In a fast food restaurant, the volume, content, and timing of production fluctuates depending upon how many customers come into the restaurant and the choices they make from the menu. Company policy requires that products be made only upon demand to ensure the freshest quality. This policy says that products must be sold within a certain number of minutes after being made; if they aren't, they must be thrown away. To avoid waste, food is produced only according to immediate demand. During busy times, managers request continuous production, which means that workers pre-prepare certain amounts of every item.

Increased demand for certain items is a result of restaurant marketing, the diversification and often localization of menu choices, the time of day, and better customer service. Thus, changes in preparing food are related to marketing strategies—a campaign to promote ninety-nine-cent menu items, for example—as well as shifts on the frontline that enhance customer service relations.

May I Take Your Order?— Technologies, Culture, and Frontline Work

Jobs in the front of the fast food restaurant typically consist of two stations: serving customers at the register and staffing the dining room.

PHOTOGRAPH 5.1   The Fast Food Counter. (Photo courtesy of Samantha Rosemellia, reprinted with permission)

(The drive-through is not a typical feature of fast food restaurants in New York City.) Customer service employees perform light physical work such as handling food, filling beverages, and operating a register;[8] more important, though, they are the liaison between the customers and the back crewmembers when orders are passed on.

The computerized register, increasingly found in fast food restaurants, is one of the most important technological developments in the fast food restaurant since its widespread use in the early 1990s (see Photograph 5.1). It has significantly affected jobs in two major ways—it places a greater emphasis on customer interaction rather than technical skills and alters the way crewmembers communicate between the front and the back of the restaurant. Because the computerized register does not require counting or calculations, cashiers spend more time exchanging pleasantries with customers and less time handling money. Jose, the general manager from the Dominican Republic and who has nine years of fast food experience, discussed some of the implications of the frontline:

> At one time when I first started [in the mid 1980s] they used to give you a math test. They discontinued that after a while. . . . I had to take a math test. The excuse was in case we need you on the register, we need to know

that you know how to count. But it [the new register] tells you everything, the change and all. You don't have to be like, "Oh, he gave me $10, how much do I have to give back?" It tells you how much to give back.

The new register consists of a key for each choice on the menu, usually identified with the item's initials, and often color coded according to type. Keys for drinks, for instance, may be blue. Burgers may be red. The register automatically computes the price of the order and the change owed to the customer when the cashier enters the amount of money given to her by the customer.

Two counter-service systems are prevalent in New York City McDonald's and Burger King restaurants: the multi-convention system, used only at Burger King, and the hospitality system, used at all McDonald's and some Burger King restaurants. The kind of system affects divisions of labor at the service counter, the kind of work each counter employee performs, and the extent to which counter employees communicate with customers. The multi-convention system is similar to the cafeteria model. The counter is divided into two areas: One half houses cash registers, usually only two, and the other half is where customers pick up their orders. Customers form one line, place their orders at the next available register, receive their receipts, then move along the counter to pick up their orders; meanwhile, counter service employees gather the orders from the "chute" and prepare beverages from soda dispensers and coffee and hot water urns located either directly behind them or on the side of the service counter. They then place the entire order on a tray and hand it to the customer. In some Burger King restaurants, the soda dispensers and coffee and hot water urns are located in the lobby. In these restaurants, counter service employees give customers the appropriate beverage cups so that customers can serve themselves.

The hospitality system consists of a line of registers covering the service counter. Customers line up in front of each register rather than forming a line. The main difference between the multi-convention and hospitality systems is that the former ensures a division of labor at the counter between cashiers and those who service the food orders; with the latter, there is only one position: a cashier who takes and services the food orders. The hospitality system got its name because it allows each cashier to spend more time with customers.

Old technology, which still exists in some New York City restaurants, uses an audio system where cashiers announce food orders through a microphone to the back area, or even face to face. This system demands that front and back workers speak the same language. Julia, the Puerto Rican manager in Chinatown, explained the importance of a common language in the Burger King restaurant that still uses old technology:

> Because when you are in the kitchen they ask you not to speak because you have to hear the customers' orders on the mike. If you are talking to one another you might miss an order. In the other store you could do whatever you want because we had a screen. You could just read it. You would just erase it when you made a sandwich. But this one you have to use a microphone so you really don't want people talking in the back.

The back employees, then, must always be not only attentive to the cashiers but also quiet so that they can hear the orders. Further, all employees need to speak a common language, which makes English a requirement for workers in this restaurant.

The new system, while transmitting the orders to computer screens at the back of the restaurant, has diminished the need for a common language between front and back workers. The language of ethnicity has been replaced by the language of technology. With the computerized register, back workers are free to socialize with coworkers or to work elsewhere in the restaurant, perhaps unload stock from trucks or help out at a less experienced coworker's station. They need only keep an eye on the computer screen. Whereas the old audio system requires a back employee to receive an order at the same time it is given, the new system provides more flexibility with time because the order stays on the computer monitor until it is no longer needed. A back worker can safely take a few moments to go to the basement to retrieve a box of frozen french fries without missing an order.

The new system also provides more flexibility in social interaction in the back because one does not have to be attentive to the frontline. This is why, for example, Charles, the Chinatown McDonald's general manager, said that "Spanish people can sing in McDonald's." There, Tina can take an order from a Mandarin-speaking customer who specifies no cheese on a Big Mac. Tina can then communicate this order to Ricardo, a Spanish-speaking Dominican who is singing in harmony with Gregorio, a Honduran, in the back. Since computer screens are positioned in several places in the food prep area, Ricardo can receive the order at Gregorio's work station, then quickly return and fill the order and never miss a beat.

Communication and technology, then, are interlinked. They influence divisions of labor based on cultural features. Technological and social shifts in the work performed bring together culturally and globally diverse groups of employees as much as the focus on service places greater emphasis on particular cultural standards, especially for frontline work.

Pretty Girls Who Attract the Customers: Gender and Technology

Technology influences a gender division as well. Like other low-wage interactive service jobs, the frontline in fast food is considered women's work. But this hasn't always been so. The fast food industry in the 1950s and 1960s was dominated by men. In his autobiography, Ray Kroc, who founded the McDonald's franchise system, describes employees of the very first McDonald's as "all men, dressed in spiffy white shirts and trousers and white paper hats."[9] John Love, who in the 1980s wrote the first comprehensive study of the McDonald's Corporation, believes that the key to the industry at that time (before 1960) was the "all male crew."[10] Robin Leidner points out that Kroc initially decided not to hire young women to work behind the McDonald's counter because, he claimed, "They attracted the wrong kind of boys."[11]

Since the 1970s, more and more women have taken fast food jobs, and their increased numbers have paralleled the adoption of advanced technology, the subsequent emphasis on service, and the social and monetary devaluation of fast food jobs. (Since the early 1970s, the buying power of minimum wage—the wage for entry-level fast food jobs—has fallen by close to 50 percent.)[12] Reflecting trends in the changing labor market at large, women tend to move into jobs perceived to require declining technical skills. Fewer skills, at least the perception of them, are invariably linked to declining wages, which, in turn, propel men out and into higher-paying jobs and leave vacancies for women to fill. The nontechnical social skills required for customer-service jobs are subsequently devalued because of their low wages and because women disproportionately occupy them.[13]

The growth of the fast food restaurant industry has paralleled the growing rate of women's participation in the paid labor market.[14] In 1940, slightly more than a quarter of all women in the United States worked outside the home. By 1998, more than 60 percent of all women worked outside the home. (This figure is higher—72 percent—among women who are parents of young children.)[15] The industry's growth can be viewed partly as a consequence of women's increasing participation in the labor force and the subsequent effect on consumer trends. Women (as well as men) have less time to cook at home when they hold jobs and pursue careers. This creates a greater demand for food service, and, especially, for convenience foods.[16] In turn, the industry takes advantage of a growing number of women willing to take low-wage jobs.[17] But the industry has also grown because we have become a culture of fast food influenced by the power of mass advertising, Hollywood movies, children's shows, and Happy Meals.

Technology plays a role in reinforcing the gender division of labor, which is based on gender and job standards, within the restaurant organization.[18] The greater emphasis on customer service and social skills created by advancing technology has helped to feminize frontline jobs. In fast food restaurants today, women, by socialization or by "nature," are considered better able to meet the various subjective standards that management demands. Women, no matter what country they are from, are thought to be enthusiastic, patient, and attuned to the needs of customers. Some managers describe them as "more meticulous" and "better speakers." Women are also considered harder workers either because they are in greater financial need, or, as one manager said, "So many women feel like they have to prove something and they just tend to be awesome because of it."

Women are also thought to be a more attractive force in the restaurant. According to one manager, consumer surveys have revealed that most customers would rather be served by a woman than a man: "A woman would rather be served by a woman, a little more intimacy they feel, more bonding, they feel more relaxed. And a man would rather have a woman serve him for obvious reasons, that it is a pretty face and they are happy." It could also be because it makes them feel as though they are at home. There is also a tendency to sexualize the position in some restaurants. "Pretty girls who attract the customers" are hired, said a Burger King employee. (This is quite a contrast to Kroc's idea that girls attract "the wrong kind of boys.") Attractiveness is invariably equated with youth and femininity. One employee said that "the girl who is not very pretty" works in the back rather than the front. A manager claimed that women over twenty-five are considered "old maids" in the industry and are usually relegated to the kitchen and dining room. This prejudice applied to me because I was twenty-six when I went to work at Burger King. Even though a general manager, in an unenthusiastic and painful-to-hear tone, once told me that I "seem to be presentable enough to be a cashier," I always remained in the back preparing food. I well remember the deflated self-image I always had when I went from my graduate school classes, where I felt quite youthful (I was a relatively young graduate student, after all!), to the social world of the fast food restaurant, where I felt as if I had already climbed into middle age.

While valuable to the organization, these same feminized features tend to be devalued by employees, especially male employees, which helps reinforce a gender division between the frontline and the back. Men often resist performing jobs in the front, a resistance that seems to be embedded in a perception of the food service cashier as not only a job for a woman but a job for the less technically skilled. As one manager commented:

> In Burger King and McDonald's restaurants you see that the women are front counter and the guys are in the kitchen. All the stores I have dealt with have tried to put guys on the front counter. But they are not out to do that. They are not motivated to stay in it. They say, "I don't want to be a front cashier. It is a girl's job." It's a women's thing. "Hi, may I take your order please?" It's a women's thing. Where that came from? I don't know.

The male perception of "front-work" is partly built on traditional conceptions of what constitutes so-called real work when real work is equated with technological skill, knowledge, or strength. According to one male employee, "Sometimes I might go in the front now and then but I don't really like the front. I hate pressing buttons all the damn time. I want to *do* something." This attitude is reinforced through the devaluation of the skills that front work entails. The general attitude among male employees is that the cashier position is not "real work," that it is "easier," and that the personal qualities valued for the cashier position are, for the most part, superficial. One employee captured a common sentiment. "Half the girls don't even know what the hell comes on a cheeseburger. Because the girls, especially if they look cute, don't let them look gorgeous, the first day they come in and work here, they be in the kitchen for about five minutes and they'll be working cash register for the rest of their lives. With the guys it is different."

Other male employees elaborated. As one said, "Cashiers think that all they have to do is stand there and look pretty while the rest of us work." Another added,

> It is like this. Mostly I guess because girls are more friendly when it comes to doing things; like the majority of guys, when they see a cute little girl in here they are going to come in here, especially if they are hungry. It is going to be the first place they stop. They see someone really nice—I want her to take my order. Plus they can have a little conversation when they are waiting for their food. And the company knows that so they keep all the girls [who are pretty] in the front.

Men play a role in excluding women from certain work required in the back, particularly from jobs that are perceived to be more technical, dangerous, or that require physical strength. Generally, women don't perform heavy work such as unloading trucks, lifting stock, taking out the garbage, and breaking down (taking apart to clean) equipment. Men don't want women to do it and women tend to accept this because it is considered some of the most undesirable work in the restaurant. One manager said, "Usually we like to have men in the grill area because if we need a box of fries that is thirty-nine pounds, it is hard to tell a woman, 'Go over there and get me a box of fries.'" Or, as a male crewmember said, "I wouldn't want a woman helping me with the equipment. They wouldn't know what to do."[19] So on the one hand, men devalue the work that women do on the frontline; it isn't "real" work, they say. On the other hand, women's feminine status is devalued if they do "men's" work in the back; they are considered "old maids" or "not pretty."

The influence of technology on the gendering of work is not uniform but mediated by other factors, including the kind of customers the restaurant targets, features of the neighborhood, and the time of day. Several managers who worked in neighborhoods that are considered "shady" or "dangerous" claimed that they preferred men to work on the frontline at night because that was when rougher customers patronized the restaurants. As one female manager said,

> Working at night, because it is more rough—you have the rough crowd coming in. So you have to be a little more rougher than you usually are. Men are usually just rough all together in the day or the night. That is the difference that I see. In the morning time when we work, we could be jolly and act all crazy. Because then we have all families and kids [as customers] so we don't have any problems. But when it comes to the nighttime, you have to change your attitude.

Women often refuse to work at night for safety reasons, and Tina is a good example. When I asked her whether she ever worked at night, she talked about living too far away and her fear of different people. "No, because I am far away in Chinatown [Flushing]. Sometimes my friend tells me that in New York City there is a lot of different skin [colors] and languages who comes here and it is not safe. My husband also does not want me to work at night. Then I would have to worry."

During night hours, then, the gendered value of frontline service roles is often reversed. The "masculine" qualities of men, such as greater physical size, strength, and aggressiveness, become assets for frontline work because the men who possess these assets can better control rough customers. But this does not mean that men always replace women in managers' and frontline jobs at night in dangerous neighborhoods. Women often adapt by changing "attitude" and taking on what are considered masculine features, such as aggressiveness. In this way, women are considered more emotionally flexible than men. They are perceived as able to adapt to changing demands at the restaurant.

The influence of technology on the gendering of work is also mediated by cultural characteristics. Restaurant work, in general, is gendered work for some immigrant groups. For example, according to an Antiguan manager, Antiguan men do not typically work in restaurants; rather, Antiguan male immigrants are concentrated in the construction trades. For this reason, most Antiguan fast food workers in New York are women. And according to a manager from India, South Asian women do not traditionally work in occupations that require the handling of food. Therefore, most South Asian fast food workers are men, and in restaurants that are dominated by a South Asian workforce, frontline workers are also usually men. Although it is likely that transnational cultural influences on gender roles in the fast food workplace in New York will eventually break down, it is less likely that the gender division in the fast food restaurant will change. Traditional gender roles are reproduced in New York City's fast food restaurants and fast food technology helps reinforce them.

As in the traditional ethnic restaurants, gender helps to construct ethnically based jobs and divisions of labor. Tina, for instance, and people like her, join a cadre of immigrant women moving into the New York City labor market, helping to feminize certain kinds of low-wage work. Yet, Tina stands out from those women in traditional ethnic enterprises because she and those like her are not valued simply for their vulnerable and co-ethnic status but for their ability to affect marketing strategies with their personal, cultural, and feminine attributes. As I discuss in Chapter 6, the value of such attributes influences the ways a workforce is managed and controlled.

6

It's Hard to Get These Kids to Smile: Managing the Fast Food Personality

Two years ago, the riots in Washington Heights, the next day, and for the next week to two, you got tons of police officers all over the place. And then, after the whole drama is over, you tell these kids to smile at their customers. . . . So, like I told my supervisor, I have to be careful how far to push because I want to be as real as possible. It is rough at times but at McDonaldland you just don't give up. You try and try and try again.

—Dominican manager working in
Little Dominican Republic (1994)

In the world of the small entrepreneur, men sold goods to one another; in the new society of employees, they first of all sell their services. The employer of manual services buys the workers' labor, energy, and skill; the employer of many white-collar services, especially salesmanship, also buys the employees' social personalities.

—C. Wright Mills (1953)

On the fast food frontline, Tina is constantly encouraged by her managers to smile and maintain an air of friendliness, a part of her job that she takes very seriously. As Tina explained, "The first time I did the work, they said 'smile, be polite.' If some customers are impolite or not kind, we have to smile to everyone." The importance of personality in service work is nothing new and has been written about for over half a century, beginning (in the American context) with sociologist C. Wright Mills.[1] But when Mills wrote about an arising "personality market" in the 1950s, he was referring to a new breed of white-collar workers in an era that was occupied with constructing the American Dream. Presumably, he was not thinking about the way the "personality market" would shape the minds, occupations, and goals of new immigrants half a century later. Mills wrote, "For in the great shift from manual skills to the art of 'handling,' selling, and servicing people, personal or even intimate traits of the employee are drawn into the sphere of exchange and become of commercial relevance, become commodities in the labor market."[2] Mills was concerned with the rise of "anonymous urban markets" in the face of a declining proportion of small independent merchants, where more people were in this position.[3]

The commodity of personal traits today is intertwined with how corporations target new cultural markets and how the "sale of ethnicity" can advance profits. Corporations are creating new roles for workers in the immigrant neighborhood and drawing more people into the personality market. Focusing on my interviews with managers, this chapter examines how managers enforce "service with a smile."

Mills said that "mass production standardizes the merchandise to be sold; mass distribution standardizes the prices at which it is to be sold. But the consumers are not yet altogether standardized. There must be a link between mass production and individual consumption."[4] This link—between corporate America and the consumer market targeting new immigrant groups—is where the immigrant fast food worker and the immigrant entrepreneur play the biggest roles; indeed, they become cultural middlemen. Because the immigrant employment literature has not focused on such consumer service industries, it has neglected to consider the role of personality in shaping employment relations.

With a shift in fast food from emphasis on preparing a customer's order in the back to serving the customer in the restaurant's front area, the greatest concern today is how to control, define, and measure service. Considerable effort has been put into grasping the abstract nature

of service. In general, a distinction is made between the physical product (the hamburger and fries) and "human relationships" (the pretty
young women who flashes a friendly smile as she hands the hamburger
and fries to the customer) as products. An article in the *Journal of Marketing* suggests that the service encounter is frequently the service from
the customer's point of view.[5] Similarly, in a fast food company memo,
distinctions are made between the physical product that is bought and
sold and the intangible value derived from the physical product:

> You don't buy circus tickets, you buy thrills.
> You don't buy the paper, you buy the news.
> You don't buy glasses, you buy vision.
> You don't buy dinner, you buy sales and service.[6]

The industry's main goal has become service enhancement—frontline behavior that makes customers glad they're at the restaurant.
Frontline employees, in their presentation of self, help shape and even
constitute the abstract service that is bought and sold. "We have to sell
the personalities, the courtesy, and the respect," one manager noted.

The role of the fast food frontline worker, according to managers I
spoke to, requires astute emotional awareness about the customer and
an ability to know when to express deference or other emotional behavior. Employees are expected to be responsive to customers' questions
and concerns, apologetic about grievances, appreciative of compli-
ments about the company, silent or tactful in the face of personal insults, and skillful at elevating the general mood of their customers.
They are supposed to involve themselves emotionally, to report to work
in a good mood, and to maintain that mood throughout the working
shift. They must also look good, be well groomed, and wear clean,
pressed uniforms.

These demands are not new to the service industry, as we have
learned from Mills:

> They sell by the week or month their smiles and kindly gestures, and
> they must practice the prompt repression of resentment and aggression
> . . . traits as courtesy, helpfulness, and kindness, once intimate, are now
> part of the impersonal means of livelihood. . . . For these intimate traits

are of commercial relevance and required for the more efficient and profitable distribution of goods and services.[7]

What are particular to the modern fast food restaurant, perhaps, are the *ways* in which the service role is defined and managed and the intensity of its application. As Arlie Hochschild found in the airline industry, service is a crucial product of the top American corporate service organizations because it shapes consumers' expectations through mass media advertising, and, in turn, employees' understanding (this includes flight attendants) of these expectations and their responses to them.[8] In fast food, economies of scale, as well as greater efficiency and better communication, enable the restaurant to cater to local customers and pay as much, maybe more, attention to the frontline as it does to production; this, in turn, affects job requirements.

The role of the host at one fast food place I visited is a good example of the ways in which fast food managers equate service with profits. At this restaurant, hosts are part of a Customer Care program designed to increase sales and solicit customers' comments. The host's looks, neatness, and attitude are such crucial aspects of service that they are explained in detail. An "acceptable appearance," for example, is defined as *"wears a proper uniform and latest promo and conducts him/herself professionally."* An "outstanding appearance" includes *"customizes crew room, front counter, store ambiance. Conducts him/herself professionally."* An "acceptable creative personality" is defined as *"Pleasant, smiles often, professional conduct."* An "outstanding creative personality" refers to *"Positive attitude, smiles are a way of life, bubbly, walking, talking, interacting professionally."*[9]

In the immigrant neighborhood, ethnicity helps shape service. As I discussed in Chapter 2, ethnicity is often sold as part of the restaurant's service and expressed on the frontline as a foreign language or ethnic appearance, features designed to unite corporate and authentic cultures over a friendly meal. But cultural stereotypes about immigrants that concern looks and personality must be modified according to the needs of the restaurant. The economic circumstances and burdened schedules of many immigrant employees, coupled with the stigma attached to fast food work, add to the problem of how to manage and control employees' personalities.

George Ritzer in *The McDonaldization of Society* assumes that workers' personalities are automatically controlled through formal means, including management and standardized routines.[10] (Formal control refers to the way automation and technology structure a worker's duties.)[11] But in the restaurants I visited most of the measures managers used, whether individual or organizational, suggested that control over fast food employees is not set in stone. The corporate management philosophy is even designed to encourage local autonomy in managing the frontline personality. This autonomy makes such a study important. But the fast food restaurant, unlike the ethnic eatery, is not based purely on informal control. (Informal control refers to social and human techniques, for example, a manager standing over a worker to make sure the work gets done.) Rather, workplace control in the fast food restaurant combines both models, formal and informal.

The advanced technology and greater capital intensity of the fast food restaurant suggest that managers rely on formal as well as informal methods. In regard to formal control, for example, the computerized register in the fast food restaurant helps determine the amount of time cashiers spend with customers and the quality of the interaction. If cashiers need only punch one button for each hamburger or Coke and do not have to make calculations, their time with customers can be spent in friendly exchange, including eye-to-eye contact and "service with a smile"; also, because service is faster, more customers can be served in a given amount of time. But indirect, subtle, and informal forms of supervision are also important to an industry that places a premium on customer service.

Workers' emotions and expressions during the customer-service exchange are supposed to appear positive, natural, and organic. But fast food workers, according to managers, do not tend to express positive and appropriate emotions naturally when on the job, partly because of their cultural and/or socioeconomic backgrounds and living conditions, but also because they simply do not buy into the corporate ethos. Fast food employees would seem to have significantly less investment in their jobs (compared to other service workers, such as flight attendants) because of their low status, low wages, and the dead-end, temporary nature of the work. They are therefore unlikely to "deep act," the term Hochschild uses for the way flight attendants internalize the values and expectations of the company they work for. Rather, fast food employees may be more inclined to "surface act," Hochschild's term for when employees emit the expressions required of them but do not feel what they express.

According to Hochschild, flight attendants sometimes cross the boundary from surface acting to deep acting. In the process, they may not only lose a sense of their real selves as they express the emotions the corporation requires them to display but also experience a fusion between their real feelings and those they display on the job.[12] One of the key differences between the flight attendant and the fast food employee is their occupational and economic status, which affects the degree to which they identify with their jobs. Because fast food workers do not invest significantly in their jobs, they may not act at all. Sometimes they may display their true feelings even when they are inappropriate; for instance, they may talk back to a customer who has insulted them or express anger at work because their apartment was robbed the day before. Therefore, a significant part of a fast food supervisor's job is to elicit organizationally appropriate smiles, positive gestures, and expressive moods from workers, even when it means that employees must go against what they really feel or what is culturally appropriate in their own ethnic communities.

Why Is This Lady Smiling?—
Immigrant Culture and Frontline Demands

The "selling of self" in accordance with fast food organizational goals is far from automatic in the immigrant neighborhood. The culture of the corporate service organization is often perceived by managers to be at odds with various immigrant cultures as well as with the conditions of work and home life. Managers are constantly trying to accommodate the organization by working around the attitudes of various cultural groups.

Smiling and saying "please" when serving a customer, for instance, are not necessarily a normal part of every culture, according to fast food managers. Pedro, the Colombian manager working in Chinatown, said, "I notice a lot of people from other countries, they don't really practice the art of saying 'please' at the end of a sentence, or 'thank you' or 'can you please do this for me.'" Alison, the manager from Malaysia working in Chinatown, explained the awkwardness within the Chinese culture regarding fast food's expectations for expressions of friendliness:

> If you are smiling to them [Chinese customers], first of all they think what is it that you want since you are smiling? Every day you are smiling to them [customers] and he or she is trying to smile with you but the first time you are smiling at them they are so shocked. They [customers] are thinking, why is this lady smiling? I receive a lot of letters. One letter asked why are they [employees] smiling here?

Tina expanded with her thoughts on the differences between Chinese and American public behavior and the difference it makes when she works as a McDonald's hostess.

> I know there are differences in my country [China]. I saw that all people that walk in they are very polite. They always say "Hi" to you when you come in and "Bye bye" to you. If you help with something, they say "Thank you." In my country [China] it is not like this. I think this is a different culture. Sometimes they [the customers] spill their water and they don't know what to do next. I tell them, "Don't worry about anything. I can give you another one." Sometimes they have to wait [in line] for a long time, so I talk to the customers. I say, "How are you? What do you do? Where are you from? Where do you live?" and maybe they forget that they have to wait a long time. I think this is more polite than my country people. In my country, I always hear that in public they always argue, sometimes about little things. . . . Like in McDonald's, maybe I bump into you, I say "Sorry." But in my country, they argue.

As much as the behavior of the Chinese is thought to work against the organization's goals of outward expressiveness, the behavior of Latinos is perceived to match them. Latino employees are perceived as more expressive and flamboyant. Alison, from Malaysia, said, "The Chinese people just work. They are quiet. They just work, and go home and punch out. The Spanish people, they love to sing. They love to talk with the people. If they are quiet, you say what happened, what happened. They will do something and they are laughing, laughing, singing." Julia, the Puerto Rican manager in Chinatown, compared the Chinese and the Spanish as customers:

> The Chinese people in this neighborhood are cold. Like I will try to have a conversation with them but I'm not going to bend over backwards either. The Spanish people are like "Wow, did you see so and so on television last night?" They want to talk. The Chinese people are like, the food, the food. They just want to get out. They don't want to smile. They want their service and they want to get out.

Fast food managers, in general, were explicit about making distinctions between ethnic groups. But they often disagreed, especially about how these differences relate to frontline jobs. Regardless of their ethnic backgrounds, managers viewed the Chinese as more polite and patient, but less expressive. They viewed the Latino and black employees as less polite and patient, but more expressive. Managers often disagreed about how these qualities affected the organization. Julia, for instance, was convinced that her black and Latino employees on the frontline exhibited positive traits. She said,

> We have three girls here all from the same neighborhood. They are from Harlem. They are terrific. There is one particular girl, Kim. She'll say, "Hi, welcome to Burger King, may I take your order please?" Every single customer. And every time she gives the order she reads it back to them. She goes, "Thank you for eating at Burger King and have a nice day." People love her. They get such a kick out of it.

In contrast, she believes the Chinese employees, while generally polite, are outwardly friendly only with other Chinese customers.

> When the Chinese girls are dealing with Chinese customers they are very friendly and talkative. When they are dealing with English-speaking customers, they are not as friendly. They are like "What do you want?" "Anything else?" That is it. You are supposed to say, "Hi, welcome to Burger King. May I take your order? Would you like some fries with that? What kind of soda would you like? May I read your order back to make sure I got accuracy?" They are like, "Next, next, next, step down."

Pedro, the Colombian manager in Chinatown, held very different views on ethnic differences among employees and how they relate to front-line jobs:

> We have a lot of girls who have a chip on their shoulder . . . usually the Spanish and blacks. . . . The Chinese girls are usually the nicest ones. I think they are more fearful mainly. They treat people nice because they want to be treated nice. Some other girls (like the Hispanic) will talk back at the customer when the customer gets cross with them. They will fight back. But the Chinese will never do that. They are not like that.

Although frontline behavior is often assumed to be rooted in cultural and ethnic differences, it is also thought to be affected by immigrants' lifestyles, standards of living, and type of neighborhood where the restaurant is located. In Little Dominican Republic, where the majority of employees are among the working poor, managers say their employees often come to work depressed. "It is hard to get employees to smile and be enthusiastic," said one manager from the Dominican Republic. Workers are burdened with financial, social, and family-related problems that affect their emotional states. Miriam, a Cuban employee in Little Dominican Republic, is an extreme example of some of the problems fast food workers battle every day.

Miriam, an only child, came to New York City from Cuba in 1985 with her parents. Her father worked as a housekeeper at a Hilton Hotel until he was laid off in 1995; her mother was a nurse's aid until her death in 1993. Miriam had planned to become a medical doctor, but when her mother became sick, she quit high school and never returned. Now she is supporting herself and helping her father on her McDonald's wages. She is simply trying to survive. "My dream," she says, "I see it [is] so far now."

Miriam earns $107 per week (take-home pay) and can't get a second job because her schedule at McDonald's changes every week. As the only woman at home, she is responsible for most of the household duties and does not have time to hold a second job. Her boyfriend, who is from Bangladesh, lives with them part-time and works as a busboy in a Manhattan restaurant. When she has a day off, "It is worse than when I am working," she says. "It is the day to wash clothes and clean the house and everything, 'cause you know how it is being with the men. It is tough."

Her financial difficulties, along with her responsibilities at home and work, affect her emotional state and attitude in the restaurant. She is constantly tired, ill, and depressed; and as a poor Latina, she is triply burdened by class, gender, and culture. Managers judge her value to the organization by her emotional state and relegate her primarily to the kitchen, where she does not have to interact with customers. Because Miriam is not usually interchangeable with frontline workers and does not elevate the overall mood in the restaurant, she is unable to get stable hours or be promoted, which simply reinforces her circumstances.

Aside from their individual difficulties, fast food workers in Little Dominican Republic constantly deal with various aspects of street culture prevalent in the inner city, such as the dangers and temptations of the drug trade and the social stigma attached to low-wage work, especially fast food work. Managers find themselves dealing with problems and conflicts concerning neighborhood crime, violence, and peer pressure. "When you have a rough clientele, it is hard to get these kids to smile and greet these customers when sometimes they come in here like they want to chop your head off. It is rough sometimes," said Jose, one of the Dominican managers in this neighborhood. He elaborated on one situation.

> Two years ago, the riots in Washington Heights, the next day, and for the next week to two, you got tons of police officers all over the place. And then, after the whole drama is all over, you tell these kids to smile at their customers. It is hard because you know all your customers are not all bad. But unfortunately, they are bad customers. Like I told you before. We are in the business to make money. Sometimes, money obscures the fact that we may be pushing these kids too far in the sense that the reality is, there are some bad customers. So two weeks later when the riots are all over, some of these bad customers who were probably out there burning tires, looting, whatever, these kids had to serve them. So like I told my supervisor, I have to be careful how far to push because I want to be as real as possible. It is rough at times but at McDonaldland you just don't give up. You try and try and try again.

The Tasks of a Fast Food Manager

The tasks of fast food managers are threefold. First, fast food managers often seek reasons for employees to invest in the values of the organization. Second, they make sure that real feelings, when negative, are suppressed. Third, fast food managers constantly need to find ways to stimulate employees' moods throughout their work shifts by means unrelated to their roles in the fast food organization.

Proud to be Employee of the Month?
Investing in Organizational Goals

The shift from a mechanical to a humanistic management philosophy reflects managers' attempts to encourage feeling invested in the organization for reasons that are unrelated to better wages, benefits, and occupational status. A McDonald's billboard advertising job openings that reads "A job that pays in many ways" is a good indication of McDonald's attempt to emphasize nonmaterial job benefits (see Photograph 6.1). This shift is reflected in one restaurant in the way corporate-level management conducts periodic inspections (company evaluations that ensure restaurants are complying with standardized procedures and policies). As Julio, the Puerto Rican manager in downtown Brooklyn, explained:

> When I first started here [ten years ago], everything was very mechanical. Everything was about numbers. We had inspections here unannounced, twice per year. But I always noticed that when I was a crewmember, that he came and checked all the equipment. But he never asked any workers any questions. He never asked any of the customers any questions. He just looked at everything we did. I felt like they didn't really need workers, they needed robots, literally. Over the past three or four years, they have gotten away from checking all the times and temperatures. They will check to make sure the food is cooked, the meat is cooked. But in their check-ups now, they almost never check the equipment. They will look to make sure the restaurant is clean, that it is sanitary. But they deal mostly with the workers. They will just sit and they will let the workers speak, possibly have a meeting, possibly have a rap

PHOTOGRAPH 6.1   McDonald's Sign Enticing People to Apply for a Job.
(Photo courtesy of Atul Talwar, reprinted with permission)

session, and ask them, "When is the last time your manager spoke with you? When was your last pay increase? The last time anyone asked your opinion?" They will go in the lobby and speak to the customers. "Has anyone ever spoken to you? Any worker ever tried to make things personal among you and your service? Does anyone come in the lobby?" They have changed it completely. Before they had very rigid standards. You must have a customer do A,B,C, and D. Now they say, "Do what it takes to make the customer happy."

Pedro, with a decade of experience in Burger King, commented on different styles of management and Burger King's adoption of a new program called People at the Leading Edge:

Some of them [managers] are just quiet and they don't even talk to anybody. They don't really relate to the employees in any way. Others are like little Hitlers. They take rules with an iron fist. That is one of the main courses in Burger King called People at the Leading Edge. They teach you how to deal with employees and customers [in a positive way], which is the hardest part of the job. Learning how to do paperwork, equipment steps, that's what you did in high school anyway, that is easy. But to teach someone management skills . . . one of the things I read was the *One Minute Manager*. It is a tiny book, like made for a third grader. But it is actually used in all the . . . it is recommended by ATT and IBM. They give it to their managers to read. Big fat words and it just teaches people . . . like when you are going to scold someone, you are supposed to give them their good points and then tell them what they did wrong. You never wait more than a day. You tell them immediately. It is that type of thing. You don't hold it inside of yourself. It has to do a lot with stress management. But it is a very, very simple book.

Charles explained what he does every day:

> We are not doing things on the negative side. We are doing things on the positive side. We catch them doing something right instead, not just catch them doing something wrong. They be looking like a mouse and seeing you as a cat, running and everywhere. It is not efficient. It is not professional. And you are not getting a good result. . . . They are human beings. They are not machines. That is why the leadership we have learned is so many different styles.

Some restaurants have adopted storewide management systems that emphasize crew empowerment and teamwork. Crew empowerment calls for workers to enjoy "democratic" involvement in decisionmaking, to take an active role in restaurant practices, and to have autonomy in how they respond to customers. The idea is to involve crewmembers through decisionmaking on how to "better satisfy customers and increase sales," to inspire company loyalty by making crew members see the "importance of their own contribution," and to provide psychological tools to crew members that enable them to deal with customers according to company policy. Crew empowerment also helps diffuse top-down standardized control over work performance.[13] A letter to regional headquarters from one fast food restaurant describes the results of this strategy:

> Our crew persons are all empowered to handle most customer complaints other than money or refund situations. All crew persons know what to do when we have a concern with spills, coupons, grill orders, incorrect orders, or smokers . . . They are all informed during their

orientation of their one and only chance to impress the customer when there is a complaint.

Some fast food managers organize staff trips to amusement parks and encourage their employees to join company-sponsored sports leagues and become involved in community events. Others offer incentives based on a reward system. An example, used widely across retail industries in the United States, is to honor an employee's good work performance by displaying a worker's name and picture on an "Employee of the Month" plaque, which is hung on a wall in the dining room. Social functions encourage employees to be loyal to the company, especially when representing the restaurant on a sports team or at a community event; socializing also diffuses hierarchical relationships and the work's low status while encouraging employees to identify with the company.

Involving customers is another technique used to encourage a positive attitude and loyalty to the company. Customers may be encouraged to evaluate the service performance through customer contact cards or 1-800 phone lines. Hochschild discusses a similar strategy used by the airline industry in which passengers are asked to fill out customer satisfaction cards. These cards are used by managers to determine good and bad work performance among their employees.[14]

Restaurant managers who solicit customers' feedback often use their own methods. One restaurant, for example, asked customers to write letters about their visits and encounters with employees. Letters come from employees of schools, the police department, and Immigrant Social Services. They also come from individual customers, including CEOs, international tourists, and neighborhood residents. Of the letters collected by managers at one restaurant, virtually all referred to the service rather than the quality of the food. One letter enthusiastically stated that an employee "gave me such fine courteous door service in a Park Avenue manner." Others said the service was "speedy," "polite," "friendly," and "concerned about my problem." The following is one such letter from a customer:

I am writing to applaud the efforts of one of your employees. My six-year-old cousin and I came into your restaurant. A young girl assisted us at the register. She was very patient with my young cousin as she made her selection. I had just left the beauty parlor, and she took the time to tell me I had hair all over my face and to compliment me on my haircut. She was very cheerful and helpful. With the war between fast food restaurants becoming more fierce, quality service should be concentrated not only on your food products, but also on the customers you serve. This girl showed excellent customer service skills. She made the effort to be personable with the customers. As a frequent visitor of fast food restaurants, one becomes used to sullen-faced, rude cashiers. This girl was a refreshing surprise. I regret I did not take her name down so she could be identified easily. Please let her know her efforts were appreciated.

This letter is from a businessman:

I have visited your restaurant with my wife and kids. An employee helped us with our trays, drinks, and napkins up three flights of stairs. She did this without having been asked with a delightful smile and personality. I am a CEO of a large company, and realize customer service is paramount in being successful. This employee is a person who truly recognizes this and acts accordingly and has great attention to detail.

Leave Your Problems At Home: Dichotomizing Feelings

Despite the attempts to persuade workers to buy into the corporate ethos, managers concede that it rarely works and that they struggle daily with maintaining enthusiasm. One of their biggest concerns is with making sure that employees' real feelings, when negative, are suppressed. Managers constantly remind their employees to "leave your problems at home" or "report to work in a good mood." These statements imply a dichotomy of feelings. They require workers to "surface act," to make a conscious effort to suppress their real feelings (when contrary to the organization's goals) and adopt organizationally appropriate "feelings" on the job. The goal is to maintain a clear distinction between home and work while ensuring that home life does not interfere with a positive mood at work.

Individual managers may develop personal ties to workers to better control employees' emotional states during nonworking hours. Such personal ties are sometimes built upon common ethnic identities and revolve around bridging the cultural gap between home and work. The West Indian workers and managers in the McDonald's in downtown Brooklyn, for instance, live in the same neighborhood and hang around together when not working. Charles speaks all the dialects spoken by his Chinese employees and is known to help out in work-related matters; these have included translating between and among employees and customers and mediating between Chinese workers and their parents who are upset because their children have taken a job instead of concentrating fully on school. (Charles sometimes speaks to the parents of the Chinese employees and explains the inherent conflicts between the Chinese and American cultures, especially the American emphasis on establishing independence and working when still a teenager.) Tina explained how she thought Chinese parents felt when their children work in the United States:

> In China, a lot of students only study their course. Their parents don't want their kids to make money. In America I think it is different. Now in China every family only has one child. So they do not want to have that child have a job. So in China when I graduated my high school and took my television course, then I found a job. It is different in America. I see a lot of kids who come here [to McDonald's] I think they are only sixteen or fifteen.

Other managers do different things that result in developing personal ties with employees. Jose, in Little Dominican Republic, makes personal loans to employees, often in cooperation with the employee's family. Managers at the Burger King I worked at also gave out loans to employees that came out of their own pockets. Such a loan was called "an advance" and was for anything from subway tokens to utility or medical bills.

Fabiola, the other Dominican manager, gives out her home phone and beeper numbers so that she can manage employees' problems outside of work:

I usually give my crew my home phone number or my beeper number. Things like that. Or if they have a problem they can't come in tomorrow I like to be notified before I come in. Because if I can fix the problem at home it helps. So they become a little more closer. I try not to have just a crew-manager relationship. I try to go a little beyond. . . . I try to become your friend instead of looking at it as "Oh I am just a manager and that is it." It is kind of hard sometimes because I come in with a bad mood myself at times.

Within the workplace, negative reinforcement, or discipline, is sometimes used when workers fail to suppress their real feelings. Inappropriate behavior may include the expression of a real feeling or need, such as tiredness or hunger. Laurie, the assistant manager from Antigua explained:

Maybe sometimes they [employees] need a break and they can't get one. Because most of the time it is very busy. We know everybody is hungry but we have to take care of the customers so they can get fast, friendly service so that they could come back again. But they [employees] think of their stomach all the time. Sometimes they get us so mad. . . . We give breaks but they are like "I'M HUNGRY" right in front of the customers. That is not nice. Or, "It is time for me to leave." I don't like when they do that because I think that is disrespectful. When they do that to me, I let them close their lines, but then I let them sweep and mop and then I will find something else for them to do before they leave.

Laurie explained that some type of discipline is required when employees do not exercise deference with a disagreeable customer.

We take them to the back and talk to them and sometimes we give them a break and explain to them that the customer is always right, even though they are wrong, they are always right. The crew person doesn't seem to understand that. There are times when the customers are really . . . they get us really mad. If it happens to me, I call another manager because I don't want to curse the customer out. I prefer another manager to take care of that customer. Then I take a walk to the back and count from one to ten.

Just Mention the Word "Sex": Stimulating Smiles

Even when managers don't feel like smiling, they try to stimulate their employees and make them want to smile by whispering jokes in their ears or offering financial incentives for every "real" smile. These stimuli must be external to the job because of the lack of intrinsic value employees find in their work roles or because it is contradictory to their cultural backgrounds. Laurie, for instance, likes to whisper messages in employees' ears to make them laugh. "Well, like myself, they like to hear rude things. So I will go to their ears and tell them something about their boyfriends. That is the only way I get them to smile. Like I, myself, I don't smile. But as my boss tells my supervisor, just mention the word 'sex' and you will see that [she] smiles." Julia uses a more direct approach. "I'll go up in their faces and I go 'What is wrong?' They look at me like they don't know what I am doing. 'What is wrong with your face?' 'I am smiling. You don't know what it is like? You have to smile right?' In fact, I have gone to the point where I have written 'smile' on the registers. Right above the numbers, I wrote 'Remember to smile.'

Some restaurants hold games based on suggestive selling, providing incentives to smile and boost the mood in the restaurant. As Jose explained:

> To get these guys to smile, we have a contest. That is the only way they have fun, most of the time. A contest to see who collects the most customers or who makes the most money, and they will get a free meal. They will put their energy into that and they will smile for those few hours that the contest is on. Nine out of ten times when we have a contest they win a free meal. Or we used to have this program who sells the most extra-value meals—meaning the fries, the soda, the sandwich. At the end of the month, they get $50. But they have to have sold at least two hundred [value meals]. The contest runs like this: We start from 11:00 to 2:00. Who makes the most money. Who has the most customers.

Who has the [least] deletions—a customer orders something and changes their mind so you have to delete it.

Buying into "Burger King Land": Personality and Work Culture

One could say that managers have little influence in shaping or altering the real personalities of immigrants beyond the workplace. To suggest that workers' feelings and personalities are fused with the projected and marketed friendliness of the McDonald's company would be as shortsighted as believing Ritzer's theory that fast food workers are reduced to mere robots. The differences between flight attendants and fast food workers are professional and emotional. Flight attendants have a professional and, therefore, emotional investment in their jobs because their profession has a relatively high status, is long-term, usually pays decently, and offers union protections. These are career jobs. Most fast food workers do not have an investment in their jobs because they are low-status, temporary, and pay miserably.[15]

On the one hand, it would seem that the demands of performance, as Erving Goffman suggests, could be a basis for solidarity among performers (in this case, fast food employees).[16] What is asked of them is so superficial that it seems likely fast food workers will join together in mocking customers, managers, and the demands for smiling. In *Race Rebels,* Robin Kelly describes how African American workers in a fast food restaurant developed a unifying sub rosa culture of resistance that mostly went under the managers' radar.[17] When I worked at the Burger King in Brooklyn, I observed various activities undertaken behind the backs of managers that united workers in resisting their status as fast food workers and recognizing their common interests.

One of these was a "putting down" ritual that entailed cooking an oversupply of food near closing time so that workers could take the food home. (The policy was that employees could consume all food left over at night; otherwise, workers had to pay for their food.) This event took place even when employees had little interest in consuming the food. Satisfaction was derived from getting away with it. (I well remember eating chicken specialty sandwiches back home in front of my computer while typing my observation notes for the night. Somehow, they tasted good just because I had taken part in a prohibited ritual.) Workers would give away food to friends who came into the store posing as customers; they would also mock customers, and even managers, whom they thought had bought into "Burger King land." One manager worked so hard and displayed so much energy that the crewmembers made fun of him by spreading the idea that he was addicted to cocaine. "How else could he give so much energy to Burger King?" they joked.

Still, resistance culture is severely limited today, and it has little potential for achieving the kind of collective experience that can bring change or extend beyond the workplace for very long. Robin Kelly's example of a resistance culture among McDonald's workers in 1978, and what I experienced in 1981 when I was a teenager working at a McDonald's, stands apart from the restaurants I examined in the mid-1990s. First, emphasis on service interaction was not as intense as it is today, partly because technology has made such an emphasis possible and partly because of the corporate-engineered policies that have resulted from it. Technology, for example (and as I discussed in the previous chapter), has reshaped work in a technical sense and commanded greater control over what workers do, particularly when building an environment geared towards customers. The more decisive division of labor now found between the front and the back eliminates the need for face-to-face communication between frontline workers and those who prepare the food.

The pay of fast food work today only reinforces the limits of a unifying workplace culture. Kelly's McDonald's workers were "kids" and earned a much higher wage (the buying power of the minimum wage at that time was considerably higher than it is today) and at a time when long-term job and career prospects were more promising for working-class minorities, particularly in government sectors and in union-shop factories. Workers in the restaurants I examined in the 1990s were not all kids; some were adults, working two and three jobs, living from paycheck to paycheck. In the Burger King restaurant where I worked, not all people took part in the "fun" and "games," especially the older workers, nor did they work with the same people every day. In general, the structural terms of fast food work (including flexible work time, high employee turnover, network recruitment, the distancing of home and work, advanced technology, and multicultural market logic) help distinguish the fast food restaurants I examined from the monocultures of the traditional ethnic workplace and Kelly's McDonald's workers.

Tina and immigrants like her, we should assume, are in little danger of having their personalities co-opted by a mega-corporation such as McDonald's. But she is also unlikely to share with her coworkers the real and intimate feelings that transcend time and the workplace and enable collective action. (On the other hand, because more and more workers today, including immigrants, depend on minimum-wage jobs for full-time work, they could band together and demand full-time status.) In Chapter 7, I explore interactions among fast food employees, particularly those constructed around racial and ethnic divisions and conflicts.

7

Problems on the United Nations Team: Ethnic Conflicts and Interactions

Haitians. They are too lazy. They are very dirty. The Dominicans. They understand you. They are ready to understand you. But they don't want to do nothing. Antiguans. You see, we work in Antigua, we gotta make coals and go to the mines and you gotta go to the grounds and plant sweet potatoes so we are used to work. Work is nothing to us. We can work.

—McDonald's employee from Antigua working in
Little Dominican Republic

Tina works with people from all over the world. Her employers very proudly refer to their McDonald's workforce as a "United Nations team" representing China, Hong Kong, Taiwan, Russia, the Dominican Republic, Honduras, Togo, Africa, and various others. This McDonald's workforce, and particularly the frontline staff, framed by an array of national flags from around the world, seems to fit the multicultural and equitable ideal represented in mass media advertising. With the upbeat ambiance and the colorful sea of smiling faces behind the counter, who would think otherwise? But I found that interactions among fast food

119

employees are often full of conflict. Given the emphasis on inter-changeability, a changing work schedule, and managers' authority to delegate desirable and undesirable work, poor morale and strained relationships are bound to occur. In the restaurants I visited, these problems often arise from racial and ethnic conflicts.

Employees in the fast food restaurant industry in New York are primarily a workforce of color. The majority of immigrants are from the Third World and most American-born workers are members of racial minorities. The "marginalization of race," as Saskia Sassen asserts, is founded on the merging of Third World immigrants, American racial minorities, and women, all relegated to the bottom rungs of the restructuring labor market.[1] Even though many of today's immigrants have successfully moved into the professional and corporate-level ranks in American society, most have not. The vast overrepresentation of Third World immigrants from South America, Asia, and the Caribbean, working for as little as $1 per hour in the city's sweatshops or as flexible labor in minimum-wage sectors such as fast food, illustrates the ethnic and racial boundaries of marginality. It also points to the way race as a social construct has been diversified at the bottom rungs of the labor market, a place beyond the black-white dichotomy that defined the color line a century ago.[2]

Studies of immigrant employment have either focused on workplaces where workers are of same or similar ethnicity[3] or examined the ethnic stratification of occupations within or across industries.[4] Little of the contemporary immigrant employment literature has examined ethnic relations among immigrants within globally diverse workplaces, particularly in the consumer services. Less work has linked ethnic relations to the structural terms of the workplace.[5]

Although I discuss what workers say about each other in this chapter, I have focused primarily on managers' perceptions of ethnic workers and how they disparage or encourage discontent among them. The distinctions typically reflect larger cultural and societal perceptions, but they also reflect the social dynamics of the restaurant's workplace. These dynamics are important because they affect hiring preferences, work experiences, attitudes about employment, and mobility. The temporary nature of fast food employment means that managers constantly hire new workers, sometimes from the same ethnic groups, sometimes from new groups.

Managers and workers in my study were often forthright about the negative and positive traits of various groups and noted explicit cultural differences. Race as a category was often broken down and reconfigured by employers who confronted conflicts, differences, or solidarity between and within racial groups. Ethnic, cultural, class, and gender distinctions and perceptions occurred within and among racial groups. Managers and workers made cultural distinctions within racial categories, especially concerning Latino and Asian groups. They were most explicit about those of African descent, including African Americans, which helps to account for what one manager described as the "fizzling out" of American-born minorities from the low-wage workplace. Stephen Steinberg[6] has maintained that prejudice against American racial minorities is still pervasive today in spite of theories suggesting that class may supersede race as a focus of discrimination.[7] The fast food restaurant provides an example of the social processes that explain such views and how prejudice and discrimination against American racial minorities develops in a global workforce of color.

Chinese, Spanish, Blacks, and Whites: Perceptions of Racial Difference

In Chinatown, where workforces are both racially and ethnically diverse, managers were emphatic about racial differences, usually including the category of "Hispanic." Pedro, the manager from Colombia, had definite ideas about racial differences:

> The Asians are the hardest workers. The whites want better. They will not stay in this job. They always want better. They always strive for better jobs. The Spanish are content with just making their money. The blacks really just want to get it over with, make their money and go home. Their spending is more toward recreation, going out. A lot of the girls just want their money to do their hair, their nails. And get home. Go out for the weekend. It is really strange how the cultures change.

Alison, from Malaysia, was also explicit about racial differences in work ethics. She said there are "white, Spanish, and Chinese" employees working in the restaurant and then explained how these groups work:

The Chinese people just work. They are quiet. They just work, and go home and punch out. The Spanish people, they love to sing. They love to talk with the people. If they are quiet, you say what happened, what happened. They will do something and they are laughing, laughing, singing . . . and the white people . . . I don't know.

But in the restaurants I examined, distinctions made within racial categories were more pronounced than distinctions based on race. This is not necessarily because managers are not cognizant of racial categories; rather, it seemed that other factors intersected with racial distinctions and broke up broad racial categories. These included ethnicity, national origin, social class, and gender. How these factors mediated racial categories was determined by local custom.

In the McDonald's restaurant in Chinatown, where the staff is mostly Chinese, managers made ethnic and class distinctions between the Chinese workers according to the region they were from and the dialect they spoke. Managers referred to workers as Mandarin- or Cantonese-speaking, and the kind of Chinese who want to "go higher" than their parents versus those who don't care. Across the street at Burger King, where Chinese constitute only a handful of the staff, they were discussed as part of one category. Managers described "Chinese" or "Oriental" people as those who "stick together" regardless of their ethnicity, national origin, and life goals, and compared them to the "Spanish," "blacks," and whites.

In the most diverse restaurant in Little Dominican Republic, which has West Indian and Latino workers, managers made a distinction between "Hispanic" and "black." Jose, the general manager, who identified himself as a "black Hispanic," discussed a common sentiment among managers. He said that the importance of the distinction in the fast food organization is cultural. Hispanics speak Spanish and blacks (West Indians) do not speak Spanish. This distinction plays an important role in the divisions of labor and social relations in the restaurant, and it is reinforced by distinctions based on racial stereotypes made in the workplace and the neighborhood at large. Workers, and the community, reinforce conventional boundaries and stereotypes between the two groups, categorizing the West Indians as a racial and inferior "other" in a mainly Latino neighborhood. Language helps define this boundary. Brenda, the employee from Antigua working in Little Dominican Republic, said that she had never experienced racism before coming to New York. Now, as she walks to and from her home in the Bronx and work in Little Dominican Republic, she experiences prejudice and discrimination on the streets and in the stores and when people call her "nigger." As she explained:

> In Antigua, we didn't know nothing about racism. Soon as you come up here . . . I experience it when I walk into a store. And I go inside. I have my wallet in my pocket. A lady was standing in front of me and thought I had something else in my pocket. I said "Hello, this is just a wallet. It is just a wallet." Everybody was just looking at me, man. . . . I just walked out. It is just a wallet. One time a guy called me "nigger." I didn't even know what word is that. I go home and tell my mother what is a nigger and she told me. In Antigua, white, black, mixed, in schools we play together, go to the beach together, everything. As soon as I come up here I know about racism.

Brenda, like many West Indians in New York, plans to return to her home country. Her plans are influenced by her racial status and economic position in New York and reinforced by her workplace experiences.

Managers and workers also made distinctions within the broad categories of Hispanic and black in Little Dominican Republic. Distinctions within the category of "black" tended to depend on ethnicity and national origin. Distinctions within the Hispanic category, on the other hand, tended towards social class, age, and gender. In the fast food restaurants in Little Dominican Republic, there was little apparent tendency to make categorical distinctions between Latino and Spanish-speaking groups based on culture or national origin, perhaps because a shared language binds a pan-Latino (or Hispanic) identity in a corporate context. The circumstances of the Latino employees are different from those of the Chinese in Chinatown. Because Chinese fast food workers do not share a common spoken language, managers tend to distinguish between Chinese employees.

Such distinguishing, particularly by managers, may be organizationally necessary to meet frontline language requirements, including accommodating the language diversity among Chinese customers. Because Chinese workers in Chinatown do not share a common dialect, their way of dealing with language differences in the fast food restaurant may be different from that of the Latinos in Little Dominican Republic, particularly in the restaurants where Spanish is imperative for frontline work. Whereas the pan-Chinese workforce in Chinatown is required to learn English to communicate, a pan-Latino workforce in Little Dominican Republic speaks the same language of origin, further reinforcing a broad cultural category of "Hispanic," inclusive of numerous national groups. In Little Dominican Republic, Spanish is the dominant language of assimilation. Other immigrants, including West Indians and Chinese entrepreneurs, often learn Spanish to function in the neighborhood. This helps to reinforce the existence and persistence of Spanish-speaking fast food restaurants and a broadly construed Latino culture.

The generalizing of the term *Hispanic* by employees to include a range of national and regional groups means that age, gender, and class become more conscious bases for distinction within the category of Hispanic. The gendered division of labor between the front and the back of the restaurant seemed to be most pronounced in Little Dominican Republic, possibly because of pan-ethnic identification among Latinos where gender, rather than ethnic differences, becomes more pronounced. Or it could be because gender roles are taken more seriously in Latino culture. Managers also stress age in reference to the way youth is equated with attractiveness and therefore the marketing value of frontline service. Social class, although a less conscious category, is intertwined with managers' philosophies about who is an appropriate worker. "Children who are having children," "high school dropouts," and "street kids" are seen as a lower and unemployable class within the Latino population.

Distinctions between groups of African ancestry were the most explicit distinctions made by managers and workers in the restaurants I visited. Employees from the West Indies generally forge alliances in the fast food restaurant, evident in the McDonald's restaurant in downtown Brooklyn where they form a majority among crewmembers and managers. But employees from different islands in the West Indies are also in conflict with each other, but the conflict is more common in restaurants where West Indians are a minority, such as the restaurant in Little Dominican Republic that employs Antiguans and other West Indian immigrants. As the quote at the beginning of this chapter shows, Betty, an Antiguan employee working at the first McDonald's restaurant in Little Dominican Republic, complained about a coworker from Haiti while comparing him to other ethnic groups. She elaborated on the source of her grievance:

> They have this one Haitian guy. I can't stand him. He is too lazy. I gotta clean the grill when he sees he is supposed to clean it. Look at me! Burns. I am dying of burns from cleaning the grill! He doesn't want to clean so I gotta clean. I tell a manager and she just tell another manager. And then they [Haitians] quit. So when they [Haitians] quit, I gotta do it.

Cultural distinctions often arise in response to job duties. Since company policy requires everyone to perform all work tasks, conflict often occurs when groups or individuals break the rules or refuse to perform certain tasks. It is not surprising that cleaning the grill might create conflict; indeed, cleaning the grills and changing the oil vats are the most undesirable tasks in the fast food restaurant. Temperatures exceeding 400 degrees make these jobs extremely dangerous. Several of my respondents showed me scars from the burns they had suffered while performing these tasks. Conflicts arise in response to other responsibilities as well. For example, as I discussed in Chapter 4, Chinese employees often refuse to work late and they tend to be less flexible with their work schedules; non-Chinese employees are then expected to compensate by being more flexible. This often sets the stage for social and ethnic divisions and rivalries within the restaurant.

Conflict also arises among employees pursuing promotion. Workplace relations between West Indian and Latino employees are generally harmonious in the Little Dominican Republic restaurant, but conflicts are said to occur when a West Indian attempts to climb the job ladder. According to my West Indian respondents at this restaurant, it is difficult to become a manager because "the Hispanics make it tough for you." Betty, for example, was promoted to manager, but lasted for just a week because the Latino workers resisted her authority. As she said, "I couldn't take it . . . because these Spanish, they don't listen to me. So I just told the manager to put me back to crew trainer. Then they will listen to me." In this case, the Latino employees used language as a means for disengaging and building a boundary between them and Betty by speaking Spanish to each other when Betty gave them orders in English. Some of the Latino employees claimed to dislike another Antiguan woman who had been a manager for several years; their explanation was that she was "too strict." But, as this same Antiguan manager told me, "You have to be strict sometimes because as soon as you let your guard down they take advantage of the situation."

The most prevalent distinctions made by managers and workers between groups of African ancestry were between African Americans and West Indians. These distinctions occurred in all three neighborhoods. Managers in Chinatown, for instance, claimed that African Americans and foreign blacks behave differently. "They [foreign blacks] come here to work," said Pedro. "African Americans are different . . . there is a lot of arguing among them." West Indian workers tend to share this view. According to Pedro, the Jamaican employees at the Chinatown Burger King often report to the managers about how African Americans take advantage of the situation when managers are out of view by "just trying to get away with something." They would stop working to "take a rest, just to take a rest . . . not that they need a rest." A Jamaican employee said, "They [African Americans] give us a bad reputation." Brenda was explicit about African Americans' reluctance to work. When I asked her whether African Americans worked at her restaurant, she responded, "I don't think so. I haven't seen any. To me, they don't want to work. . . . I worked here with some when I first started and in the next few months they are out. They don't want to work. . . . Some of them are drug dealers, whatever they want. Some of them are in drugs. And I keep far from them."

African Americans, in general, do show various forms of resistance, according to managers. They not only stop production when managers are out of view but refuse to perform certain tasks. Some managers have also observed gender differences among African American workers. Pedro claimed, for example, that African American women refuse to clean the bathrooms. "When asked to check the bathrooms, they quit. Any other group, including African American men, don't refuse." He no longer asks African American women to clean the bathrooms, but this not only creates problems for managers committed to employee interchangeability but also stirs conflict among the workers who must compensate.

Resistance in the workplace may be a product of ethnic tensions rather than a cause of them. It is not difficult to imagine that African American workers may receive biased treatment in the workplace. During my interviews, most managers revealed a much greater sympathy toward their foreign black workers. This favoritism may reflect whom they assign to perform the most undesirable tasks, such as cleaning the bathrooms. Perceptions may be based on what is experienced in the workplace, but they may also be shaped by direct and subtle forms of communication between managers and workers. Hostility is often perpetuated by long-established perceptions and prejudices.

My first day on the job at the Burger King restaurant was memorable. At the end of the work shift, while I was mopping the dining room floor after the store closed, a manager approached me and said, referring to three young African American women crewmembers leaving the restaurant, "These niggers are so fuckin' lazy. They don't care about their work. They are just going to go home, sit on their fat asses, and watch television." These African American women believed that they had a legitimate right to leave when they did; their shift was over, at least according to the posted schedule. But so was mine. If I had also left, the work would not have been done. To ensure my continued subservience, this manager had to distinguish us, to provide a reason to me why they (the black women) went home and I was left to do the work. In other words, on my first day, he did not want me to think that they went home for a legitimate reason: Their shift was over and they didn't want to stay later into the night because the restaurant is located in a dangerous neighborhood. These reasons, he thought, would appeal to me, too; after all, perhaps on my second night, I, too, would leave before the mopping was done. Rather, he wanted me to think that the African Americans went home because they are black, and blacks are lazy.

A few days later, I recorded that one of these women commented during a shift that "they treat us like slaves." This is a good example of what is called "positive and negative reference group theory" in the discipline of sociology. The main idea is that "many attitudes and beliefs get instilled in the minds of social actors by their taking some persons or groups as a natural reference."[8] In other words, this manager needed a way to distinguish my "good" behavior from their "bad" behavior so that he would not appear to sanction their actions. His distinction took a racial and cultural form.

It is not difficult to imagine here how negative management-crew relations are cultivated. It is likely that this manager held prejudicial attitudes toward African Americans. It is also likely that these women had certain ideas about what their jobs should entail, how they should be treated according to established legal codes, and the monetary value of their work. The small numbers of African Americans who work in the restaurants I visited can be explained by simultaneous processes, including resistance-type behavior by African American employees and prejudicial attitudes by managers of who constitutes a "good" worker. It may also be explained by African Americans' getting jobs in sectors where they are treated better.

African Americans in fast food jobs may be resisting coworkers who denigrate them, the managers (who form biased perceptions against them), and the conditions of the work itself. These are interrelated factors. Resistance is most likely when social relations become antagonistic and workers perceive a bias against them by their superiors. It becomes, as one manager said, "a vicious circle." As African Americans come to be viewed as poor workers compared to others, they are less likely to be hired over others. And as it becomes more difficult to get a job, they are less likely to want these jobs and apply for them. The result, as Pedro says, is that African American workers eventually "fizzle out," as does their recruitment chain. Given this scenario, it is unlikely that a manager will ask an African American to recommend a friend or relative as a candidate for a job opening. As Pedro said, "It is really strange how the cultures change. I think the black Americans, if they don't change their attitudes they are really going to affect the job market. They are going to be pushed out of the job market."

We cannot help but acknowledge that the biases that have evolved between different West Indian groups may be intertwined with the stereotypes that plague African Americans. It is the African American stereotype that foreign blacks try to escape, even if the process of escape means building up ethnic and racialized boundaries between them. It could be that West Indian employees are projecting blame onto African Americans for the racism they are subjected to in the United States. Like most immigrant groups who are aware of the stereotypes that have historically afflicted African Americans, foreign blacks, perhaps, should not be expected to be different. In so far as they believe the stereotypes—that African Americans don't want to work and are drug traders and the like—then they may continuously feel the need to distinguish, the need to show that they are willing to work. Even if they do not believe the stereotypes, they must live in constant acknowledgment that much of society does believe in them.

This is consistent with how Malcolm Gladwell, a writer for the *New Yorker*, characterizes West Indians' relationship to black Americans: West Indians *depend* on "remaining outsiders . . . on being distinct by custom, culture and language from the American blacks they would otherwise resemble."9 As Gladwell explains, "It is the means by which discrimination against American blacks is given one last, vicious twist: I am not so shallow as to despise you for the color of your skin, because I have found people *your* color that I like. Now I can despise you for who you are" [emphasis added].10

Fizzling Out: American Workers vs. Foreign Workers

The distinctions made between African Americans and foreigners of African ancestry is exacerbated by a tendency to make a further distinction between the American-born and the foreign-born. This broader distinction, rooted in nationality, crosses categories of race, ethnicity, social class, and gender. While voiced by both managers and workers in all three neighborhoods, it was most prevalent and explicit in downtown Brooklyn, perhaps because American racial minorities, especially African Americans, have historically been the dominant labor supply to low-wage sectors here. With more West Indians and other immigrant groups coming to downtown Brooklyn in competition for these jobs, distinctions are based predominately on the categories of "American" and "foreign," where race is broken down by nationality.

In Little Dominican Republic and Chinatown, on the other hand, "American," as a broad category that crosses race and ethnicity, is not as clearly defined; in part, this is because the American-born do not represent a large part of the restaurant workforces. In addition, other categories work to obfuscate "American" as a social category. Second-generation Latinos in Little Dominican Republic, for instance, are not necessarily distinguished from first-generation immigrants, particularly by employers. A common language of origin and similar ethnic origins contribute to an identity based on culture rather than national origin. In Chinatown, the American-born are subsumed within their respective racial and ethnic categories rather than separated from these categories to form a distinct category of "American." African Americans are the exception because they are recognized in these two neighborhoods as a distinct social group. As opposed to Asians and Hispanics, African Americans do not have common roots in these neighborhoods or strong representation in management. In general, first- and second-generation Chinese and Latinos have more in common with each other (the same or similar origins, recency of arrival, etc.) than West Indians and African Americans.

In downtown Brooklyn, the African American category is merged with the broader American category. The explanations provided by employers for the American versus foreign distinction are rooted in U.S. versus Third World culture rather than in race or ethnicity, class, or gender. Nonetheless, in practicality, and given the composition of job seekers in the area, the category of American has become a euphemism for an inner-city underclass, distinguished from what is perceived as an upwardly mobile immigrant population predominately from the West Indies. In other words, when managers refer to "American," they are invariably referring to poor African Americans, Latinos, and to a lesser extent, whites, who were born in the inner city. (Middle-class Americans, regardless of their race and ethnic backgrounds, do not tend to work in minimum-wage fast food jobs. They have better opportunities and can be found in more upscale retail franchises, including Starbucks, the Gap, and Urban Underground.)

Loren, the African American manager in downtown Brooklyn, was born and raised in New York City, and he was explicit about the foreign versus American distinction.

> People who are born here, they are more into saying "I don't need this." There is not the same pride in their work as much as people who come from somewhere else and say, "Hey, this is my life. I have to start from

somewhere. And when I get to this place, I will move to the next place."
That is what I am seeing from people who are coming from other places.
Believe it or not, I see those kinds of people being hired in the future
than the ones who are just saying, "I don't need this job. I don't need
you. I am just here for the paycheck." And there is a lot of that going on
by people who are born here.

He linked this attitude to what he considers a comfortable lifestyle and
a lack of a future orientation even though this "comfortable" lifestyle
means a resignation to living in poverty.

> They live with their parents. They have boyfriends or girlfriends, they
> are pretty stable. They are just comfortable at minimum wage and work-
> ing twenty hours a week and doing this for the moment. They are not
> looking ahead. That is what is unfortunate about people who are born
> here. That is what I am recognizing at this store. Not all. But a majority.
> They are not looking ahead. That is where the problem starts.

Loren implied how the company philosophy involving motivation and
loyalty, values embedded in nineteenth-century Protestant conceptions
of work, are influencing managers' preferences for immigrants. This
conception of work is founded on a neoconservative moral structure
where values are linked to the traditional family, self-reliance, hard
work, and civic mindedness.[11] "I am just here for the paycheck" is, to
this manager, an unacceptable purpose for working. Employees must
not only work. They must be proud of their work and exhibit this pride
while working. Further, employees must be upwardly mobile, or at
least believe they are, by "looking ahead."

Julio, the New York City-born Puerto Rican manager in downtown
Brooklyn, was also explicit about differences between immigrants and
the American-born:

> The big difference I do notice is that a lot of the foreign-born come here
> knowing mopping or sweeping because they have done it before. The
> ones who are born here are not used to mopping, cleaning . . . like they
> have had everything handed to them. It is a lot more frustrating some-
> times because like you got people in orientation that you explain to them

mopping and sweeping and they get up and say, "No, I am not going to work here because I don't mop and sweep." I find that rather strange sometimes.

Julio related it to a lack of good parenting and a greater interest in partying than working.

Most of the ones who are foreign-born, they come here and their parents push them because it is the American dream. Like I brought you to America to seek the American dream. And a lot of people who were born here, they think the American dream is something that is given to you. People who come here, they realize that the American dream is what you work for. You reap what you sow literally. So they push themselves hard because they know—a lot of people tell them it is a waste of time to go to school—but they know that all the sacrifices now have to pay off sooner or later. . . . A lot of kids who are born here, I notice that . . . they don't want to come to work, they want to leave early. Fridays and Saturdays are very difficult for them. Friday evening rolls around and people try and call in sick. Partiers. I try and tell them that a party is nothing. You don't understand, they tell me—that I am not of their generation. I try to tell them when I was your age I was in your same place.

In general, the negative traits of Americans are juxtaposed with the positive traits of immigrants. The foreign-born "come here knowing mopping and sweeping" and the Americans "don't mop and sweep." To the foreign-born, the "American dream is what you work for," and to the Americans the "American dream is something that is given to you." The foreign-born "know that all the sacrifices now have to pay off sooner or later." The Americans, on the other hand, are "partiers" and "not looking ahead." In this way, it seems that the traits of immigrants have come to reflect employers' expectations and labor requirements for all workers.[12]

Managers said that a poor work ethic among the American-born affects the way they work. Loren linked the "no pride in their work" to an inability to be flexible; he also believes that they are less capable of meeting the spontaneous demands of the work, including fluctuating demands from customers:

Some people are automatic. The ones who are automatic have that pride. Again, if there is something on the floor, pick it up. If something spills, you gotta mop it. If a customer is sick, you try to encourage them. Some people have this naturally and that comes from the way they are brought up. Others are quick to say if something comes off the wrong way or bumps you, "What is your problem?" as opposed to "Excuse me." A lot of people make a big issue out of a customer coming back and saying, "My french fries are cold." "Well I didn't give them." That is not the point. The person at Burger King has to accept this. [They say] "You didn't get nice hot french fries? This has to be changed." Maybe the customer sat twenty minutes under the air conditioning and the french fries got cold. But Burger King states that they want the customer taken care of regardless.

One manager explained that the skills associated with successfully interacting with people are not traits learned in the workplace. Rather, these features should be integral parts of a person's upbringing. In other words, employees should already be trained and conditioned to deal with customers. Although immigrants are able to do this, he said, the new generation born in America is not.

Me trying to explain that to some people, they really don't understand. They say, "She didn't have to tell me that way." Yes, yelling and screaming is not the way to go all the time. But she (customer) has a reason to be upset. There are people who can really understand and there are those who can't. The ones who can't have never been around that surrounding.

Good socialization is also reflected in one's demeanor. As he explained:

I know for a fact. I see the guys here. I look at them. The way they carry themselves. I know you don't wash dishes, you don't clean. I know for a fact. I know your mother does all your laundry and everything else. I know. The majority who come here are like that. The ones who have the pride in their work are under some situation where they really feel the need to grow and grow and grow and grow. Until these guys [American-born] get it, they are going to be that way anyway. "I don't need to do this."

This lack of pride and motivation, which is linked to a weak work ethic among the American-born, is also perceived by some managers as reflecting "outside forces," such as the drug trade, that offer more prestige and more money. According to one manager, "We have a lot of outside forces where you can make a quick buck doing things illegally. Unlike here where everyone starts at minimum wage. So you make minimum wage and you got to wear that uniform and there is a lot of pressure. So why do they want to take a job like this?" "Outside forces" particular to the youth generation raised in the United States include a bent toward individualism, which constrains the development of social skills, according to managers. Television, Walkman radios, and video games contribute to social isolation and the inability to deal with the pressures workers confront when dealing with the public. As Julio suggested,

> There is a lot of stress in this job at times. As you came in yourself, you see the front counter. There are a lot of customers. Some of these customers get on you. A lot of these young kids are not used to dealing with pressure. Being heaped and being heaped. A lot of them put on their Walkmans. The bigger (newer) generation, I was telling people, they watch television, play video games. They are locked in a room most of the time where everything comes to them. So then when they deal with the public it is harder for them to deal with them. I come from a different generation. We would go on the street and we had to invent our own games and invent our own fun, our imagination would go wild. But now things are in such a way that you can isolate yourself and it is a lot harder to deal with the public.

Managers implicitly suggested that those from countries where modern technology is not widely affordable are better prepared to use the social skills that fast food work requires.

The social stigma of working in fast food restaurants is an added pressure on American-born youth. This peer pressure affects the work ethic and creates a problem for managers in assigning American-born workers certain tasks. Sandeep, the downtown Brooklyn manager from India, said, "A lot of them, if they are working here in uniform in back and you want them to go in the lobby or go to another store to pick up something, they want to change their clothes. They want to change everything completely. Like they don't want their friends to see them. A lot of people just look down on working here: 'Oh, you are just a burger flipper.'" Julio tried to explain why this social stigma affects the American-born more than immigrants. "It is the picture that was probably painted for them, on advertisements, maybe in comedy clubs, maybe throughout the years. Maybe they are those customers who were turned away. . . . Again, someone who is from somewhere else, not listening to all the things that people are saying—they haven't been associated with it—'You are hiring? Hey, great.' When they come here to work, they appreciate it." According to the managers in downtown Brooklyn, their foreign-born employees are less vulnerable to the peer pressure prevalent in American youth culture. As Sandeep said, "You got workers here, most of the workers who come from other countries, come to work in their uniform. They get here and just take their jacket off." These workers are more likely to run errands willingly outside the restaurant or to work in the dining room.

Managers further claimed that the foreign-born are more geared towards the future and willing to delay immediate gratification, such as going to parties when scheduled to work. The foreign-born, then, are thought to be more adaptable to the industry's scheduling and flexible assignment of tasks and they place a priority on work over play. Looking out for the future seems to carry intrinsic value in this industry and earns fundamental respect from employers; this is partly because it has been a major source of self-respect by many managers, especially the American-born racial minorities who consider themselves successful and self-made. They attribute their success to a work ethic built on being mindful of the future or, as Weber describes it, "transvaluations of earlier Protestant conceptions of America."[13]

These managers seemed intolerant of those who don't have this orientation, and some of this intolerance reflected their inability to influence youth. As Loren noted:

I tell young kids today when they get here, "Let me tell you something. All your Whitney Houstons, all your Sylvester Stallones, and all your Donald Trumps have worked in fast food before, so you just take note of that. Try to find out why and be aware of what people really have been doing and what they've been against . . . all the young basketball players

. . . maybe those are skills that don't have to use so much brains, but all the people who do have to use brains have worked at Burger King or McDonald's. They joke about it now because they remember the days. I try to tell kids today that they should be getting a start somewhere. You can't just be an engineer one day. And nobody is going to give you the keys to any corporation without knowing you a little bit. So you are going to have to work, buddy, whether you like it or not.

Managers identified more with and held greater respect for their foreign-born employees. Julio spoke highly about several former coworkers who immigrated to this country:

One person, George Willis, he is a doctor and for four years, he literally just went to college and worked here. He had no social life whatsoever. He was born in Jamaica. He had no social life for four years. Now he is an anesthesiologist at Lennox Hill Hospital. He has all the time in the world. Much more relaxed. It paid off. He is only twenty-six years old, also. He has everything ahead of him now. Another one is a teacher. The third one, she is a registered nurse. There are a couple of nurses. The biggest thing about them is that none of them were born here or their parents were not born here. They all came from different countries. They came from other countries, they went to school here, they worked here, and they busted their behinds in order to make it. Doctors, lawyers. We also have some that went into the police force.

While these managers distinguished between foreign-born and Americans, they also distinguished themselves from American youth. Both Loren, as an African American, and Julio, as a Latino American, have had similar experiences. They both started out as crewmembers while they were teenagers in high school. They both aspired to and climbed the fast food job ladder while they were young, and they have both worked in the industry for nearly a decade. When I asked Loren what makes him different from other American-born employees, he said,

I was born in Brooklyn. But I will tell you one thing. I got all my thought patterns and all my everything from my family. My family is strictly hard work, serious business. If I talked back at my mother it was like I had swung at her. I see kids with their parents now: "Ma, shut up. You don't know what you are talking about." What? If I said that I'd be history. I think it comes from the home. What they see their parents doing. What they see their parents' friends doing. What they see their brothers and sisters doing and getting away with. Parents. I believe in them.

Although he acknowledged different societal forces influencing today's American youth, he also believes that, at some level, it is the parents' responsibility to counteract these forces.

No. It is not always their fault. There are a lot of hard-working parents who have nothing against their children. But it is not the majority, unfortunately. A lot of what I have seen is coming from the parents. Look at the language he is using. Look at the way she is carrying herself. And it is no wonder. And again, you talk about someone coming from somewhere else, they are raised from hard work, I'm sure. Hard work, whether it is McDonald's or sweeping the streets. They better be the best garbage picker-upper you can be to get ahead. Hey, there is no pride in the work when it comes down to other people saying, "I don't need this."

Managers often blamed bad family values for poor work ethics among American youth, but one manager referred to the changing structural conditions of the family:

Some of the people who were born here, they are at a disadvantage because their parents don't push them as hard [as immigrants]. And then some of them, their parents both have to work. Some have to work two jobs. So they are not home. So you have a child who goes to school, he may be all by himself in the day at home. Nobody asks him how he do in school, what did he do for the tests. So, a lot of them are unmotivated. But you can't blame the parent either. Sometimes it is just the system. You get caught in the cycle that never ends. And it is very difficult to break that cycle.

In explaining his own success, Julio referred back to an explanation of family values.

My parents made sure I did my work. Made sure I studied hard. Made sure I was accessible to a library. My mother bought me an encyclopedia set. So I didn't have to go breaking my neck in a library. . . . So I think the blame must be shared between the system, and among the family. Somehow, they have to work together to try to knock down this barrier that seems to be preventing kids from getting a good education.

Many of the distinctions employees made between themselves and other Americans referred to family values. But their explanations tended to reflect changing structural conditions in society at large— changes they have seen and experienced since they started in the industry. So-called outside forces, such as the drug trade, media influences, technological developments, and peer pressure were said to affect "attitude," work ethics, and work performance. Family values were regarded as necessary, and even obligatory, to counteract these outside forces. But families were also viewed as structurally constrained by changing economic conditions that force, at minimum, both parents into the workplace, or, at worst, break them apart when material tensions escalate. In general, employers recognized a growing contradiction between family values and the ability to abide by these values in the changing American workplace. Still, they usually failed to convey this understanding to their employees.

What managers said about their American-born employees was never wholly consistent with what these same workers said about their own experiences and work values and with what I have observed in the workplace.

I Hope His [the Manager's] Car Blows Up

Employees reflect some of these same family values regarding work and family. As expressed by many employees I spoke to, these values include the idea that work itself should carry intrinsic social value, that workers should earn a "breadwinner wage," and that work should be a means for social elevation. A belief in these values, however, embodies certain expectations in the workplace that are usually not met, such as earning a higher wage and being respected for doing "honest work." When these expectations regarding work, family, and social mobility are not met, employees display signs of discontent, helping to reify employers' stereotypes regarding a negative "attitude."

One African American employee working in downtown Brooklyn explained how managers' insensitivity to workers' social conditions affect a negative reaction on the part of employees.

> If a company does not care about their employees, then the employees are not going to care about the company. . . . I think the main reason I don't like [the main manager] is that he really doesn't care about the employees. They are breaking the equipment. One of the ladies one time she hurt herself. She fell on the steps and twisted her ankle. He said, "Well, she should have noticed the step. She should have been careful." I believe with the New York City safety code you are supposed to be wearing protective gear when you are doing equipment like that. All we have are gloves that come up to here. So if oil splashes on our hands it is fine. But if it splashes on our faces, we are fucked. They don't care. That is why we hate him. When people take food, they don't give a fuck and I don't blame them. I hope he [the main manager] goes back [to the country where he came from]. I hope his car blows up. I wish he would just drop dead.

This comment implies that one should not expect employees to have pride in their work or respect their employers or their jobs, as managers suggest, if the employers do not have the same respect for the employees. This employee is saying that employees value their jobs as much as managers value their employees. Sociologist Elliot Liebow, three decades ago in *Tally's Corner*, pointed out that it made perfect sense that "street corner men" would hold little value for low-level jobs such as dishwasher or janitor. As he said, "He cannot draw from a job those social values which other people do not put into it."[14]

Edward, a second-generation Antiguan who identified himself as African American, is a production leader in downtown Brooklyn, and he explained his rationale for employees' resistance behavior.

> I have seen them take money, take food. But in a way I can't blame them because they are not getting enough money in here. A lot of people in here have families and children and they are not making enough to sup-

port them. And, plus, it is bad enough they are going through that. They are getting stressed out. They want you to do everything in here in such little time and for nothing. So I can't really blame them when they want to take money from the cash register and get over.

His comment suggests that taking money from the employer to "get over" is rational and legitimate in the workplace because employees are trying to make a living from wages that do not provide enough to do just that. He makes a distinction between "robbing from people," the activity of the "handicapped," and "taking" from the employer, the activity of the employees. It is different and legitimate because they are performing work that is worth more than what they are being paid. In other words, employees are taking what is rightfully theirs.[15] It is not difficult to understand how Edward feels. He was involved in the drug trade and rejected it for what he considered a more socially legitimate path. Now, after years of fast food experience, he has burns and permanent injuries on his hands and arms. He had planned to become a manager at Burger King but changed his mind because of what he has experienced in the industry. It seems that unfavorable work conditions compounded by poor material and living circumstances and lack of job alternatives help shape a particular work ethic, or set of values among employees in the restaurant workplace.[16]

Giving Them a Break

Whether resistance to organizational goals is accommodated or disparaged largely depends on the ethnic makeup, experiences, and personal traits of managers. It also depends on the particular restaurant environment and culture. The inflexibility of Chinese employees' schedules, for example, is now accepted at the McDonald's restaurant in Chinatown. But managers in other restaurants, such as those in downtown Brooklyn, chastise their employees for refusing to stay later than scheduled and for showing unwillingness to work on a day off. A Chinese majority at the Chinatown restaurant has changed ideas regarding flexible work not only by accepting inflexibility but by rewarding employees who stick to Chinese custom when it comes to the division between work and study. Employees at this restaurant, regardless of ethnicity, are more apt to be dismissed or suspended from their jobs for having poor school grades than for refusing to work when not scheduled. Charles, the general manager, suspended Lila, the Honduran employee, because her school grades were dropping. As Lila explained:

> I was doing good [when I first worked here] but then my mind was too much on this job. I worked from 3:00 to 10:00 and that is all I would do. I would come here, go to work, and then I would be so tired so I wouldn't do my homework. I would just go to sleep, go to school. Be tired in school, sleep every class. All I was worrying about was coming to work. So my grades started to drop. I didn't study for no test.

She was told that when her grades improved, she could return to work. In this restaurant, inflexibility is not an expression of resistance but of conformity. It is legitimized and reinforced because it adheres to values embedded in the Chinese culture and in American society at large. The Chinese division between work and study conforms to American ideology concerning social mobility and the fundamental role that education plays in it.

American ideology, then, reinforces values asserted by the Chinese in the fast food organization. But the way these values are played out is largely determined by the organization. In Chinatown's garment factories and Chinese restaurants, employees' lives are wholly organized around the workplace. Social mobility in such workplaces depends on savings accumulated from long hours of work for a long time, or else on moving up the job ladder. Or it happens through intergenerational mobility. The fast food restaurant is different. The temporary and part-time nature of fast food work offers little chance to build savings, nor is there much hope of promotion. Therefore, the fast food worker's social mobility depends on human capital and pursuing professional careers through a college education. Only a few move up the fast food job ladder to a manager's position. Many Chinese employees who choose to work in fast food restaurants are not like Tina because they tend to pursue professional careers outside the industry.

Other forms of nonconformity, regardless of the reasons for it, do not have the same amount of influence and legitimacy in the fast food workplace. Those who object to changing the oil in the oil vats, such as

the Haitians in Little Dominican Republic, or the African American fe-
males who refused to stay late to mop the floors in downtown Brooklyn,
often end up quitting or being fired. Instead of being viewed as justified
in not performing work that causes injury or may be unreasonable to
them, they are labeled lazy or accused of harboring an "attitude." The
most undesirable tasks end up being performed by the least resistant
workers—such as the Antiguan female employee in the Little Dominican Republic restaurant. These employees do not blame the organization at large but rather those who refuse to do the work. The Antiguan
employee does not blame her scars and burns on her employer; rather,
she blames them on "the Haitians." She takes her frustration home to
her mother, who reinforces her compliance in the workplace and tells
her to "ignore them" (the Haitians). As the employee said,

> I do that a lot. Just ignore them and if the manager tells you to do some-
> thing just do it. Just stay away from them. I just come here. I ask the
> manager to punch in, work, and every time he needs me to do some-
> thing, I do it. And then when he tells me to go, I go. And then I put on
> my coat and I am out until the next day.

Individual managers do sometimes accommodate and even reinforce
employees who resist certain tasks, such as cleaning the bathrooms,
mopping, and sweeping. But such accommodation and reinforcement
is not customary in the restaurants I examined and among the managers I interviewed.

My interview with Julia, the female manager from Puerto Rico working at the Chinatown Burger King, indicates the way sensitivity to the situations and social conditions of their employees can lead to a favorable
interpretation of work performance and work ethics despite dominant
stereotypes to the contrary. Julia believes that American racial minorities
have good reasons for their actions and attitudes on the job. She believes
that resistance in the fast food restaurant is rooted in a history of oppres-
sive social conditions. "We shouldn't expect otherwise," she said.

The anger, the "chip on their shoulder" Pedro referred to, implies to
Julia a reaction to the general social conditions minority women have
historically been subjected to. As she sees it, women often want to be
managers more than men do; they are more aggressive about it with

managers, whom they believe harbor prejudice toward them. This prejudice, in itself, creates a barrier to their mobility in the organization. Therefore, they "act out" by refusing to perform certain tasks. One type of resistance, partly symbolic, is refusing to clean the bathrooms.

The differences in the way managers interpret the same behavior are partly rooted in managers' own ethnic origins and cultural experiences, as I discussed in Chapter 6. They are also explained by managers' different supervisory responsibilities in the restaurant, as well as their history in the industry. Julia, for instance, started out in the industry as an entry-level frontline worker. She eventually became a head cashier, and then an assistant manager. Because of this trajectory, she may be especially attentive to the service relations between cashiers and customers and to the subtle interactions that occur between them. Pointing out the differences between Chinese, Latinos, and blacks, she says that the "Chinese girls" are friendly with the "Chinese customers," but they are not so friendly with the "English" customers (see Chapter 6). Pedro, on the other hand, thinks of the restaurant as a "come and go" kind of place, where speed of service is much more important than the friendliness of the cashiers.

As an assistant manager, Julia must make sure the restaurant is appropriately staffed for the day. This usually requires calling employees at their homes before their shifts. The Colombian manager is more focused on the overall operation of the restaurant, including food preparation in the back, where he had his own crewmember training. Also, as a female member of a racial minority group and as a single mother, Julia may show a greater sensitivity to both women and minorities. This sensitivity would not automatically lead to a different perception of gender or race; but it has become important in the way Julia communicates with her staff. Such sensitivity becomes reciprocal, cultivating good and bad work performance. What she perceives is actual, but her perception is embedded in the social relations that she cultivates. A sensitivity to the particular situations and social conditions of workers may lead to a favorable interpretation of work performance and work ethics. Perception and actuality shape each other through subtle forms of communication that express such sensitivity.

Sensitivity to one social group, nonetheless, can mean insensitivity toward another group, reinforcing conflict rather than quelling it. The

Puerto Rican manager is especially sensitive toward Latinos and African Americans, particularly women. Yet Julia favors the Chinese less. She is also less tolerant of male employees, especially those who exhibit what she refers to as "male chauvinism" embedded in the Latino culture. Such intolerance further exacerbates conflict between social groups. Her favorable relations with Latino and black women are partly a result of the kind of role model she is, principally in respect to breaking down traditional gender roles in the fast food organization. She has risen in the all-male ranks to become a manager, she performs traditional "male" tasks, and she feels that, especially as a Latina, her success is due in part to her aggressive attitude and way of being.

Julia reinforces this attitude and way of being in her female employees. But it also helps account for the "chip on the shoulder" demeanor used by Pedro to describe these same employees. This demeanor fuels conflicting relations with the male employees, including managers. As Julia claimed, many men were threatened by her actions. One quit. Some reported negative things about her work performance to the general manager. At times she had problems with her male crewmembers. As she explained:

> I had an employee yell at me because I gave him an order. He was a male, Spanish guy. I said I don't care what they do in Argentina. I don't care what you tell your wife to do. When you are here, you do as I say. If you don't like it, if you can't deal with it, because I am a woman, then go home to mommy. Because I am not going to be intimidated by you or any man. I am like—I hate to use the word—but, the bitch. The girls love it, though. The other girls are like, "Yah!"

Accommodating resistance in the fast food organization implies exhibiting sensitivity to workplace conditions as experienced by different social groups or subscribing to cultural custom that characterize entire ethnic groups. But it can also reinforce conflict in the organization when it implies intolerance toward another social group.

In general, managers' and workers' perceptions of different social groups may reflect dominant stereotypes in the society at large. They are also rooted in managers' and workers' perceptions and interpretations of what they observe and experience in the restaurant. How a perceived cultural characteristic is interpreted to fit into the fast food organization often varies among individual managers. But it is also interpreted according to neighborhood marketing strategies. Stereotypes, workplace observations, market forces, and actuality are intertwined and shape each other, and have different implications for different social groups.

8

Up the Ladder or Down: A Question of Mobility

All my skills were mom-and-pop style. . . . I was not being able to expend my talent. I was trapped in [the Chinese restaurant that I owned]. Day in and day out operation. I did not have anyone else to run it for me. I found out that this system is not really working well. I work like a dog. . . . KFC gave me the first opportunity to go into the fast food industry. McDonald's gave me a very strong foundation to start realizing how they become number one in the fast food industry. . . . I am coming out of the little league to a big league.

       —General Manager from Taiwan working in Chinatown

My situation is a pathetic, pathetic story.

       —Assistant Manager from India working in Brooklyn

My girlfriend, also Chinese, worked five days a week. She told me to work and got me the job here. . . . Because she said everybody, every student in the United States has a part-time job. Only you don't have it.

       —Assistant Manager from Malaysia working in Chinatown

Tina dreams about becoming a manager at the McDonald's restaurant where she works because this is the most promising avenue she has for obtaining a salary, health insurance, and higher status in the mainstream economy. She may very well achieve her goal. As she said, "I work hard, I want to change my place [status]. I want to learn the whole McDonald's system. This is my purpose. I want to do it. It is up to my ability." One often reads about the opportunities the fast food restaurant provides for those who stick it out at the bottom and hold fast to their dreams of climbing the hierarchy. The *Wall Street Journal*, for instance, wrote in a front-page story in August 1995 about Phil Hagans, an African American owner of four McDonald's restaurants in Houston, who started out as a burger flipper: "[He] settles behind the wheel of his gray Mercedes sedan, flips on his cellular phone and drives past the ramshackle houses of his old neighborhood . . . a role model for black teenagers."[1] In a March 1994 article, the *New York Times* described Sally Allen, the daughter of factory workers in Georgia, who began as a burger flipper to help support her children and later became a franchise owner in Kerville, Texas.[2] And in July 1995 it wrote about Mark Ishaya, who went from being a child laborer in an oil filter factory in Lebanon to a McDonald's manager in Chicago.[3] According to Parcel and Sickmeier, who studied the fast food organization, "A major avenue to higher management involves upward mobility through the ranks of operating a store or stores."[4] Is this really true? Given that corporate sectors such as fast food are expanding in the immigrant neighborhood, it is important to know whether they represent real avenues for social mobility.

I found that one cannot approach the question of social mobility from a conventional standpoint in the fast food industry because the structure and concept of mobility vary. Restaurant and ownership structures differ and immigrants employed in them are diverse. Immigrants join the industry for many reasons and with various goals; but for most, fast food is a temporary stopgap. Immigrants from many backgrounds enter, and most of them leave, on their way up or down the American social ladder. But some immigrants do aim for and rise on the fast food job ladder, and in these cases, the industry represents upward mobility. For Tina and crewmembers like her, who compare fast food employment to conditions in the underground economy, or Brusso, who compares it to being a taxi driver, becoming a fast food manager is an ambitious social and financial step up. And for Charles, who began on the high rungs as a general manager in one of the biggest fast food corporations in New York City, it was a significant career shift that came with the financial and social benefits rare in this industry. But owning one of the biggest restaurant franchises—a McDonald's or a Burger King—is merely a pipe dream for those who start out as "burger-flippers" or "basket-fryers," despite a few well-publicized examples to the contrary.

Fast Food in the New York City Labor Market

The fast food restaurant industry, in general, is pivotal to our understanding of how the changing labor market is affecting immigrants' chances for mobility. Despite the economic boom of the late 1990s, most job expansion has been at the low-end of the labor market, such as in fast food, and we know little about the long-term implications, or even expectations, for people who work in industries such as fast food. The city, indeed, has experienced overall job growth since the 1980s, showing a net gain of over 400,000 jobs. But this growth must be examined in respect to jobs lost as well as created during the last two decades.

New York City has experienced a significant erosion of manufacturing industries, where half a million jobs were lost between 1980 and 1999. Sectors that account for the greatest job growth include the services (such as health and security services), and finance, insurance, and real estate (FIRE). But although more than 600,000 jobs have been added in the service sector, where jobs are apt to be low-wage, temporary, and part-time, only slightly more than 50,000 jobs have been added in FIRE, where jobs command high salaries and good benefits (see Table 8.1 below). Certain sectors categorized under retail trades, including clothing stores and restaurants, also account for a significant amount of New York's net gain in employment. In restaurants alone, nearly 43,000 jobs were created in New York between 1980 and 1999, and fast food restaurants account for a large portion of this growth.

The growing yet polarizing economy has resulted in a downward career shift on the New York population at large. More people are turning to minimum-wage jobs, as in fast food, to sustain livelihoods and families. According to fast food employers, those turning to fast food employment for the first time in recent years include displaced blue-collar workers, single mothers, adults helping to support households, the

TABLE 8.1   Distribution of Jobs Across Employment Sectors in New York City, 1980 and 1999

Employment sector	1980		1999		Change	
	Number of Jobs (in thousands)	Percentage of Total Employment	Number of Jobs (in thousands)	Percentage of Total Employment	Change in Number of Jobs (in thousands)	Percentage Change
Manufacturing	586.6	15.7	302.1	7.3	-284.5	-48.5
Transportation, Public Utilities	280.3	7.5	234.3	5.6	-46.0	-16.4
Wholesale/Retail Trade	716.0	19.1	727.6	17.5	-11.6	-1.6
Finance, Insurance, Real Estate	469.7	12.5	522.6	12.6	+52.9	+11.3
Services	1002.0	26.7	1575.3	37.9	+573.3	+57.2
Government	596.0	15.9	650.8	15.6	+54.8	+9.2
Other misc.	97.1	2.6	143.7	3.5	+46.6	+50
TOTAL	3747.7	100	4156.4	100	+408.7	+10.9

SOURCE: New York State Department of Labor, Nonagricultural Wage and Salary Employment from the Current Employment Statistics Program in New York State, 1980 and 1999.

elderly, and young people trying to make an independent living. Increasing numbers of them, like Tina, are immigrants.

These trends, exacerbated by the economic downturn of 2001, contribute to and help shape a highly competitive and volatile job market in New York City. Jobs in fast food restaurants, in particular, have become more of a perceived job alternative among New Yorkers in recent years not only because such jobs are growing but also because they have traditionally had high turnover rates. Fast food jobs are among ten occupations in New York City that have the most openings every year.[5] Because fast food jobs are obtainable without job skills or a high school education, virtually anybody is eligible to apply. Most New Yorkers (more than 75 percent) do not have a college degree.[6] According to the New York State Department of Labor, fast food jobs are one of only nine growth occupations in New York City that do not necessarily re-

TABLE 8.2   Poverty Rates, Household Incomes, and Educational Attainment by Race in New York City, 1990

Group	Family poverty rates	Median Household Income	% with BA degree	Percent of total NYC workforce	Percent in top occupations
White (non-Hispanic)	9.6	$36,464	61.1	48	65.6
Black	25.3	23,820	12.4	21	15.2
Hispanic	33.2	20,402	8.2	16	8.2
Asian/Pacific Islander	16.1	31,860	33.4	6.7	6.3

SOURCE: U.S. Bureau of the Census (1990). *1990 Census of Population, Social and Economic Characteristics, Metropolitan Areas, Release CP-2-1B*. Washington, D.C.: Author.

quire more than a high school diploma. Four out of these nine growth occupations (including fast food jobs) are food-related jobs.[7]

People of color—both immigrants and native New Yorkers—are disproportionately affected by the polarization of New York City's economy.[8] Demographically, people of color represent a growing proportion of New York City's population due to ongoing white flight and a constant inflow of immigrants from the Third World.[9] Compared to New York City's white population, certain groups—especially blacks and even more so Hispanics—are at a significant disadvantage in occupational status, education, income, and standard of living. There are also vast economic disparities among groups of color. Asian populations, for example, are significantly better off, on average, than black and Hispanic populations[10] (see Table 8.2).

Table 8.3 illustrates the racial and gender composition and stratification of New York City's lowest-paid food-related workforce (excluding occupations in restaurants that provide table service such as waiters, cooks and bartenders). Although fast food occupations are only one of many occupations included in the broad categories listed by the Department of Census,[11] the table is helpful to view because the broad racial and ethnic diversity of the fast food workforce is reflected in this larger portrayal of the food industry. Moreover, it depicts a racial hierarchical stratification in the food industry that reflects the larger demographic features shown in Table 8.2.

TABLE 8.3   New York City Food Workers and Supervisors (Includes Fast Food Occupations), 1990: Percentages by Race and Gender

Level		White		Black		Hispanic		Asian/ Pacific Islander	
		M	F	M	F	M	F	M	F
Supervisor	% of all supervisors	28.0	11.6	11.2	10.2	17.7	4.4	13.8	2.8
	% of overall labor force (by category)	.2	.08	.2	.13	.3	.01	.6	.15
Food worker	% of all food workers	12.9	13.1	12.0	9.7	35.7	8.5	8.9	2.1
	% of overall labor force (by category)	.3	.4	.7	.5	2.2	.7	1.5	.5

SOURCE: U.S. Bureau of the Census. *1990 Census of Population, Social and Economic Characteristics, Metropolitan Areas, Release CP-2-1B.* Washington, D.C.: Author, 1990.

Hispanics, for example, account for nearly half of all food workers. They also have the highest representation of food workers within their racial group—2.2 percent of all Hispanic men and 0.7 percent of all Hispanic women in the labor force are food workers. Yet, compared with whites, Asians, and even blacks, their representation in supervisory positions is far less than their representation at the bottom rungs of the hierarchy. Although Asians have the second highest representation in food occupations within their racial category, they are far more represented in supervisory than in nonsupervisory positions. The white labor force as a whole has the lowest percentage of employees in low-level food occupations (only 0.3 percent of men and 0.4 percent of women). Yet whites account for nearly 40 percent of all supervisors.

The social and racial stratification within the food service industry should be viewed in the context of larger occupational inequalities in the labor market at large. Food service managers and supervisors are among the lowest-paid managerial positions in New York—even though these earnings are considerably higher than the wages of entry-level employees such as food sales clerks, counter attendants, fast food workers, and fast food cooks who earn, on average, between $170–$200 per week. Fast food managers in New York City earn an average weekly

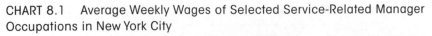

CHART 8.1 Average Weekly Wages of Selected Service-Related Manager Occupations in New York City

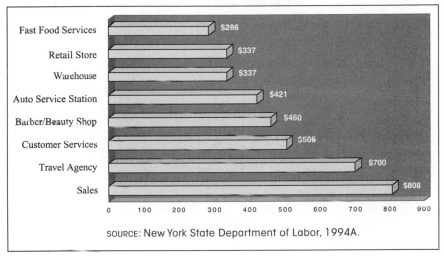

SOURCE: New York State Department of Labor, 1994A.

salary of $286. These earnings are lower than those of every other kind of manager, even managers of retail stores and gas stations (see Chart 8.1), and considerably lower than the earnings of managerial and professional specialty occupations across New York City that pay an average of $552 per week.[12] It is important to note, however, that these figures do not capture variations across the management hierarchy. For example, the average salary of a general or top-level fast food manager in New York City is $16.24 per hour, significantly more than the average fast food manager's salary.[13] But these figures also do not capture variations between restaurants concerning wages or opportunities for managers.

The Fast Food Hierarchy

Despite the common assumption that fast food restaurants are all alike in the kinds of opportunities they offer, the job ladders of individual McDonald's and Burger King restaurants can vary considerably. McDonald's and Burger King have about eight positions from entry-level crewmember to general manager or owner-operator (see Chart 8.2), with slight differences between McDonald's and Burger King and even

CHART 8.2   Typical Fast Food Restaurant Social Hierarchy

Owner/Owner Operator

Store Supervisor

General Manager

Associate Manager

First Assistant Manager

Second Assistant Manager

Manager Trainee/Swing Manager/Production Leader/Head Cashier

Crew Trainer

Crewmember

some differences between restaurants within the same company. Differences include how many people in each position at each restaurant, the extent of upper-tier management opportunity, especially opportunity that extends beyond the restaurant, and wages and benefits.

The extent of opportunity depends on the size of the restaurant, the type and size of ownership, manager turnover rates, ratio of managers to crewmembers, and employers' practices regarding promotions. Not all restaurants have a promote-from-below policy. Those most likely to hire managers from outside the restaurant are large-scale, corporate-owned restaurants such as the corporate-owned McDonald's in Chinatown. Their size and profitability enable them to provide upper-tier management opportunities and prospects to grow within the firm. Consequently, they tend to draw on a professional class of immigrants who are largely from Asia, such as Charles, from Taiwan, and Sandeep, from India. These immigrants are unlikely to join the industry on lesser terms.

From an entry-level employee's standpoint, internal job ladders appear accessible, especially in those establishments with a strong promote-from-below policy. But the low ratio of managers to crewmembers (usually about one to ten), combined with lower turnover rates among managers than among crewmembers, make salaried managers' positions difficult to obtain. In addition, those restaurants that do have a strong promote-from-below policy tend to provide the least amount of upper-tier management opportunity. Numerous low-paid middle-level positions—between crewmembers and salaried managers—help create the illusion of good opportunity. David Gordon, the late economist and the author of *Fat and Mean,* wrote that this kind of layering of managers in today's society is widespread and indicative of corporate restructuring trends.[14] Gordon explained that managers often attempt to reduce turnover and improve workers' morale by adding extra rungs to the ladder. These "extra rungs" are what Gordon calls "frontline" managers, or those responsible for supervising workers at the bottom of the corporate structure.[15]

Every restaurant that I visited except one had this social hierarchical structure or something similar to it. The exception was a Burger King restaurant that had a nonhierarchical management team. This store employed five salaried managers (one "manager" and four assistant managers) and sixty crewmembers. According to one of the assistant managers, they all had extensive McDonald's management experience when they started out together at this Burger King. They all knew how to do everything, which eliminated the need to create a hierarchical division of labor. Salaried managers at each restaurant ranged from four to eight depending on the size of the workforce and restaurant. Generally, the percentage of managers of the total workforce is between 8 and 10 percent; but several swing managers and crew trainers can make up another 10 to 25 percent.

At McDonald's and Burger King, the entry-level position is that of crewmember. As a crewmember, one can become a crew trainer—one of the middle-level, lower-tier positions—and expect to be paid twenty-five or fifty cents more per hour. A crew trainer's additional responsibilities include training newer crewmembers. At McDonald's, a crew trainer can participate in the SIT program (Swing Managers in Training); upon qualification, the crew trainer is certified to become a swing manager. The equivalent in Burger King is a production leader (in the back) and a head cashier (in the front). These mid-level positions are the nearest equivalent to those of a foreman in a factory—a kind of liaison between managers and crewmembers. They account for the most numerous as well as most stressful managers' jobs in the restaurant.

When asked the main difference between a crewmember and a swing manager, Ria, a swing manager of Puerto Rican descent, said,

> A swing manager has more responsibility than a crewmember. A crewmember has to take care of customers. I will be behind them, making sure they do their job. I manage the floor. If I see someone doing something wrong, I make sure I correct them. That way they can get it right. I don't tell them in front of the crew. I pull them aside and let them know what they are doing wrong.

When I asked a production leader, Edward, the second-generation Antiguan in downtown Brooklyn, the same question, he responded by explaining how stressful the position is.

> It is like . . . I am basically friends with everyone. Everyone knows me here. It is kind of stressful because sometimes I have to put my foot down and say look, I need you to do this. If they don't like it, I can tell them to go home or I can request that they punch out. Or for them to get written up. A few people I have requested that they get terminated and they did. It is kind of messed up when you are friends with someone and they try to use your friendship against you. When I try to look [out] for some of my crew and the management don't like it, and I have to cover for them. If the big boss comes in and the managers did something messed up, they will be like, James, what happened. I be like, what are you talking about? Oh, well, I am sorry, I made a mistake. I took off the equipment a little too early. To cover it up. So when I need it they will cover for me. Either way, I am caught between a rock and a hard place. I am dead in the middle. I am not crew and I am not management. I just have a little more authority than they do and know a few more things than they do. But either way it is messed up.

To become a swing manager, one has to study what crewmembers in McDonald's refer to as the "Big Book" or "the Bible"—the McDonald's operation manual. This may take several months to review and must be completed before promotion and usually during one's free time. A crewmember may receive pre-promotion training on-site to learn the intricacies of the restaurant's operations. This training also usually occurs during an employee's free time. There are three levels of swing manager. At McDonald's, the levels refer to degrees of responsibility. Level three is part-time availability with a set schedule and never running a shift alone. Level two is full-time fixed availability (being on-call during certain days and times) with a set schedule and possibly being allowed to run a mid-shift alone. Level one is full-time "open availability" (being on-call at all times) with a flexible schedule while possibly being allowed to run any shift alone. The pay for these positions ranges from seventy-five cents to $4 per hour over the minimum wage. The pay for the equivalent positions at Burger King is about the same.

After reaching level one at McDonald's, a swing manager can enter the MIT program (Managers in Training). Upon passing an exam, the swing manager becomes a second assistant manager. The hurdles to advancement then become increasingly difficult. As a second assistant manager, one can take the BOC (Basic Operations Course). Following the BOC is the BMC (Basic Management Course), and following that is the IOC (Intermediate Operation Course). One then becomes a first assistant manager, followed by associate manager through exemplary performance. These courses are usually conducted in a local headquarters office of the company. Associate managers travel to Illinois for two weeks of intensive training and instruction at Hamburger University, after which they become candidates for general manager. When several restaurants are under the same ownership, usually a store supervisor above the general manager is responsible for supervising more than one restaurant. Above the general manager and the store supervisor is one (or more) owner-operator. The corporate-owned restaurants usually have opportunities at the corporate-level ranks.

Poverty and Wealth: A Look at Income Disparities

Crewmembers in New York City are typically paid the minimum wage. All my crewmember respondents were paid minimum wage or slightly above, and none received significant material benefits such as a health insurance policy. McDonald's assistant managers are usually paid an annual salary. The lowest assistant manager's salary among my respondents was $15,000 a year. General managers among my McDonald's respondents earned an annual salary ranging from $30,000 to $50,000. The

Burger King managers had a wider range, assistant managers making as little as $7.50 per hour to some making a claimed $1,000 to $10,000 per week. (Some restaurants have profit-sharing systems in place.) Salaried managers are typically provided with medical and other benefits.

Even though the average fast food manager's salary is extremely low, the range is extreme. Corporate-owned restaurants tend to have more upper-tier positions than restaurants owned by small-scale proprietorships. The disparity in income and benefits does not pertain only to hierarchical differences: Disparities rooted in ownership structure and the size of the restaurant exist within positions across restaurants.

The following descriptions by two managers clarify this distinction. They are both first assistant managers but work at different Burger King restaurants. The first assistant manager is Julia, the Puerto Rican woman whose restaurant is owned by the small-scale businessman from Vietnam. The second is Loren, the African American whose restaurant in downtown Brooklyn is owned by a large corporation. The first manager stressed the importance of a new tax bill introduced during the Clinton administration to help alleviate her difficult living conditions.

Julia: I make $7.50 per hour. They pay you biweekly. The taxes kill you. And I am just hoping that Clinton actually goes through with it (new tax bill). I pray to God it happens fast. Because you feel so run down at times and you want to go to see a doctor and you can't afford it. A few months ago, I was feeling really run down and I wanted to see a doctor. She told me it was $55. I paid. When I came out they charged me an extra $25 for the urine. Then I got a bill from the lab: $120 for the blood samples. I was like "Oh, my God." Then it turns out I had a stomach ulcer. Eighty-one dollars for the medication. So I paid more than $300 on that visit. And I am still paying it off. I can't afford it. I have been told I could apply for Medicaid, but that is such a hassle. That is such a hassle. I have worked so many years. I have been working since I was fourteen. Always on the books.

Loren: I needed vacation time, they gave it to me. I never had to ask for a raise. They give it to me. I mean I earned it. Everything I need. Benefits. Me and my family are covered. Medical and dental. I pay $10 per week. I get a monthly bonus program right now. It probably brings in $1,000 extra every month. Just bonus on how much sales we do and how

much we receive. If we receive $40,000 more than we expected, then I
get a percentage of that. My weekly check and depending on how hard I
work, I get $1,000. It could be $2,000 or $10,000.

Particularly striking are the disparities in income across the hierarchical corporate structures, from entry-level crewmembers to CEOs.
Chart 8.3 identifies the range of earnings my respondents reported for
each position in the McDonald's and Burger King organizations. According to these figures, the average McDonald's owner earns annual
take-home pay of $150,000 for each restaurant owned. This is seven-
teen times the earnings of a crewmember working full-time at minimum wage. An owner of three McDonald's restaurants earns about fifty
times the wages of a full-time crewmember. And the chairman of
Grand Metropolitan, the British company that owns Burger King, was
paid the equivalent of $1.5 million in 1995, one hundred and seventy
times the income of most Burger King crewmembers in New York City
(based on minimum wage and full-time, year-round employment).
Such disparity in income is indicative of trends among most giant
corporations today, where earnings disparities are growing. Howard
Botwinick writes in *Persistent Inequalities* that "while real wages declined and working people scrambled to make ends meet, the incomes
of the top 1 percent of the population rose by a stunning 74 percent,
and the salaries of corporate CEO's grew by 19 percent."[16] Yet earnings
disparities in the corporate fast food industry appear even more extreme than they are in the average major corporation. Botwinick cites a
Business Week report showing that the average CEO of a major U.S.
corporation made eighty times more than the pay of a typical factory
worker in the U.S. in 1990.[17] (The earnings gap between the chairman
of Grand Metropolitan and the average New York City crewmember is
more than double this figure!) What is important, and consistent with
Gordon's findings, is that earnings disparities between nonsupervisory
workers (or crewmembers) and onsite, restaurant-level managers are
not nearly so extreme as those between crewmembers and owners or
CEOs. The highest salary among general managers that I was able to
obtain the figure for is only about four times a crewmember's pay. The
disparity between an owner of only two restaurants and the highest-
paid general manager is much greater than the disparity between a

CHART 8.3   Disparity of Earnings Across Fast Food Restaurant Industry Occupational Hierarchy

Position	Range of annual earnings based on full-time employment
Crew member	$8,840 to 10,546
Crew trainer	$9,360 to 10,920
Swing manager/production leader/head cashier	$9,880 to 16,640
Second assistant	$14,560 (w/out benefits) to 15,000 (w/benefits)
First assistant	$15,600 (w/out benefits) to 40,000 (w/benefits)
General manager	$20,000 (w/out benefits) to $40,000 (w/benefits)
Store supervisor	$25,000 (w/benefits) to $100,000+ (w/benefits)
Owner operator	$150,000 (owner of 1 restaurant) to 2,850,000 (owner of 19 restaurants). Take home on average for each restaurant (based on McDonald's figures) is $150,000.
Corporate executives	The chairman of Grand Metropolitan was paid 907,000 British pounds (equivalent to about $1.5 million) for sitting on the board of directors in 1995. (McDonald's does not include CEO pay in its annual report.)

SOURCE: Interviews with respondents and corporate memos and reports, 1995.

general manager and a crewmember. The CEO of Grand Metropolitan was paid forty times more than this general manager was paid, a stunningly larger gap than the earnings gap between the general manager and the crewmember.

Moving Up? Hopes, Dreams, Expectations

Given the limits to mobility and the seeming lack of rewards at the bottom of the management ladder, one would not expect many people to pursue positions in management. Indeed, less than one-third of my crewmember respondents desired or planned to become managers, or even considered management a serious option. Employees' goals in the industry are invariably linked to their education and plans. No crewmembers I talked to had a four-year college degree, although one crewmember had a vocational degree. About half the crewmembers were planning on obtaining a two- or four-year college degree. Three were already attending college, twelve were planning to attend college, and five were planning to pursue a vocational degree. Seven crewmembers considered fast food management as a career choice and were among those who were not planning to attend college (see Chart 8.4). This may reflect their lack of alternatives, or ambitions, in the larger labor market as much as a realistic plan to make a career in the fast food industry. Four other crewmembers were considering pursuing positions in management for as long as they remained in the industry while preparing for a career outside the industry.

According to managers, certain kinds of people are more likely to pursue and win the opportunity to join the managerial ranks from an entry-level position. These include immigrants with some form of cultural capital,[18] women,[19] and young people living in financially stable households. Employers commonly claim that the younger an employee is, the more that person can be shaped and cultivated according to the organization's image, structure, and management styles. Young people are more malleable: "There is a difference when you hire someone from the street and you raise a manager from McDonald's . . . someone from the street, high-power person, has an 'I'm the boss attitude,'" said Jose, the Dominican manager in Little Dominican Republic. "Growing up in McDonalds" is the kind of language used to describe the teenager who starts out at sixteen or seventeen and develops his work ethics and attitudes within the fast food restaurant, as several of my manager respondents did. Young people are also believed to have more energy and enthusiasm, fewer problems, and more stamina—qualities needed to keep up with the strenuous physical demands of the job, including the long and fluctuating hours. They are also better able to relate to and supervise young crewmembers.

Various requirements must be met before an employee is considered for a promotion, and these have a direct bearing on one's socioeconomic status. First, those respondents promoted from the entry level

CHART 8.4   Crewmembers' Goals (n=40)

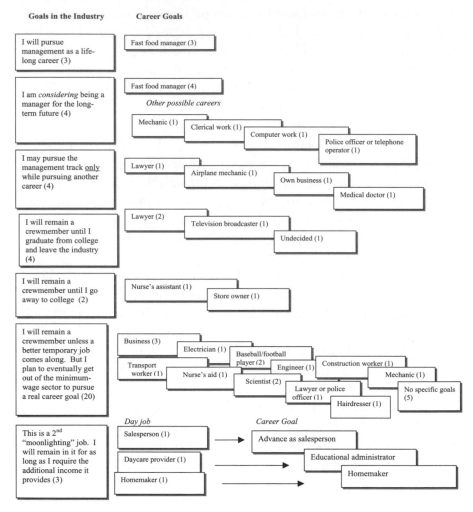

Goals in the Industry

I will pursue management as a life-long career (3)

I am *considering* being a manager for the long-term future (4)

I may pursue the management track <u>only</u> while pursuing another career (4)

I will remain a crewmember until I graduate from college and leave the industry (4)

I will remain a crewmember until I go away to college (2)

I will remain a crewmember unless a better temporary job comes along. But I plan to eventually get out of the minimum-wage sector to pursue a real career goal (20)

This is a 2nd "moonlighting" job. I will remain in it for as long as I require the additional income it provides (3)

Career Goals

Fast food manager (3)

Fast food manager (4)

Other possible careers

Mechanic (1)   Clerical work (1)   Computer work (1)   Police officer or telephone operator (1)

Lawyer (1)   Airplane mechanic (1)   Own business (1)   Medical doctor (1)

Lawyer (2)   Television broadcaster (1)   Undecided (1)

Nurse's assistant (1)   Store owner (1)

Business (3)   Electrician (1)   Baseball/football player (2)   Engineer (1)   Construction worker (1)   Mechanic (1)

Transport worker (1)   Nurse's aid (1)   Scientist (2)   Lawyer or police officer (1)   Hairdresser (1)   No specific goals (5)

Day job   *Career Goal*

Salesperson (1) → Advance as salesperson

Daycare provider (1) → Educational administrator

Homemaker (1) → Homemaker

had worked as crewmembers, on average, for at least a year and a half, well above the industry's average tenure among crewmembers. Some were not promoted for several years. The Dominican general manager in Little Dominican Republic, for example, worked as a crewmember for four years before being promoted. But people do not remain in this industry at the entry level for years at a time unless other household members significantly subsidize their wages. Managers claim that when it comes to job tenure, their workforces have become polarized: More than half of all employees quit or are fired from their jobs within three months. The others remain for significant periods, lasting, on average, between one and four years.

Those who are promoted from the entry level are usually financially supported by relatives and, which is important, do not have another job. A criterion that bears a direct relation to socioeconomic status is having *free* and *flexible time*. Before being considered for a promotion, an employee has to invest free time to study company material. An employee also has to invest time during off-hours to study the intricacies of the restaurant's operation. The free time needs to be flexible because training for promotion usually takes place when the pace of business (which is usually unpredictable) slows down. This training is usually unpaid and offers no guarantee for promotion. The training for promotion, then, favors young people who live in, at the very least, financially stable households. They live with their parents, spouses, or other wage-earning relatives, and are unlikely to have dependents.

But most crewmembers (nearly two-thirds) do not plan to pursue a position in management. They plan to remain crewmembers but view their jobs as something to endure until a better job comes along or until they do not need the income anymore, or as a source of income while they are in school or until they go away to college. No one plans to make a career as a crewmember. Most have a specific career goal that is higher in occupational status than their fast food job, ranging from lawyer and doctor among the college bound to construction and transport worker for those not planning to attend college.[20]

Despite higher occupational goals, those with the least ambitious educational plans show a pattern of hopping around from one low-wage job to the next, often lingering in a particular low-wage job for as long as three or four years until fired or attracted to a few advantages a new job might bring—a more convenient schedule, the opportunity to work with friends, or a "nicer" supervisor. Table 8.4 demonstrates a correlation between education, plans, and the length of time a crewmember holds the job, suggesting a greater dependence on fast food work among the least educated and least upwardly mobile.

Fast food employees, with a few exceptions, do not believe that their fast food jobs will enhance their ability to find a better job. Peter, a

TABLE 8.4   Crewmembers: Educational Status and Plans and Length of
Time in Current Crewmember Position (in months)

	College degree	In college	Planning to go to college	Planning to go to vocational school	Not planning to go to college or vocational school	Don't know
Number of respondents	0	3	12	5	19	1
Average number of months in current crewmember job	---	5	9	13	15	1

crewmember in downtown Brooklyn whose parents are from Puerto
Rico, thinks that putting his Burger King experience on a resume may
hurt him when applying for an office job. As he said, "If I am applying
for an office opportunity, I certainly wouldn't put Burger King. I would
put my other job [salesman]. I would make up a good lie—that I had
my other job instead of this. It is more prestigious." Getting a better
job, according to crewmembers, depends on acquiring a better education, making the most of other jobs, and/or getting "hooked up" with
someone who has connections in another workplace.

Managers' Expectations: A Bridge to the Middle Class?

Managers, like crewmembers, also vary in their expectations in the industry and in their career goals (see Chart 8.5). In general, those who
plan a lifetime career in the industry are those who predict opportunity
to continue rising in the ranks. Invariably, they have already experienced some success in the industry and work for a company with a large
ownership. No one plans to remain in the industry if it means continuing at the same rank. Anyone who occasionally visits a fast food restaurant has probably observed that managers are rarely older than forty. It

CHART 8.5   Managers' Goals (n=16)

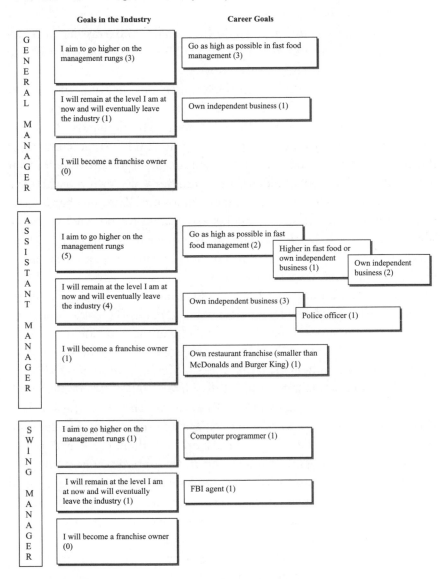

Goals in the Industry   **Career Goals**

GENERAL MANAGER		

I aim to go higher on the management rungs (3)

Go as high as possible in fast food management (3)

I will remain at the level I am at now and will eventually leave the industry (1)

Own independent business (1)

I will become a franchise owner (0)

| ASSISTANT MANAGER | | |

I aim to go higher on the management rungs (5)

Go as high as possible in fast food management (2)

Higher in fast food or own independent business (1)

Own independent business (2)

I will remain at the level I am at now and will eventually leave the industry (4)

Own independent business (3)

Police officer (1)

I will become a franchise owner (1)

Own restaurant franchise (smaller than McDonalds and Burger King) (1)

| SWING MANAGER | | |

I aim to go higher on the management rungs (1)

Computer programmer (1)

I will remain at the level I am at now and will eventually leave the industry (1)

FBI agent (1)

I will become a franchise owner (0)

was made quite clear by my respondents that no one reaches "old age" as an onsite fast food manager.

Some managers said that it would be socially embarrassing to be an onsite manager beyond the age of thirty: "Move up or move out" is the general credo for a career in this industry.

Managers' ranks are directly correlated with job conditions: pay levels, responsibilities, levels of stress, and social pressures. According to managers, part of the pressure is simply physical. The demands of the job become too strenuous. Pedro explained, "I don't think someone in their thirties or forties can take this job anymore. Standing on your feet for ten hours per day. A lot of older gentlemen, thirty-five or forty, who have been in the system for ten years, are like dinosaurs. They can hardly deal with the job." The physical demands are related to the neighborhood. The job tends to be harsh and dangerous, especially in certain neighborhoods in New York City. All the restaurants I visited are located in areas with relatively high crime rates and where violence is common. Managers recounted numerous stories of harassment by customers and the dangerous situations they had to deal with every day. The older one gets, they believe, the more difficult it is to handle crime and violence.

Another cause of stress on the job is the age difference between managers and crewmembers. The pressures of dealing with young kids are too great, said one manager; those thirty-five or older "are dealing with kids who are twenty years younger than them. They have raised their kids and now they have to raise more? They have no patience anymore at that age for young kids." Constantly present, then, is a social, physical, and financial pressure to move up in the organization as one gets older. With the promise of advancement, managers often linger on in their jobs; and the higher they go, better salaries and less direct supervisory responsibility lessen the pressure to leave the industry and make upper-level opportunity that much more competitive.

Those with college degrees or postgraduate training among my respondents occupy the highest and best posts in management. For instance, three out of four general managers I spoke to (Charles, from Taiwan; Jose, from the Dominican Republic; and Gitu, from India) envision a lifetime career in the industry. Significantly, all three work for large companies with job ladders extending into the corporate ranks.

They each have a college degree, and two of them (Charles and Gitu) have postgraduate training. In contrast, the fourth general manager (Pedro, from Colombia) has only a high school education, works for the small-scale businessman from Vietnam, sees no opportunity to move beyond his current position, and plans to leave the industry eventually and open a mom-and-pop restaurant. The distinction between managerial conditions may say less about educational requirements for upper management positions than it does about the competitive nature of "good" opportunity in this industry and the roles human capital and ownership play in deciding fast food careers.

Cultural capital may also be important at the upper rungs, as is evident with Charles, the Taiwanese manager, and his successful drive to integrate McDonald's into the Chinese community. But ownership size and human capital are the defining features that distinguish between people in the best and worst managerial positions. The distinction between Julia and Loren (described earlier in this chapter) is a good indication of the importance of ownership in determining wages and opportunities. Additionally, Table 8.5 demonstrates a positive link between educational goals and attainment and aims in the fast food industry. The more highly educated employees—those enjoying human capital—are promoted sooner from entry level positions, are more apt to be hired as managers rather than crewmembers, and are quicker to leave the industry because they have more alternatives.

Those having a college degree or postgraduate training have been with their current employer for an average of sixty months (five years) versus ninety-six months (eight years) for those who do not have and do not plan to pursue a college degree. (In other words, employees having only a high school degree tend to linger longer in the industry, often take longer to be promoted, and have difficulty competing at the highest rungs of the job ladder.) For instance, only one out of twelve assistant and swing managers have a college degree and only five others are pursuing or planning to pursue one. Three lower-level managers consider the fast food job ladder as a possible career path, although only one is studying for a college degree. Their choices may reflect a lack of opportunity in the larger labor market as much as a real desire to remain in the industry.

TABLE 8.5   Managers: Educational Status and Plans and Length of Time in Current Crewmember Position (in months)

	College or postgraduate degree	In college	Planning to go to college	Planning to go to vocational school	Not planning to go to college or vocational school
Number of respondents	5	3	2	0	6
Average number of months working for current employer	60 (5 yrs.)	60 (5 yrs.)	30 (2.5 yrs.)	----	96 (8 yrs.)

The possibility of obtaining another job outside the industry largely depends on human capital, particularly college degrees and social contacts. The distinctions between Julio, the Puerto Rican assistant manager, and Jose, the Dominican general manager, make this clear. In some ways, they are similar. They both have bachelor's degrees, they are both Hispanic, and they are both in their late twenties. Jose, a general manager who works for a growing company that owns other restaurants, plans to stay in the industry indefinitely. Therefore, he has an opportunity to become a store supervisor, and, perhaps, to climb even higher. He also has a bachelor's degree to fall back on or build upon if and when he does leave the industry. Julio, on the other hand, will probably not be able to climb higher than his current position. The general manager at his restaurant has been there for fourteen years and has no plans to leave; moreover, the ownership is a small proprietorship that does not offer opportunities beyond the restaurant site. In the meantime, Julio is working towards a master's degree so that he can leave the industry and pursue another career.

It is more difficult to secure a future outside the industry without having a college degree. The lack of a college degree, however, may be compensated for by the amount of social capital one has accrued while serving as a fast food manager. Loren, the African American assistant manager in Brooklyn, for example, has only a high school degree and no other work experience outside the fast food industry. This constrains his opportunities both within and outside the industry. Still, as a fast food manager, he has developed close personal ties with owners in the same area. During the writing of this book, Loren was allegedly fired from Burger King; but he was immediately hired as a manager at a store directly across the street from the restaurant—a discount electronics store chain. It appears that horizontal mobility exists in the low-wage world. Such mobility is determined not only by management experience but also by social capital. Management experience, in itself, provides the opportunity to build social capital.

Horizontal mobility has little or no correlation with movement between same-franchise businesses. Managing a Burger King does not necessarily put you in a better position to get a job at another Burger King if it has a different owner. One would be more likely to find a job at a different kind of establishment owned by the same person, say a Dunkin Donuts also owned by the Burger King owner. In general, and as Pedro said, when those without any "real" credentials leave the industry, they often fall into jobs of lower status and pay and sometimes even start all over again in an entry-level position. One such manager, according to Pedro, "went to work at Genovese Drugs and she was just a regular employee." Another manager, he said, went to work "at some dinky restaurant as a waiter or something."

Some of the lower-level managers are opting for careers in law enforcement or the computer industry and are in the process of earning a college degree (Ria, the Puerto Rican swing manager, is one of these). Those not planning to attend college but who are planning to leave the industry want to own their own businesses. Loren plans to own his own restaurant franchise, one considerably smaller and less expensive than a McDonald's and Burger King franchise. Several managers expressed interest in opening their own restaurants in the future—from mom-and-pop eateries to small franchises. Lower-tier managers generally believe that their fast food management experience is good training for eventual restaurant ownership, but finding the investment capital is usually beyond their earning power. In contrast, upper-tier managers, particularly the few who own company shares and earn bonuses through profit sharing, claim that their earnings will allow them some day to invest in a small franchise restaurant.

Becoming an owner of one of these larger franchises is not a realistic possibility for the average manager or minimum-wage worker. It is not a position one moves up into because it requires enormous financial capital, not work experience. The price of a franchise restaurant varies considerably. McDonald's and Burger King restaurants are among the most expensive. To open a McDonald's restaurant in 1995 required an investment of over $600,000, 40 percent of this in personal resources, as well as years of training (for owners-to-be), some of it unpaid.[21] It is not difficult to imagine that the capital required is beyond the reach of the average manager who earns a modest salary. It is not realistic to expect that a crewmember earning minimum wage would be able to buy a franchise. Those managers who aspire to be restaurant owners consider only mom-and-pop establishments, or smaller, cheaper, and less prestigious corporate franchises.

These patterns show the expectations held by immigrants holding jobs in this industry. But even within these broad patterns there exists nuance pointing to the ways fast food workers view their jobs in the larger context of their lives and goals.

Beyond the Underground Economy

Bettina, for instance, is from the Dominican Republic, and is considering pursuing a fast food managerial position. Like Tina, Bettina settled down in an ethnic neighborhood to live among relatives, including many who worked in the underground employment sectors. Like the Chinese, many Dominicans, who make up one of New York's poorest and least-educated immigrant groups in New York, rely on the lowest-paid jobs, often sub-minimum-wage, in the underground economy.

As a small child, Bettina came to New York with her mother. But like many of the city's Dominican people, including Jose, the Dominican general manager in Little Dominican Republic, Bettina spent much of her childhood traveling back and forth between New York and the Dominican Republic. Bettina and her mother now live in a tiny apartment in Little Dominican Republic, only a few blocks from the McDonald's where Bettina works, and on a street known for its drug dealing and frequent shootings. Her mother, who speaks only Spanish, is a seam-

stress who works at home making little girl's dresses as part of a contractual agreement with a local businessman. This kind of work
arrangement is what social scientists call "outsourcing" or "home working." It is a deregulated form of garment production that cuts production costs and increases profit levels by eliminating onsite factory costs
such as rent, capital outlay, taxes, and supervisory staff. Bettina's
mother does not want her to follow in her footsteps. She is proud of her
daughter's employment at McDonald's, and encourages her to continue
even though she is often harassed and made fun of by neighborhood
peers. Bettina has worked in fast food restaurants on and off for five
years, since she was fourteen. Her fast food paycheck, in a small way,
helps pay the rent and other household expenses. Becoming a salaried
manager would bring an increase in income, a steady paycheck, health
insurance, and a boost in status.

Young women like Tina and Bettina have been helping to fuel the
burgeoning underground economy for decades, particularly in downscale garment manufacturing. Their movement into fast food restaurants is representative of those who are breaking out of enclave employment and joining the mainstream in the hopes of long-term gain. But
they are doing this with the support of family members whose earnings
from the underground economy provide the household with a meager
yet relatively stable income.

Managers were well aware that many of their employees live in
households that have long depended on jobs in the ethnic enclave's underground sectors. But not all of them are looking for a career in the industry. Charles, the manager from Taiwan, who hired Tina in Chinatown, has observed that many Chinese youth join the industry for other
reasons. He believes it is a generational phenomenon.

> The kids, when they go into a real hard-working environment, they can't
> handle it. Because they have parents, family here. For most of us that
> came in fifteen to twenty years ago, we came alone. We didn't have any-
> thing to fall back on. We had no choices about working hard to make a
> living. To support ourselves. The kids now, they don't need that. A hard
> working environment, twelve to fourteen hours a day working. They
> don't need that. What they want to do is make some more experiences.

They want to get to know more and different people. They want to make a little spending money on the side. That is why we are getting all these people. They want to learn something in their first job. By living in the community they know Chinese restaurant already is a very difficult job.

Alison said that those who work at McDonald's tend to be the upwardly mobile.

Here [McDonald's] they feel good. After they graduate college they want to find a job five days a week and after four hours have a break. They don't want to work in a factory. If they want to work in a factory they will keep going to work in factory because you can make a lot of money. When you feel you have made a lot of money you are not going back to school. But here you work hard. You have a little money but you will go to school. Because you say you don't want to work at McDonald's all my life. Those who choose to go to a higher level work here.

Among the elderly in Chinatown, working in a fast food restaurant is a kind of haven away from the harsh conditions of Chinese factories and restaurants. Comparing the factory conditions to McDonald's, Alison, the Malaysian manager said, "The factory conditions are very dirty. Some there is no air conditioner. It is no good for them." Jose believes that fast food employment is a more secure and validating alternative to traditional restaurant jobs in the Dominican community.

A lot of these kids, like the ones who talk around the neighborhood and the Dominican kids come in from the Dominican Republic or from another area, they know here that in McDonald's in general, if they work they are going to get paid for what they work. They have benefits. They have rights. They are not going to get abused. On the other hand when they work in certain restaurants, I don't know which ones, they know from heresay they are going to get abused. Maybe if they don't pay their taxes or whatever, but in the long run it is going to catch up with them. So they don't want to, for the most part, take that risk. It just is not worth it. If they are legally here, that is.

Middle-Class Children:
From "Jordon Sneakers" to Building Careers

Wendy is so far removed from the underground economy that she barely knows it exists. She came to New York from the Dominican Republic with her parents when she was fifteen, two years before I interviewed her. They came because her father, a journalist, had found a job with a Spanish-language newspaper in New York City. Wendy's family represents a small percentage of the Dominican population that enters the United States with professional legal status.

Instead of settling in an immigrant neighborhood, Wendy's family rented an apartment in a middle-class neighborhood in the Bronx. Wendy is a college student majoring in communications, and she is hoping to make a career in television. Her mother is a registered nurse. After being in the United States for only a year, Wendy took a job at a Burger King close to home. Later, she got a job at a McDonald's located in Little Dominican Republic. This job is close to her cousin's house and some of her friends work at the restaurant.

In many ways, Wendy fits the traditional stereotype of the American fast food worker. She began working to earn pocket change, not out of necessity. In other ways, Wendy's experiences in New York reflect those of scores of teenagers who emigrate to the United States and find themselves negotiating between the culture from back home and the youth culture in their new country. Wendy decided that she had to work to fit into a highly competitive teenage culture that stresses independence, consumerism, and conformity. Such pressure does not exist in the Dominican Republic. As Wendy said, "The difference is, right there [Dominican Republic] I can't have a job. Right here [New York] I can. Right here I have to work and I have to study. Right there, I just have to study. I don't need to work. . . . There you can go to school. You can hang out. You can stay at home and you can have money. But here it is different."

Wendy was struggling to fit into a new youth culture not only by acquiring a taste for American consumer goods but also by claiming an independence from her parents, who disapproved of her working and her new spending habits.

As she said,

Oh, yah, you have a Jordon sneakers? Oh, you have ruffy? I am going to buy something like that. That is what my father don't like. If I see a sneaker, I say, "I like that sneaker. I want to buy that sneaker." I tell my father, but he says, "I don't want to buy that stupid thing because it is ugly." That is why I work. Because if I work, I can buy the shoes. . . . But he doesn't want me to work.

In the same way, and as the quote at the beginning of this chapter implies, Alison felt a great deal of pressure from her school friends, who insisted that she get a job. She explained why she eventually gave in:

At 1:30, I left the school. I had nowhere to go but home. I was too lonely. . . . She said, "Do you want to hang out together after work?" I said, "How can I hang out together when I just came to this country? My father doesn't allow me to go out." She said, "If you work at McDonald's, we can hang out after work." I always opened, like 5:30 in the morning. And after 1:30, I hung out on the street with my friend, going to the movies. After 6:00, my father would pick me up. My girlfriend went back to China.

Wendy and Alison represent a relatively new type of labor supply in New York—middle-class teenage immigrants who fit the traditional American stereotype of the upwardly mobile fast food worker. They are, as described by managers, ideal workers: young, upwardly mobile, and true to the immigrant work ethic. They also do not plan to stay in the industry and are unlikely to organize a labor union. They often enjoy their jobs, particularly the excitement that comes from working in an "American" institution in a new country while proving themselves capable in a competitive youth culture.

Brusso, the young Russian worker in Chinatown, also comes from a middle-class background. But he is somewhat less fortunate than Wendy and Alison because he is the sole income earner in a household of five people. Brusso's father was an architect in Russia, a draftsman of museums and restaurants, and his mother a housewife. Brusso's parents are both jobless after more than two years in the United States. In Russia, Brusso was familiar with American fast food restaurants and remembers the enormous publicity surrounding the first McDonald's opening in Moscow in 1990. Besides being too young (fifteen) at the time to think about applying for a McDonald's job, Brusso lived too far away, in another city. Brusso first visited a McDonald's after he arrived in New York in 1992. He emigrated with his family to escape the political turmoil and economic crisis following the collapse of the Soviet Union in 1991.[22]

Brusso's family is typical of those with professional backgrounds who arrive in the United States without English-language skills and the human capital required to find an equivalent professional position and the social status it brings. They are still financially dependent on relatives. Brusso' low wages are not enough to pay the rent, but are a necessary contribution. Brusso has forsaken plans for college so that he can help support his parents and younger siblings. Though he earns just above minimum wage, he aspires to a career at McDonald's and plans to move up the manager rungs to the corporate level, where he believes he can earn a "respectable income."

The Socially Mobile Working Class: One Rung at a Time

Fabiola, the twenty-four-year-old assistant manager from the Dominican Republic, is a good example of the way those from lower-class backgrounds, particularly women, have effectively moved into fast food's management positions, helping to establish women as managers in what Fabiola describes as a "male-centered" Latino culture.[23]

Fabiola began working at McDonald's "for fun" when she was eighteen. She began moving up the management ranks after one year of being hired and while she was earning an associate's degree in management. Her husband, whom she met while they were working together at McDonald's, is also a fast food manager (at another restaurant). Fabiola aims to become a general manager and make a career in the McDonald's company. Although Fabiola believes that being a fast food manager is a step up in social status from her parents' occupations (a nurse and an ambulance driver), she acknowledges that the compensation does not match up. "It is not easy to make an independent living," she said. Fabiola and her husband have a one-year-old son and the three of them live with her parents in a Bronx apartment. The only way she is able to work, she said, is because her mother (who is retired) cares for her son, "every day and every night that it is necessary." Because her work schedule changes weekly, Fabiola finds it difficult to make other childcare arrangements. Besides, she said, "It would be hard to afford it."

Peggy, the eighteen-year-old Jamaican employee in downtown Brooklyn, is a good characterization of West Indian immigrants who are successfully moving up the American social ladder and going to work in fast food jobs. Her parents' careers are typical of the trajectories taken by West Indian immigrants in New York. Her mother is a nurse's aide in a hospital and her father attends a technical school to learn refrigeration repair. Peggy lives with them. Joining the mainstream economy has been easier for many West Indian immigrants, particularly those from former British colonies, partly because English is their native language. They also tend to live in households that pool resources. Peggy plans to go to college, become a lawyer, and practice in the United States. She claims that her part-time status at McDonald's provides her the time she needs to study.

Aiming High; Returning "Home"

Not all West Indian employees are destined to successful careers. Some of my West Indian respondents, particularly the Antiguans in Little Dominican Republic, have fallen into the industry as a job of last resort and plan to return to the "home" country to build a better life. Their plans are influenced by their economic position and racial status in New York. Laurie, the Antiguan manager who works as Jose's assistant manager, is a good example. Laurie, whose dream was to become a teacher, left Antigua with some of her siblings when she was a teenager. They joined their aunt, who lives in the Bronx. Their parents stayed behind in the rural farming village where they grew up.

Once in high school in New York, Laurie's aspirations to become a teacher began to wane. As she said, "It started changing. I wanted to be a word processer, and then the money to go to college and working, I couldn't do it. So I decided just to finish high school and that is it." She had never heard of American fast food restaurants before arriving in New York City. She started as a part-time crewmember and, as she said, "I kept moving up so I decided to become a manager. Why? I don't know." Laurie is the only one among her immediate relatives in New York with a job in the formal mainstream economy. Her aunt and sister babysit at home and her brother is a mechanic off the books, common occupations for Antiguans in New York. Laurie has another brother and sister in Antigua; the brother is also a mechanic and her sister "works [as a clerk] in the labor department."

Her family is very proud of her rise in the managerial ranks. She is the first person in the family to become a "manager." But Laurie is not happy with her job, a feeling influenced by the racism she claims to encounter both at the restaurant and in the neighborhood where she works. She plans to return to her home country, where she aspires to start her own business. She sends a small part of her paycheck home to her parents, who are saving it for her return.

Betty, the Antiguan crewmember in Little Dominican Republic, also plans to return to her home country. Betty lives with her mother and sister in the Bronx, a thirty-minute walk from Little Dominican Republic and the restaurant where she works. Like Peggy's mother, Betty's mother is a full-time nurse's aid. Her sister is an entry-level cook at a Friday's restaurant. And like Peggy and Laurie, Betty had higher ambitions. She earned a degree from the IBM business school and aspired to "work with computers." After an unsuccessful search for a job in her field, she went to work at McDonald's. As discussed in the last chapter, Betty even had aspirations to move up the fast food ranks. But her promotion to crew trainer failed when her Hispanic coworkers resisted her authority. Unlike Laurie, Betty "could not take it" and asked to be demoted.

Betty and Laurie are representative of scores of immigrants who have fallen into the industry as opposed to those who are using the industry as a stepping-stone to something better in New York's labor market. But Betty and Laurie are different from other low-wage workers because they plan to return home to Antigua, where they have an opportunity to build a better life. Betty also sends part of her wages home so that her family can save them for her eventual return; this money helps elevate her socioeconomic status in Antigua.

These stories help us understand how race shapes "temporary migration."[24] In Antigua, they were poor, but they were part of a racial majority; in New York, they are still poor, but they are associated with a racial minority, a poor black population. Being subjected to racism and discrimination without the material means to alleviate this racialized experience in New York helps shape their desire to return "home."

The Professionals: Reaching the Top?

Sandeep, the manager from India working in downtown Brooklyn, is a good example of the unique and varying ways immigrants of professional backgrounds fall into this industry. Sandeep came to the United States to join his sister, who encouraged him to sell his tourism business in India and reinvest the money in the United States. He was en route to becoming part of the growing number of entrepreneurial immigrants in the United States. He was also a Ph.D. candidate in philosophy in India, although he abandoned work on his dissertation several years ago. Shortly after arriving in New York, he lost all his money in a failed investment plan. Now, he says, he cannot return to India, even for a visit, while he is a Burger King manager because he feels ashamed of his position and cannot face his family in India; this shame typifies how some immigrants today, especially those from elite backgrounds, see their fast food status in the United States as a personal failure.

Unlike Laurie's relatives, who are proud of her success in becoming a manager, Sandeep says that his family would consider his current manager's position a disgrace, very low in social and economic status. He describes his situation as a "pathetic, pathetic story." In the United States, his lifestyle has changed drastically from what it was in India. He works at Burger King ten hours a day or more, five days a week. "This is America," he says. "[It is] entirely different with bad social conditions." He does earn enough to help support two children in college and his wife on his Burger King salary. He does not plan to leave the industry until his children have graduated from college, at which time he hopes to start his own business. In the meantime, he says, "If you don't have time to laugh, you cry, and half my life is over, so I try to be satisfied with my life."

Hiring managers externally (rather than from the ranks) is more likely to occur in restaurants that are owned by large local corporations. Because of their large size, they offer more positions in upper management and are therefore able to draw from a professional group of immigrants, particularly those who have not found jobs in their own fields. Opportunity in upper management and an ever-growing number of immigrant professionals in New York City have increased the growth of ethnic niches at these upper rungs. South Asians, well-endowed with human capital, account for the largest ethnic niche in fast food management in New York. But not all are as bitter as Sandeep.

Gitu, for instance, has been a manager at Burger King for seven years and has managed a Burger King restaurant in Little Dominican Republic for nearly two years. He has a physics degree from India and moved to New York to join family members. Although he never imagined working in a fast food restaurant in New York, he is now pursuing a career in the industry. He obtained his job as a "manager trainee" through a friend from India who was working in a fast food restaurant. Gitu aspires to become a district manager, where he will be in charge of several restaurants under the same ownership. He is not particularly proud of the industry he works for, but he sees it as the best of available alternatives and takes it seriously.

Charles, the Taiwanese manager, has been in the food business for nearly two decades, even though he has an engineering degree. He immigrated to the United States from Taiwan to pursue graduate studies. While studying, Charles worked at his sister's Chinese restaurant, doing "everything . . . dishes, busboy, waitering, and bartending." He then managed her restaurant for three years and eventually ventured out on his own as the owner of a successful Chinese restaurant. His background is unique relative to other fast food manager respondents in this study. As the quote at the beginning of this chapter suggests, his movement into the fast food industry on the management rungs represents an upward career shift into the corporate world.

Like Gitu, Charles plans to become a store supervisor and oversee four or five restaurants under the same ownership. Ultimately, he would like to move into the corporate ranks and enjoy a good salary, fringe benefits, a five-day work week, and vacation time—what he considers "luxuries" compared to running an independent enterprise.

The New Poor: From One Job to the Next

Marco, a thirty-six-year-old Cuban immigrant, represents the growing number of downwardly mobile workers who have found themselves trapped in the "cycle that never ends." For several years he has been "hopping around" from one low-wage job to the next without improving his job status and working conditions. He is a father, a divorcee, and former member of the U.S. Marines who claims that his only alternative "is to become a cop," but his parents are against the idea because of the perceived danger. He tried to join the marines again but they said he was too old. He tried college, but he "couldn't take it." During the interview, he said to me jokingly, "Do you have anything? I will clean your house, wash your clothes, anything."

Marco is an example of many men without college degrees who are willing to work hard and live a simple life of going to work, doing the job, and being done with it at the end of the day. These are men who a generation earlier would be doing semiskilled manual work in a factory. They are finding little or no place in today's service economy—no place, that is, that provides a decent standard of living for a family, with job security, a good income, and health insurance. As Marco described it, his precarious job situation put too much pressure on his marriage, which led to divorce. Now he barely makes enough to pay his part of the rent for an apartment he shares with a stranger. He works most days, and spends most evenings at home watching television. He cannot afford a telephone. The only thing he claims to look forward to is the one day every week he spends with his son. If Marco did not have a supportive family structure, if he could not depend on his parents to be there for him during times of crisis, he would be only one step away from living on the streets.

As an older person in a youth-oriented workplace culture, he often finds himself socially isolated. Like other "older" employees, he is assigned to the most undesirable work in the restaurant: wiping tables, mopping floors, and taking out the garbage. On the night I met Marco to learn about his job, one of his coworkers was having a party for all the employees. But Marco felt uncomfortable about going because, as he said, "It would be all young kids." He is motivated in his work by the fear of losing his job.

For someone like Marco, the possibility of becoming a manager is virtually nonexistent. Either you start out young, like Pedro, Julio, Loren, and Alison, or you enter with other credentials, such as a college degree, as did Sandeep, Gitu, and Charles. While Marco claims that he does not want to pursue a management job because the "hours are long and requires responsibility beyond just a job," this could be a rationalization in the face of an impossibility: a resignation to a position he is finding harder and harder to climb out of as he grows older. Without moving up, he ends up shifting from one low-wage job to the next, accruing work experience that holds marginal value in each new job. Before his current Burger King job, for instance, he worked at McDonald's for several months, where he was paid minimum wage. After eight months at Burger King, he was earning twenty-five cents above minimum wage.

On a broader level, and what is significant here, is that the amount of job experience one accumulates at the bottom rungs of the service and retail economy has little influence on vertical mobility in the service and retail sectors at large. No matter how many years of experience they had, or how many jobs they had previously held, my employee respondents began working every new job at the entry level, and, by and large, at minimum wage. Roy, my crew trainer during my participant observation at Burger King, for example, and as I mentioned in Chapter 1, started at minimum wage in his current job, even though he had previously become an assistant manager at a McDonald's restaurant.

A recent finding by the nonprofit Community Service Society illuminates the importance of the tendency to hop around from one low-wage job to the next. Between the late 1980s and late 1990s, the rate of poverty rose, particularly among those who have long been considered immune to poverty: those who work (and even those holding more than a high school degree). They are labeled the "New Poor." That over half (twenty-one out of forty) of my crewmember respondents currently attend or plan to attend college is no longer a sure indicator that they will escape future poverty.[25] But that nearly half (nineteen out of forty) of my crewmember respondents do not even have plans to go to college or even vocational school would seem to be a more frightening indication that many people in this industry are falling into an even deeper cycle of poverty, even though nearly all of them have higher job and career aspirations[26] (see Table 8.4 and Chart 8.4).

9

Flipping Burgers in a Melting Pot? Looking Ahead to a More Multicultural Society

As more and more immigrants like Tina become our nation's burger-flippers and basket-fryers, we need to reconstruct our vision of the fast food industry as a rigidly standardized institution and understand the ways in which immigrants influence how restaurants such as McDonald's and Burger King operate, and the various meanings and social uses that are related to fast food work.[1] With the presence of such institutions in ethnic enclaves, too, we need to move away from the image of immigrant communities as homogenous and ethnically segregated. In so doing, we cannot apply a single framework that would help us understand what this industry implies in the long run for immigrants' adaptation to American society.

Tina, for instance, personifies a conventional "melting pot" understanding of immigrant adaptation to American society. Stepping out of the ethnic enclave, Tina joined an American institution where she is learning to speak English and associating with people outside of her own ethnic group. She dreams of becoming a manager so that she can gain higher social status, a salary, and health benefits in the American mainstream economy. Tina works in Chinatown, a globally diverse neighborhood, in a restaurant that targets a diverse clientele, including international tourists, a pan-Asian residential population, and a multicultural mix of New Yorkers. The labor force reflects this global diversity and affirms a kind of melting pot phenomenon.

But immigrants' experiences in this industry are not uniform. Restaurants are situated in various cultural contexts, have different types of ownership, and considerable autonomy in decisionmaking, and hence, they vary at the local level. This is despite old-school wisdom that posits the fast food restaurant as an "ideal type" for modern society's mass standardization and simplification.[2] The geocultural context in which Tina works, for instance, plays a significant role in shaping her work culture.

This means that fast food work cultures in other geocultural contexts can play very different roles in shaping the cultural adaptation of immigrant workers to the American workplace and American society. Restaurants in Little Dominican Republic, such as the one where Wendy works, tend to re-affirm Latino identity and culture (constructed within a pan-Latino context) rather than a melting pot or Anglo identity. In some restaurants, workers are required to speak only Spanish and do not speak English. Although most workers live outside the Little Dominican Republic, they are drawn from other Latino neighborhoods in New York City and therefore live, work, and go to school within the boundaries of Latino communities.

American fast food restaurants in this neighborhood help reinforce aspects of ethnic culture within the Latino community while reconstructing what it means to be an American mainstream enterprise and altering the requirements for employment. In this way, the culture of ethnic communities is reinforced. Latino workers gain experience in an American mainstream enterprise but do not necessarily learn English on the job. But as the Spanish language is absorbed into the mainstream job market, it, too, is reengineered as a commodity to be bought and sold, interwoven in the exchange between customers and workers. On the other hand, these restaurants may come closest to resembling Portes's and Bach's ethnic enclave model and the ethnic resilience it creates.[3]

The Global Workplace

The fast food industry does not typify traditional work forms in the immigrant neighborhood. The kinds of people employed by the industry and the structural terms of employment are considerably different from the traditional conception of the ethnic neighborhood firm. These differences affect the way immigrants identify themselves as exploited or upwardly mobile workers. Employee relations and the values immigrants are confronted with in the workplace are also affected, particularly as they affect the way immigrants see their working conditions.

First, in New York City, workforces are socially and globally diverse in this industry, and their chances for success vary. Employees include those seeking a professional career change, like Charles, the Taiwanese manager in Chinatown, and those like Marco, the thirty-six-year-old Cuban, who feels exploited and trapped. In this way, the fast food workforce is not uniform in the way it identifies its position in the industry. Second, although many employees like Tina seek upward mobility within the industry, most do not. Given the stigma associated with fast food work (which is internalized by some immigrant groups and individuals more than others), employees are not likely to identify with the industry socially and personally. Immigrant fast food workers may be ethnically stratified and organized in this industry according to geocultural context, hierarchical position, and so forth. But no fast food restaurant workforce in this study represents the kind of ethnic and social class homogeneity characteristic of the ethnic economies model.

Such diversity, from an industry perspective, derives from job requirements that stress cultural diversity as well as customer-related job skills. Fast food employers are not concerned about hiring a vulnerable co-ethnic workforce; they are more concerned with shaping an image and ambiance that merges geocultural features with corporate traditions. In this way, immigrant cultural capital and social skills are more important than co-ethnicity and vulnerability, which are important in the ethnic economies model. It is important to understand the hiring decisions and cultural preferences built into these decisions as local negotiations built into the corporate organization.

Cultural preferences are not simply products of stereotypical conceptions of ethnic groups, or even a tendency to "hire your own." They are intimately linked to the structural features and marketing practices of this industry, which determine the local adaptability of certain immigrant groups versus others. Gitu, the manager from India, hires only Latinos in Little Dominican Republic because they can speak in Spanish to the customers. Loren, an African American, refuses to hire "his own" because he believes their attitude does not fit the corporate organization's emphasis on providing friendly and courteous service. This says as much about how managers perceive the traits of different groups as how they negotiate the interaction between cultural features and organizational goals.

Technology also influences the diversity and social organization of a workforce. Employing the most advanced communication technology in the restaurant, for example, enables managers to hire diverse groups of people. Tina, who is from Shanghai, can take an order on the frontline from a customer in a Chinese dialect that they share and then communicate this order to Ricardo, a Dominican immigrant speaking Spanish to a coworker from Honduras in the back. The requirement for "harmonious human relations" in the restaurant industry, as William Whythe described it nearly a half century ago, now transcends the need for a common spoken language. Language of ethnicity has been replaced by language of technology in the most technologically sophisticated restaurants. Technological standardization allows for a global workforce. In turn, diversity helps deter a collective identity among employees.

The Irony of Minimum-Wage Work

Fast food employee relations are not always harmonious in this industry, despite conventional thinking that equates standardization with rationalization and human complacency,[4] and despite other fast food studies that show a uniform culture of worker resistance.[5] I saw conflicts in the fast food restaurants I examined, and these conflicts, ironically, are endemic to the industry's structure and contribute to social divisions within the fast food workforce. Flexible work time, including interchangeability in the assignment of work tasks, represents a break from the rigidity and routinization implied in our usual understanding of low-wage work. This "usual" understanding is associated with the past century's models of production, including Fordism, where the modern assembly line came to represent what we know about routinized work. But if the routinization of shop-floor auto work was compensated for by the $5 a day wage (equivalent to $120 a day today), it would seem that today's comparatively low wages should be compensated for by not-so-dull work. Despite common thought that has long insisted that fast food work is easy and requires little skill, I have found from both experience and what workers tell me that it is difficult, often challenging, and does require skillful labor. But it has acquired low social status in society at large, and includes a good deal of dirty and dangerous work.

Fast food work comprises both desirable and undesirable work, which forms and reinforces status distinctions within the restaurant. A woman in the job of cashier gains as much respect as a woman cleaning the bathrooms gains disrespect. Preparing french fries is as safe as changing the 400-degree oil in the vats is unsafe. (Dangerous work has low status because it often results in injuries.) Being assigned a cashier's position, for a woman, is a symbolic gesture implying attractiveness and competence. Being assigned to clean the bathrooms is a statement of marginal social status in the restaurant. Making french fries requires a simple gesture—pouring frozen potato slices into a machine. Cleaning oil vats often results in burns, injury, and scars.

Given the industry's emphasis on interchangeability and managers' authority to delegate various restaurant tasks, including the most undesirable work, distinctions between workers are inevitable. Distinctions based on ethnicity are the most common and explicit. The ethnic antagonisms that I have identified in this book should not be viewed out of context because they are local and structural.

On the one hand, ethnic distinctions may be used as tools by managers to ensure that the undesirable and dangerous work gets done. The racially divisive tactics employed by a manager on my first day on the job at a Burger King restaurant illustrate this point. Giving labels of "nigger" and "lazy" to the workers who refused to mop the floors implied an elevation of my status as white because I didn't refuse to mop the floors. More important, it suggested that the increased burden of having to mop the entire floor on my own was caused by the "laziness" of the African Americans. If I had played into the manager's logic, I would have gone home feeling a racially-based anger toward the African American teenagers.

Negative sentiments toward social groups that take an ethnic or racial form are often constructed as rationales by workers for explaining their own subjugation to work they feel is unfair, such as cleaning bathrooms, changing oil vats, or mopping floors. It is easier to explain why someone does not do the dirty work than to explain why one conforms to unfair work. Betty, the Antiguan worker disgusted with the Haitian coworkers because they left her to clean grills that burned her arms, blamed her coworkers' irresponsibility rather than her manager. Instead of thinking about seeking protection from dangers in the workplace, workers create social boundaries between themselves. Managers may help incite these boundaries or simply respond to them through reinforcement.

Fast food workers are constantly in search of validation for what they do. Invalidating the behavior of a particular social group is one source of self-validation. Validation, in general in this industry, has to come from external sources because the work carries negative social status. The fast food organization does not encourage a long-term commitment to honest work because it does not reward long-term employment. Fast food employees claim to work honestly because their work is legitimate and not illicit; and, more often than not, they seek long-term and stable work, even though temporary jobs are expanding at a faster rate than permanent jobs in today's labor market. But workers do not necessarily receive societal respect, or equivalent social status, for conforming to these traditional social values in the fast food restaurant.

Herein lies the great irony of minimum-wage mainstream work in the twenty-first century. As Richard Sennett points out in *The Corrosion of Character*, the values of working, of maintaining a job and a commitment to it, do not necessarily correspond with the values embedded in the work itself.[6] Validation for working in a postindustrial minimum-wage job is found off the job, not on it. As one manager said, "They [values] come from somewhere else." Values are rooted in the family and in the internalization of neoconservative versions of a work ethic that stress conformity, hard work, and delayed gratification. These values may be reinforced through religion, the family, or ethnic culture.

They are partly shaped by reference to others and by constructing boundaries between "good" and "bad" workers. They are not shaped by references to the organizational structure, or the structures of power that engineer the organizational structure. The values embedded in workers' private realities do not coincide with the values promulgated in the public workspace. Although employees may receive public recognition for good work through such things as an "employee of the month" plaque or positive customer feedback, these do not necessarily result in improved work conditions such as significant pay raises, promotions, or health insurance.

In this way, the fast food industry departs from the strategies employed by the most prominent mainstream sectors of our past industrial era. The fast food industry is unable to convey a complementary set of values to its workers as Henry Ford did to his assembly line workers. However tedious and alienating assembly line work was, Ford stressed company loyalty, life-long commitment, and an income that bought enough material status to gain societal respect.[7] The fast food industry stresses temporary status, the contingency of industry need, and an income that gains societal contempt rather than respect. No wonder workers behind the counter suffer harassment from customers, feel that they are not respected, and rarely wear their uniforms in public.

The premium placed on customer service, the shaping of personality, and the dichotomizing of feelings between work and home further widens the gap between private life and work life and poses a contradiction for the fast food organization. The more the gap widens, the more managers are required to gain control over the private lives and emotions of their workers. In the hope of encouraging laughter and smiles in the workplace, Laurie, the Antiguan manager, whispers jokes to her workers about their private lives. Fabiola, the Dominican manager, maintains contact with her workers outside of the workplace by giving them her home phone number. Julia makes rounds of calls every morning to make sure her employees are out of bed and getting ready for work. Some of this control is aided by co-ethnic relations; for example, Charles mediates conflicts between Chinese teenagers and their parents, and Jose makes personal loans to his workers but negotiates the terms with the families. Gaining a degree of control over employees' private lives helps to mediate personal problems among workers so that they may be better prepared to present a "good mood" when they are at work.

The dichotomizing of feelings and the construction of a work-type personality also may imply that relations between employees in the workplace are not necessarily shaped by the expression and communication of private reality. The emphasis on a customer-oriented environment represses the expression of the private self, and, in the process, fragments relations between workers. This does not mean that workers lose a sense of their "real" selves as much as it means that workers have less opportunity to share their feelings with coworkers. In this way, emotional fragmentation has structural roots more than anything else, and it is reinforced through the flexible terms of fast food work. Temporary and contingent work status and a constantly changing schedule mean that workers are unlikely to work with the same people every day or for very long. Therefore, the fast food restaurant in the immigrant neighborhood embodies a different set of work relations and values than those that characterize the traditional ethnic enterprise.

From Behind the Counter to the Living Room: The Link Between Private and Public Ethnic Life

In the time that Tina's husband, Paul, has been in New York City, he has lived and worked in the Chinese enclave, associated almost exclusively with Chinese people, and spoken only Chinese. Although we may view his conditions as exploitative, he has nonetheless been reinforcing the link between his private and public ethnic life; this is important because it represents a dynamic different from that experienced by Tina. By working at McDonald's, Tina may be helping to break down the ethnic link between work and home.

In some ways, we can say that she is building a new link, one between the ethnic community and giant corporate America. If we take Paul's advice, this link has a lot of promise: a chance to learn the language of the dominant society, a chance to build mainstream social capital, a chance to work in a safe, legal, and reliable environment. Paul has in many ways lived a hard and pious existence in New York. It is important to understand his advice to Tina in this context. Still, Tina is trading in a set of values and social relations for this mainstream opportunity. She is unlikely to have the opportunity to build a long-term relationship with a coworker, at least not the kind of sustained co-ethnic relations her husband has established during his years in New York City. Few people she works with will ever know Tina for more than three months at a time. She will rarely work with the same people from day to day. Presented with her cheery smiles and uplifting mood, few people she comes in contact with at work will ever know about the ups and downs of her life.

Tina's ethnicity, a commodity to be bought and sold in the corporate quest for new cultural customers, will cease to perform the traditional economic function in sustaining the ethnic community. Tina's ethnicity in the McDonald's restaurant has been divorced from an authentic community and re-engineered to fit the market logic of corporate capital.

Still, we cannot ignore the sentiments workers expressed concerning the bonds they have managed to build with coworkers in the fast food restaurant. The shaping of an ethnic environment among West Indian workers at a restaurant in Downtown Brooklyn and the expressed closeness it fosters between workers needs to be recognized. This restaurant is unique because most of its employees are West Indians who live in one area of New York City. The closeness between these West Indians may represent some of the most intimate connections that exist among workers in this industry. Nonetheless, we do need to question the way the organization's emphasis on a customer-oriented ambiance and flexible work terms undermines such closeness.

We can safely argue that the fast food restaurant in the immigrant neighborhood represents, by and large, a breakdown of ethnic persistence as defined in the ethnic economy literature. Ethnic communities have indeed made inroads into the American fast food industry by helping define and shape its organizational culture, its job requirements, and its opportunities. But the terms by which this happens are mediated by corporate organizational logic, market principles, and a continuing system of inequities. The values embedded in fast food work are market values premised on workplace flexibility. They include putting work life over family life to meet the flexible demands of the fast food restaurant. They include the discontinuity between work relations and community relations, a result of the temporary nature of the work and the distancing of home and work. They include a repression of real

feelings so that the organizational goals for a customer-oriented, upbeat, and enthusiastic environment can be met.

We could argue that the breakdown of ethnic and community relations would not matter so much if the industry aided upward mobility
into American society for immigrant groups. In any case, for many employees, the limited job ladders within the restaurant don't even matter.
Unlike the traditional ethnic enterprise, the fast food restaurant draws
on a labor force comprised of all classes of people. Children of professional middle-class parents do fast food work for pocket change and
work experience, not to pursue upward mobility. They are in or en
route to college. They are banking on professional careers themselves.
They have a preference for part-time and temporary work at certain
stages of their lives. For the most disadvantaged, we need to have more
concern. As we begin the twenty-first century, we need to recognize
that fast food work is no longer fringe work within a booming manufacturing economy, as it was in the middle of the last century.

Today, the fast food restaurant industry epitomizes jobs in the expanding low-wage service sector, where more people without college
degrees, as well as those not planning to attend college, are becoming
dependent on employment. But a minimum-wage job does not provide
enough income to support an independent living. Most of my respondents live in households supported by multiple incomes. Several of
these households, including Tina's, draw on incomes from the underground economy. Moreover, the fast food industry offers little hope for
those who cling to the idea that hard work alone pays off in the long
run. Few restaurant employees are able to take advantage of the little
good opportunity it does offer.

The increasingly competitive nature of "good" opportunity has
tended to hike up hiring and promotion requirements so that those
with college and even postgraduate degrees are found wearing fast food
management uniforms. There is little indication that fast food work experience is valuable in the labor market at large, particularly for getting
a better job. There is every indication that the industry contributes to a
growing phenomenon of horizontal movement across low-wage job sectors, what one manager called "the cycle that never ends," and contributes to a growing population of "new poor." For those of modest
means, breaking this cycle of working poverty, or not getting entangled

in it in the first place, depends upon whether families are able to support higher education and job training as well as the strength of an internalized value system to cope with the contradictory features of minimum-wage postindustrial work.

What is important is that the ethnic community is held together by its links to ethnic economies and enclave firms. The fast food restaurant industry does not necessarily foster this link and therefore does not support the family and community values this link represents: long-term relationships with coworkers (the kinds of relations that extend into the community), flexible hours for workers (to allow women to juggle family and work responsibilities), and rewarding company loyalty with long-term, full-time work status (the kind that is predictable and reinforces family stability). The fast food restaurant industry not only offers little opportunity for upward mobility in its own ranks but defies the family and community institutions that could aid upward mobility or create a better united front to respond to adverse conditions in the industry.

Although it does not make sense to apply only one framework for understanding what this industry means for immigrants' adaptation to American society, it would also be shortsighted not to acknowledge that this industry is wholly representative of major trends in the postindustrial economy at large. We need to be attentive to the ways in which more and more immigrants are being absorbed into the corporate consumer world, whether they are flipping burgers at McDonald's, serving cappuccino at Starbucks, or taking movie tickets at Sony Theaters. And as these institutions become more numerous in immigrant neighborhoods—places thought to be immune to corporate growth—we need to be increasingly critical of the theories that isolate "ethnic economies," no matter whether fast food restaurants and corporate franchises are inextricably linked to ethnic economies or are their ultimate successor.

NOTES

Chapter 1

1. Vivian Huong, "Immigrants Tell Tales of Brutal Sweatshops," *New York Daily News*, 20 April 1995, 10. The *New York Daily News* quoted the director of the Chinese Staff and Workers' Association (CSWA), reporting that Chinese restaurants in Manhattan's Chinatown employ Chinese immigrants who work seventy hours a week and are paid less than $1 per hour. This article also noted that a Chinatown New York garment factory worker earns $20 per day after working fifteen to eighteen hours. Scholars, too, have documented the adverse working conditions in New York's Chinatown, where Chinese people work for low wages, often under the legal minimum with no material benefits such as health insurance. See Peter Kwong, *Forbidden Workers: Illegal Chinese Immigrants and American Labor* (New York: New Press, 1998).

2. Ivan Light and Steven J. Gold, *Ethnic Economies* (San Diego: Academic Press, 2000).

3. Gabriel Escobar, "Immigrants' Ranks Tripled in 29 Years," *Washington Post,* January 9, 1999, A01; Leon Kolankiewicz, "Immigration, Population, and the New Census Bureau Projections," Center for Immigration Studies (June 2000).

4. George Ritzer, *The McDonaldization of Society* (London: Pine Forge Press, 1993).

5. Alejandro Portes and Robert L. Bach, *Latin Journey: Cuban and Mexican Immigrants in the United States* (Berkeley: University of California Press, 1985); Min Zhou and Regina Nordquist, "Work and Its Place in the Lives of Immigrant Women: Garment Workers in New York City's Chinatown," *Applied Behavioral Science Review* 2, no. 2 (1994): 187–211.

6. Ivan Light et al., "Beyond the Ethnic Enclave Economy," *Social Problems* 41, no. 1 (February 1994): 65–80.

7. Zhou and Nordquist, "Work and Its Place in the Lives of Immigrant Women."

8. Studies of employment in the immigrant neighborhood, particularly the ethnic enclave, have cited the importance of ethnic and spatial factors in shaping the way labor markets work. The ethnic enclave is characterized as a concentration of immigrant-owned firms that enjoy social and economic advantages through their

195

links to the immigrant community. In a critique of dualistic labor market models, Portes and Bach characterize the ethnic enclave as a third labor market, distinct from the general economy. In some ways, they reflect what dual economy theorists refer to as the "secondary labor market." See Portes and Bach, *Latin Journey*. The distinction between primary and secondary labor markets derives from dualistic theories of the labor market, for example Doeringer and Piore's dual economy theory and Gordon, Edwards, and Reich's segmented labor market theory. Dualistic approaches have postulated a labor market divided between "core firms" and "periphery firms"; these divisions help us understand the various social inequalities in wages, conditions, and opportunities for advancement engendered by structural differences among employers. Core firms, or "monopoly firms," are large, employ large numbers of people, earn large profits, employ advanced technologies, and have a geographically unlimited consumer market. Jobs in core firms, usually called "primary jobs," consist of good wages, safe, clean, and stable working conditions, and opportunities for advancement. Core firms disproportionately employ white men. Periphery firms are characteristic of the traditional immigrant enterprise. They are small, less profitable, and labor intensive; they have lower levels of technology and sell to a geographically limited consumer market. Jobs in periphery firms, usually called "secondary jobs," pay little and are low in status; these dead-end jobs often provide poor working conditions. Periphery workers are disproportionately women, minorities, immigrants, and the young. A dual labor market engenders workforce inequalities not only as a result of the structural imbalance between core and periphery firms but also because there is little or no mobility between the two sectors. Ethnic economy and ethnic enclave theories claim that alongside the secondary and primary sectors of the general labor market, there exists a third sector that has dynamics of its own, particularly "ethnicity," an economic function that mobilizes immigrant resources. See Peter Doeringer and Michael Piore, *Internal Labor Markets and Manpower Analysis* (Lexington, Mass.: Heath, 1971); and David M. Gordon, Richard Edwards, and Michael Reich, *Segmented Work, Divided Workers: The Historical Transformation of Labor in the United States* (Cambridge and New York: Cambridge University Press, 1982). Using what Ivan Light refers to as ethnic solidarism or what Roger Waldinger refers to as ethnic encapsulation, immigrant owners are able to draw on and control same-ethnicity resources in the immigrant neighborhood. See Ivan Light, *Ethnic Enterprise in America* (Berkeley: University of California Press, 1972). These resources include labor, cultural managers (who share the same ethnic origin as the workforce), and political and financial support. The geographical concentration of firms lends itself to a kind of hyper-efficiency due to their ethnically networked forms of integration and location-bound consumer markets; all this is reinforced through a combination of entrepreneurial capital and an extensive division of labor within the ethnic community. "Ethnicity" in this context acts as a motor for economic growth and helps perpetuate traditional ethnic culture in the immigrant community. In this way, the ethnic community is held together by its economic functions, and begins to break down only when "ethnicity" ceases to be a profitable mechanism for economic growth. Although a contending theory argues that ethnic solidarism is based upon fundamentally exploitative class relationships within the ethnic community, ethnic enclave theory argues the opposite. See Edna Bonacich and John Modell, *The Economic Basis of Ethnic Solidarity: A Study of Japanese Americans* (Berkeley: University of California Press, 1980); and Peter Kwong, *Forbidden Workers*. Ethnic solidarism, it says, functions through reciprocal obligations and provides opportunities for immigrant entrepreneurs who, in turn, often rely on the newest and least advantaged immigrants, offering them jobs and occupational mobility reserved primarily for members of their own ethnic group. See Portes and Bach, *Latin Journey*.

9. Whereas Ritzer believes that corporate power and the inevitable rationalizing of the capitalist system dominates this integration, and the ethnic-economies position argues that immigrant enclaves are untouched by these processes, Watson notes that the reciprocity of the global-local link points to local actors. He believes that globalizing processes join the global with the local. See James Watson, *Golden Arches East: McDonald's in East Asia* (Stanford: Stanford University Press, 1998).

10. B. Elango and Vance H. Fried, "Franchising: An Overview with Suggestions for the Future" (paper presented at the Academy of Management Meetings, Las Vegas, Nevada, 1992); J. T. Doutt, "Comparative Productivity Performance in Fast Food Retail Distribution," *Journal of Retailing* 66, no. 3 (1984): 98–106.

11. Arlie Hochschild, *The Managed Heart* (Berkeley: University of California Press, 1983).

12. Robin Leidner, *Fast Food, Fast Talk: Service Work and the Routinization of Everyday Life* (Berkeley: University of California Press, 1993).

13. Situated between global corporate structures and immigrant economies, the fast food restaurant transforms ethnic relations rather than preserves cultural homogeneity and ethnic persistence. Although in some respects fast food restaurants reinforce traditional ethnic linkages between immigrant communities and labor markets by using ethnic resources, they also help transform these linkages, contributing to globalizing tendencies within the immigrant neighborhood. Such processes are important in understanding the new cultural categories being formed at the bottom rungs of the global economic ladder. As these processes broaden the traditional models of ethnic segregation and persistence that have long characterized the immigrant neighborhood, they shed light on larger questions about the role of corporate capital in the shaping of America's cultural framework. This includes the terms of immigrant adaptation to American society and the role the immigrant neighborhood plays in this adaptation.

14. I started interviewing fast food workers in 1992 and continued until 1996, although the interviews were only a part of my ongoing research.

15. See the lists of respondents in Appendix A.

Chapter 2

1. Variations between restaurants result from the autonomy exercised by local franchise owners when they hire employees to reflect the "customer oriented" environment typical of each neighborhood. Such variation suggests that perhaps the ubiquitous corporate franchise no longer represents the epitome of standardization. See George Ritzer, *The McDonaldization of Society* (London: Pine Forge Press, 1993). These variations also point to the way industry or occupation-based "niche" models, including the "queuing theory"—all of which explain immigrant labor market incorporation—are not broad enough to capture the interindustry variations in major growth sectors of the economy.

2. Alejandro Portes and Robert L. Bach, *Latin Journey: Cuban and Mexican Immigrants in the United States* (Berkeley: University of California Press, 1985); Ivan Light and Steven J. Gold, *Ethnic Economies* (San Diego, Tex.: Academic Press, 2000); Ivan Light, *Ethnic Enterprise in America* (Berkeley: University of California Press, 1972).

3. Jan Lin, *Reconstructing Chinatown: Ethnic Enclave, Global Change* (Minneapolis: University of Minnesota Press, 1998).

4. Ibid.

5. Peter Kwong, *Forbidden Workers: Illegal Chinese Immigrants and American Labor* (New York: New Press, 1998).

6. McDonald's has also contracted with the Chinatown Holiday Inn to provide Holiday Inn employees with food vouchers (McDonald's meeting memo, 1993). As the McDonald's general manager said, "They can't afford to feed their employees so it is cheaper to do it through us." It is interesting to see how corporations cooperate to minimize their labor costs. Holiday Inn restaurants serve more expensive food than McDonald's; with the food voucher program, hotel and restaurant staff must go to McDonald's after their work shifts to trade in their vouchers for cheeseburgers and Cokes.

7. These organizations include the Chinatown Manpower Project, Inc., the Chinatown YMCA, local public schools (P.S. 1, P.S. 2, P.S. 110, P.S. 124, P.S. 130), the Chinatown Chinese School, the Chinatown Transfiguration School, the New York City Transit Police, the Coalition of Concerned Medical Professions, the Chinatown Head Start Program, the Chinatown Day Care Center, Immigrant Social Services, The Chinese American Planning Council, Inc., the Hoy Ping Hong Hing Association, and the Chinese Methodist Center Corp.

8. Another example of local community involvement is McDonald's "Orange Bowl," a large container filled with McDonald's orange drink that is often served at community functions. While the golden arches represent McDonald's overarching global omnipresence, the orange bowl has become a symbol of McDonald's local commitment.

9. Letters from the community are sent to the company office and rewards are handed out accordingly: Managers receive certificates, recognition pins, and

chances to win shares of McDonald's stock. The following is a typical letter written to the Chinatown McDonald's from community directors: "I wish to thank you for the generous donations and the use of your orange bowl at our first Open House. The event was a huge success. Many families visited our site with questions about our programs. The familiar sight of McDonald's was inviting and encouraged them to stay a little longer to learn more about the activities available in our YMCA. The added presence of Linda and yourself was very important to us. We are very fortunate to have McDonald's community support. We are looking forward to the use of the orange bowl again. It has proven to be a valuable part of our planning." Such letters are often requested by managers from clients; they represent a particular relationship built between the general manager and the community director, where the letters' function—to promote the manager's reputation within the corporation—is implicitly acknowledged. Shared ethnicity among community leaders is a significant help in shaping these community relations, which work to promote the McDonald's manager's reputation within the McDonald's company as much as it promotes McDonald's among community leaders.

10. From 1993 to 1994, McDonald's in Chinatown increased its sales by 40 percent. It makes approximately $9,000 in sales per day and, in 1994, made $3 million in sales revenue. It now belongs to a new club in the company—the "40 Percent Club." As the club's name implies, membership is conditioned upon making profits of at least 40 percent. The Chinatown McDonald's earned annual profits, then, of around $1.2 million. Profitmaking depends in part on keeping labor costs low. This McDonald's restaurant projected pulling in an average of $250,000 per month during 1993 while maintaining labor costs at about 12 percent (meeting memo, 1993). Such low labor costs are not necessarily industry wide (across the fast food industry); at this McDonald's, they have been gained through efficient production and marketing: adopting the latest technology, exploring new techniques in management, and applying strategies aimed at local marketing. This restaurant is unique because it has managed to lower its labor costs consistently; even so, it manages to pay wages that are higher than industry average (for New York City)—at $5.07 per hour (when the minimum wage was $4.25 per hour) for crewmembers—and it also created nontraditional jobs.

11. The thousands of Chinese dialects are all rooted in the same written language. According to McDonald's general manager, the majority in greater China speak Mandarin, including the northern Chinese and Taiwanese, and Cantonese is the language of southern China. See Gwen Kinkead, *Portrait of a Closed Society* (New York: HarperCollins, 1992).

12. Brighton Beach, also known as Little Russia and Little Odessa, has become the word's largest community of immigrants from the former Soviet Union. In 1987, Brighton Beach was home to more than 25 thousand immigrants from the former Soviet Union. See Annelise Orleck, "The Soviet Jews: Life in Brighton Beach, Brooklyn," in Nancy Foner, ed., *New Immigrants in New York* (New York: Columbia Press, 1987), 275–304.

13. Comparing the general managers at both restaurants helps capture the relationship between credentials of personnel and job conditions. For instance, unlike Charles (the Taiwanese general manager at McDonald's) who is of professional origin and has an engineering background, Pedro (the Colombian general manager at Burger King) is of working-class origin with only a vocational high school degree. Pedro earns less than half of Charles's annual salary. And while Charles has an opportunity to move higher and into a corporate-level position, Pedro has already reached a glass ceiling.

14. There are two exceptions: An employee from Venezuela does not speak English, and neither does an older woman, an employee from China. She obtained her job because her children begged the manager to hire her. Because of her age she cannot handle the stresses of factory work. Both employees perform the most undesirable tasks in the restaurant: cleaning the dining room, the lounge, and the bathrooms.

15. Patricia R. Pessar, "The Dominicans: Women in the Household and the Garment Industry," in Nancy Foner, ed., *New Immigrants in New York* (New York: Columbia University Press, 1987), 103–129.

16. Ira Katznelson, *City Trenches: Urban Politics and the Patterning of Class in the United States* (New York: Pantheon Books, 1981).

17. The Latino population has increased by 85 percent and the white population has decreased by 44 percent since 1970 in Washington Heights. Irish and Germans make up 7 percent each. Dominicans comprise the largest Latino group, about 80 percent. Cubans and Ecuadorians make up the other large Latino groups. See Garcia et al., "Spanish Language Use and Attitudes: A Study of Two New York City Communities," *Language and Society* 17, no. 4 (1988): 475–511; L. Georges, *New Immigrants and the Political Process: Dominicans in New York: Occasional Papers 45* (New York: New York University Press, 1984).

18. Katznelson, *City Trenches.*

19. Cubans were a large presence in Washington Heights as both residents and entrepreneurs during the 1950s and 1960s. Although Puerto Ricans and Dominicans later took over several local enterprises, Cubans still own many of the bodegas, meat markets, and restaurants.

20. In this case in Little Dominican Republic, the Indian manager oversees a Latino workforce, many of whom are Dominican; this reflects disparities between Asian Indian and Latino groups in respect to educational and professional backgrounds. In 1990, 76 percent of Asian Indian immigrants twenty-five years and over in New York City had high school degrees, 57 percent had some college experience, and 40 percent had bachelors' degrees. Yet Dominicans are among the least educated immigrant groups, and indeed, usually join fast food jobs at the entry level because they don't have the skills needed for higher-level positions within the industry or in the labor market at large. In 1990, only 39 percent of immigrants from the Dominican Republic had completed high school and only 6 percent had

college degrees. See the U.S. Bureau of the Census, *Socioeconomic Characteristics of the U.S. Foreign-Born Population Detailed in Bureau Tabulations, Release CB84–179* (Washington, D.C.: Author, 1990), tables 49 and 52.

21. As a group, Asian Indians have one of the highest proportions of individuals working in professional or managerial positions. Among various other fast food restaurants I examined, including in those downtown Brooklyn, highly educated Indian immigrants from professional family backgrounds joined fast food restaurants because they obtained jobs as managers. In 1990, 30 percent of all Asian Indians in the labor force in New York City were in managerial or professional specialty occupations. In the same year, only 10 percent of Dominicans in the New York City labor force were in managerial or professional specialty occupations. See the U.S. Bureau of the Census, *Socioeconomic Characteristics,* table 50. For further breakdown of Latino immigrant educational characteristics, see Frank D. Bean, Jorge Chapa, Ruth R. Berg, and Kathryn A. Sowards, "Educational and Sociodemographic Incorporation Among Hispanic Immigrants to the United States," in Barry Edmonston and Jeffrey S. Passel, eds., *Immigration and Ethnicity: The Integration of America's Newest Arrivals* (Washington, D.C.: Urban Institute Press, 1994), 73–100.

22. This was the only restaurant in Little Dominican Republic where I was asked for my order in Spanish. It was also the only restaurant in Little Dominican Republic where I interviewed respondents in Spanish because they did not speak English.

23. A study of language use in Washington Heights revealed that slightly less than half (49 percent) of Hispanics in Washington Heights described their spoken English as "very good." More than 50 percent described their English as "not good" or "not at all." See Garcia et al., "Spanish Language Use and Attitudes."

24. Waldinger points out that there are few black-owned businesses of significance, especially businesses offering expanding employment potential. See Roger Waldinger, *Still the Promised City? African-Americans and New Immigrants in Post Industrial New York* (Cambridge and London: Harvard University Press, 1996).

25. The term *gypsy cab* symbolizes its sometimes unregulated status.

26. Robert Emerson, *The New Economics of Fast Food* (New York: Van Nostrand Reinhold, 1990).

27. The food court is owned by another of the city's biggest restaurant corporations. Like the other big corporate owners, they employ South Asian immigrants as managers. The South Asian managers, in turn, hire co-ethnics (other South Asians) for entry-level positions because their native tongue matches the dominant language in this neighborhood: English.

28. The restaurant was opened by the parents of the current co-owners. The father was a salesman in the wholesale carpet business when he decided at the age of forty-six (over twenty years ago) to buy a McDonald's franchise after becoming dissatisfied with the company he worked for.

Chapter 3

1. Roger Waldinger, *Through the Eye of the Needle* (New York and London: New York University Press, 1986); Alejandro Portes and Robert L. Bach, *Latin Journey: Cuban and Mexican Immigrants in the United States* (Berkeley: University of California Press, 1985).

2. Mark Granovetter, *Getting a Job: A Study in Contacts and Careers* (Chicago: University of Chicago Press, 1995).

3. George Ritzer, *The McDonaldization of Society* (London: Pine Forge Press, 1993).

4. Roger Waldinger, *Still the Promised City? African-Americans and New Immigrants in Post Industrial New York* (Cambridge and London: Harvard University Press, 1996).

5. Ibid.

6. Phil Kasinitz, "Missing the Connection: Social Isolation and Employment on the Brooklyn Waterfront," *Social Problems* 43, no. 2 (May 1996): 501–519.

7. Other areas of Chinese concentration in New York City include the southern part of Brooklyn and the Jackson Heights, Flushing, and Elmhurst sections of Queens; see Bernard Wong, "The Chinese New Immigrants in New York's Chinatown," in *New Immigrants in New York,* ed. Nancy Foner (New York: Columbia Press, 1987).

8. U.S. Bureau of the Census, 1990 Census of Population, Social and Economic Characteristics, Metropolitan Areas, Release CP–2–1B (Washington, D.C.: Author, 1990).

9. Katherine Newman and Chauncy Lennon, "The Job Ghetto," *American Prospect* 22 (summer 1995): 66–67.

Chapter 4

1. Among some theorists, Michael Piore and Charles Sabel among them, flexibility is heralded as the answer to declining national productivity and the wage squeeze that is hurting the common American worker. Corporations must compete in an international market having spontaneous, unpredictable demands. See Michael J. Piore and Charles Sabel, *The Second Industrial Divide: Possibilities for Prosperity* (New York: Basic Books, 1984). But for Barry Bluestone and Bennett Harrison, flexibility is a management strategy that creates a more compliant and disposable workforce while exercising maximum and international geographical mobility. See Barry Bluestone and Bennett Harrison, *The Deindustrialization of America: Plant Closings, Community Abandonment, and the Dismantling of Basic Industry* (New York: Basic Books, 1982).

2. This is different from the occasional use of "flexibility" in the ethnic enterprise literature. Min Zhou and Regina Nordquist, for example, argue that co-ethnic employers often cater to their co-ethnic employees by offering "symbolic com-

pensations." For instance, they may be responsive to their needs outside the work-place, including their family responsibilities, by offering flexible work hours or allowing their children to accompany them in the workplace. But such flexibility in the enclave firm is normally organized around full-time, long-term, and consistently structured work tasks and schedules. This is quite different from the part-time, temporary, and constantly fluctuating terms of American fast food employment. The difference affects the kinds of immigrants who are eligible for and attracted to such employment in terms of age, socioeconomic status, and family responsibilities. It also affects the kinds of social relations that form in the workplace, and the way immigrants' work lives are linked to their home and family lives. See Min Zhou and Regina Nordquist, "Work and Its Place in the Lives of Immigrant Women: Garment Workers in New York City's Chinatown," *Applied Behavioral Science Review* 2, no. 2 (1994): 187–211.

3. Harry Braverman, *Labor and Monopoly Capital* (New York: Monthly Review Press, 1974); Edward C. Kirkland, *Industry Comes of Age: Business, Labor, and Public Policy, 1860–1897* (Chicago: Quadrangle Books, 1961).

4. At some New York City McDonald's restaurants, labor costs are less than 12 percent of all costs (Management Memo, Meeting Summary, 1993). This is compared to independent unionized restaurants, where 72 percent of revenues go to payroll; and independent nonunion restaurants, where 29 percent of revenues go to payroll. See Bryan Miller, "Tempest in the Kitchen," *New York Times,* March 15, 1995.

5. Karl Marx, *Economic and Philosophic Manuscripts of 1844* (New York: International Publishers, 1844), 76.

6. George Orwell, *Down and Out in Paris and London* (New York: Harcourt, Brace, 1950, c. 1933).

7. This goal is attained through cross-training. When workers are first trained to make hamburgers and cheeseburgers, they undergo cross-training for another station, such as specialty sandwiches. Cross-training, according to fast food managers, makes fast food work less mundane, more challenging, and more fulfilling. It requires workers to maintain mental concentration by learning new parts of the production process for a period that could last several months (more time than the average tenure among crewmembers). Moreover, cross-training enhances the social value of workers in the organization.

8. Managers generally agreed that their workforces were divided between a more full-time, permanent, and more experienced staff and a part-time, more temporary, and more inexperienced staff. But a full-time, permanent status refers only to a year or two of employment; a temporary status refers to a few weeks to a few months. One manager said that about half his workforce stays more than a year or two and half is temporary. One said that "you will probably have 70 percent turnover [in a year]."

9. Even though fast food work is considered *unskilled* work, a hierarchy of social value exists among employees. The neoclassical concept of skill assumes that

knowledge is obtained through education, training, or on-the-job experience. See Gary Becker, *Human Capital* (New York: National Bureau of Economic Research, 1975). Job skill can be viewed as a relative concept (rather than a neoclassical positivist concept) especially when we examine the relationship between emphasis on service aspects in the fast food organization and the increasing value of social and cultural features such as personableness and cultural capital. But it is still instructive to use the neoclassical version in an attempt to measure the possible relationship between on-the-job training and experience and employee value. See Paul Attewell, "What Is Skill?" *Work and Occupations* 17, no. 4 (November 1990): 422–448. In this way, we can view skill in the fast food restaurant as corresponding with how many stations a worker can competently perform, a competence gained through on-the-job training and experience. Employee value, then, is partly associated with employees' *flexibility* to shift from station to station, or their levels of interchangeability. The levels of proficiency and skill as such are gained through on-the-job training and experience. Training is usually conducted by crew trainers (experienced crew members) in a process called cross-training. It consists of observation, trial attempts, and practice in the restaurant while the restaurant is in operation. (Initial training in most restaurants I examined also consists of watching a video in the employee lounge.) Respondents at the restaurants I examined widely varied in the amount of time it takes for an employee to be trained. Proficiency at a single station was considered to take between fifteen minutes and two weeks. One manager said that "when it comes to working the cash register, it will take you three straight hours, uninterrupted." A cashier (at this same store) said that it took "about a week." Yet, cashiers in this store are given a two-week training period before they are given their own registers. Two weeks is given for all stations in this store; as one manager said, "With a trainee, we put you to work at one station only, and they have two weeks training process we give them in the store." Proficiency in all stations was considered to take between "thirty days" and "one-half year." Such variance among respondents in the time it takes to become proficient could be explained by differences between stores such as the degree to which the store emphasizes cross-training, the kinds of technologies that have been used in the store, and how the store interprets "proficiency." It can also be explained by differences among individuals, such as employee work experience, natural aptitude, and motivation for learning. In any case, the amount of time it takes to reach the organizational ideal of complete interchangeability would also seem to challenge long-held assumptions that fast food work is unskilled or low-skilled work. It is worth noting that this does not *necessarily* contradict the assumption that fast food work is unskilled work. This assumption has been partly based on the minimal skills needed to perform any function in the restaurant when one first begins the job. The technical division of labor is so highly specialized that anyone can perform any number of basic routine tasks without training. For example, a worker can be put to work placing frozen burgers on the Burger King grill without any training. But it is not in the organization's long-term interest for an entire workforce to perform only parts of a station. On the other hand, it requires training and experience to be able to perform a whole station competently. Therefore, the fast food restaurant takes on unskilled workers, and, gradually, they become skilled. And workers are disposable only to the extent that they can be replaced by someone equal in skill level. Therefore, as long as the restaurant continuously hires new and inexperienced employees, it is assured of achieving consistent productivity levels. Becoming interchangeable, then, is a requirement in many restaurants. As one manager said, "After two weeks, if they haven't learned anything, or they seem not to absorb, then we have to replace them." Because the restaurant tends to hire new employees continuously, the restaurant is comprised of workers who have a wide range in levels of "interchangeability." In this way, a fast food worker is disposable only to the extent that the organization is able to replace him or her at that level of interchangeability. The fast food workforce as a collective whole, on the other hand, is far from disposable without an enormous setback to the organization. The fast food restaurant cannot afford to lose all of its workers at once and to hire a completely new workforce. Newly opened stores tend to have a workforce that has already been trained in another restaurant. A newly opened New York City Burger King restaurant, for example, had spent from four to eight weeks training both experienced and inexperienced fast food workers in another restaurant under the same ownership. Interchangeability and employee homogenization is enhanced by social and aesthetic work criteria. These refer to various criteria that *all* employees are expected to follow, including back workers. This is important because even though frontline employees are those who engage in service interaction, back workers are still at least visible to the customers. Interchangeability and cross-training, then, help shape demands for a flexible workforce that turns out to be hierarchically skilled. And various social and aesthetic criteria demanded by all employees, as well as emphasis on the social division of labor rather than the technical division of labor, help to reinforce at least the tendency toward workers' homogenization in their job roles.

10. According to Zhou and Nordquist, female employees in Chinatown's garment factories enjoy a certain flexibility that enables them to juggle family responsibilities and cultural traditions while working. They may bring their children to work to relieve the burden of finding good child care, or perhaps celebrate a coworker's marriage in the workplace. See Zhou and Nordquist, "Work and Its Place," 187–211.

Chapter 5

1. George Ritzer, *The McDonaldization of Society* (London: Pine Forge Press, 1993).

2. Harry Braverman, *Labor and Monopoly Capital* (New York: Monthly Review Press, 1974).

3. Peter Applebome, "Employers Wary of School System: Survey Finds Broad Distrust of Younger Job Aspirants," *New York Times,* February 20, 1995, A1.

4. Robin Leidner, *Fast Food, Fast Talk: Service Work and the Routinization of Everyday Life* (Berkeley: University of California Press, 1993); George Ritzer, *The McDonaldization of Society*; Ester Reiter, *Making Fast Food: From the Frying Pan Into the Fryer* (McGill-Queens University Press, 1991); Barbara Garson, *All the Livelong Day: The Meaning and Demeaning of Routine Work* (New York: Doubleday, 1975).

5. Braverman, *Labor and Monopoly Capital,* 371.

6. Ibid.

7. Most registers in fast food restaurants today are computerized and relatively simple to operate. See Leidner, *Fast Food, Fast Talk;* Garson, *All the Livelong Day;* and Ritzer, *McDonaldization of Society.* As in every other kind of national chain in retail trade, computerized registers in fast food restaurants increase the productivity of the cashier, almost doubling the number of customers each cashier can handle. See Braverman, *Labor and Monopoly Capital.*

8. Ray Kroc, *Grinding It Out: The Making of McDonald's* (Chicago: Contemporary Books, 1977).

9. John Love, *Behind the Golden Arches* (New York: Bantam, 1986).

10. Leidner, *Fast Food, Fast Talk.*

11. Lawrence Mishel, Jared Bernstein, and John Schmitt, *The State of Working America* 2000–2001 (Ithaca, New York: Cornell University Press, 2001).

12. Jane Jenson, Elisabeth Hagen, and Ceallaigh Reddy, eds., *Feminization of the Labor Force* (New York: Oxford University Press, 1988); Rosemary Crompton and Kay Sanderson, *Gendered Jobs and Social Chang* (London: Unwin Hyman, 1990); Alice Kessler-Harris, *A Woman's Wage: Historical Meanings and Social Consequences* (Lexington, Kentucky: University Press of Kentucky, 1991).

13. Cynthia Epstein, *Deceptive Distinctions: Sex, Gender, and the Social Order* (New Haven and London: Yale University Press and New York Russell Sage Foundation, 1988); Saskia Sassen, *The Mobility of Labor and Capital: A Study in International Investment and Labor Flow* (Cambridge and New York: Cambridge University Press, 1988); John P. Walsh, *Supermarkets Transformed: Understanding Organizational and Technological Innovations* (New Brunswick, New Jersey: Rutgers University Press, 1993).

14. U.S. Bureau of the Census, 1985 and 1991; U.S. Department of Labor, Bureau of Labor Statistics, *Report on the American Workforce* (Washington, D.C.: GPO, 1999).

15. Walsh, *Supermarkets Transformed.*

16. Price and Blair found a greater gender gap in wages in nonmanual, service-oriented work than in manual work. See D. G. Price and A. M. Blair, *The Changing Geography of the Service Sector* (London and New York: Belhaven Press, 1989); Guy Standing, "Global Feminization Through Flexible Labor" (Geneva: International Labor Organization, 1988).

17. Elaine Hall, "Waiting on Tables: Gender Integration in a Service Occupation" (Ph.D. diss., University of Connecticut, Department of Sociology, 1990).

18. Historically, women have resisted the gendering of masculine work for financial reasons: Much blue-collar manual work has been higher-paying, unionized, and has brought benefits not typically found in traditional female work. See Ann Stromberg and Shirley Harkess, "Women, Work, and the Labor Force," in Ann Stromberg and Shirley Harkess, eds., *Women Working: Theories and Facts in Perspective* (Palo Alto, Calif.: Mayfield Publishing Company, 1978). Thus, women have proved their physical ability and moved into these jobs primarily for economic and social benefits. In fast food, on the other hand, all entry-level crew work brings the same benefits and same pay, which may account for women's accepting, and even reinforcing, the gendering of heavy work, especially when "masculine work" is undesirable.

Chapter 6

1. C. Wright Mills, *White Collar: The American Middle Classes* (New York: Oxford University Press, 1953).

2. Ibid., 182.

3. Social science has been concerned with the "selling of self," or the so-called commodification of self for several decades, even before C. Wright Mills's writings in the 1950s. German sociologists in the 1930s, Crozier, Kracauer, and Dreyfuss among them, referring to an emerging class of white-collar workers in the Western world, claimed that not only the work but also the person was treated as a thing by the capitalist system. See Michel Crozier, *The World of the Office Worker* (Chicago and London: University of Chicago Press, 1965); Simon Kracauer, *Die Angestellten aus dem neuen Deutschland* (Frankfurt, 1930); Carl Dreyfuss, *Beruf und Ideologie der Angestellten* (Munich and Leipzig, 1933). Mills was the first American sociologist to study the selling of self. He was concerned with the condition of the white-collar worker, or the "new Machiavellians," as he called them, who practiced "their *personable* crafts for hire and for the profit of others." Mills introduced the concept of psychological manipulation and exploitation of workers and was concerned with the way in which workers' personalities (or authentic selves) were affected. More than three decades later, Arlie Hochschild was the first to examine the selling of self in the modern corporate organization in her study of Delta airline flight attendants. Her work identified a particular kind of service worker in modern society—the "public contact" worker—whose main job entailed interacting with customers and performing "emotion work"; work roles were standardized and commercialized according to corporate-defined and publicly propagated criteria. The "selling of self" literature is partly based on a limitation of Karl Marx rooted in his neglect to consider not only how workers in advanced capitalist society are alienated from the products they produce but also how in the performance of "interac-

tive service work" workers can become alienated from themselves. Alienation from self, according to Hochschild and Mills, occurs because employers require workers to behave and present themselves according to corporate or standardized policies rather than according to how workers feel like behaving and presenting themselves. See Arlie Hochschild, *The Managed Heart* (Berkeley: University of California Press, 1983); and Mills, *White Collar.*

4. Mills, *White Collar,* 185.

5. Mary Jo Bitner, H. Booms Bernard, and Mary Stanfield Tetreault, "The Service Encounter: Diagnosing Favorable and Unfavorable Incidents," *Journal of Marketing* 54 (January 1990): 85–101.

6. McDonald's management memo, 1993.

7. Mills, *White Collar,* xvii.

8. Hochschild, *The Managed Heart.*

9. Management meeting memo, 1993.

10. George Ritzer, *The McDonaldization of Society* (London: Pine Forge Press, 1993).

11. Richard C. Edwards, *Contested Terrain: The Transformation of the Workplace in the Twentieth Century* (New York: Basic Books, 1979).

12. Arlie Hochschild makes a distinction between "surface acting" and "deep acting" when assessing the extent to which employees resist or identify with their job roles in the consumer service organization. In surface acting, an employee deceives others about how she really feels, but she does not deceive herself. In deep acting, there is no clear distinction between how the employee really feels and the feelings he is required to display on the job. Deep acting is encouraged by managers in customer service organizations because the expression of a "real" feeling is more marketable. It is believed that customers prefer being served by someone whose smile is genuine rather than fake. But one may expect varying degrees of surface and deep acting by customer service employees, depending on the individual, as well as the kind of work one does. See Hochschild, *The Managed Heart.*

13. Company memo, 1994.

14. Hochschild, *The Managed Heart.*

15. Ironically, immigrants' authentic self is a valued commodity in the immigrant neighborhood. But the authentic self is often perceived as needing to be molded in accordance with organizational goals. Perhaps the greatest problem is not the effect on the immigrant personality; rather, the greatest influence may be on immigrant work culture. According to the ethnic enclave theorists, in the traditional ethnic enterprise, an internal and ethnic work culture evolves that is not necessarily influenced or mediated by outside forces. The work culture in the fast food restaurant, in contrast, is mediated not only by customers' interactions but also by managers' attempts to alter employees' emotions, control personalities, and maintain a façade of friendliness. Fast food workers may leave the workplace with their

real emotions intact, but they are not as likely to have shared with their coworkers a real feeling of collective work.

16. Erving Goffman, *The Presentation of Self in Everyday Life* (Garden City, New York: Doubleday Books, 1959).

17. Robin Kelly, *Race Rebels: Culture, Politics, and the Black Working Class* (New York: The Free Press, 1996).

Chapter 7

1. Saskia Sassen, *The Global City* (Princeton, New Jersey: Princeton University Press, 1992).

2. Howard Winant, *Racial Conditions* (Minneapolis: University of Minnesota Press, 1994).

3. Alejandro Portes and Robert L. Bach, *Latin Journey: Cuban and Mexican Immigrants in the United States* (Berkeley: University of California Press, 1985); Min Zhou and Alejandro Portes, *Chinatown: The Socioeconomic Potential of an Urban Enclave* (Philadelphia: Temple University Press, 1995).

4. Roger Waldinger, *Still the Promised City? African-Americans and New Immigrants in Post Industrial New York* (Cambridge and London: Harvard University Press, 1996).

5. Nonetheless, labor market research increasingly examines employment practices among low-wage mainstream employers in U.S. cities. These studies show that employers explicitly generalize about race and ethnic differences in the quality of their workforces; in doing so, they help form hierarchies of ethnic and racial preferences across entire sectors of the labor market. These generalizations are often inextricably linked to the social class and national origins of employees. Although the studies provide insight on hiring practices based on employers' perceptions of various social groups, they are limited because they do not examine workplace social relations, including the structural factors that account for manager-worker relations. Moreover, they do not take into account the unique features of the customer service workplace and its local context in defining and shaping ethnic relations. See Joleen Kirschenman and Kathryn M. Neckerman, "'We'd Love to Hire Them, But . . . ': The Meaning of Race for Employers," in Christopher Jencks and Paul Peterson, eds., *The Urban Underclass* (Washington, D.C.: Brookings Institution, 1991), 203–232; Joleen Kirschenman, Philip Moss, and Chris Tilly, "Employer Screening Methods and Racial Exclusion: Evidence from New In-Depth Interviews with Employers," working paper #77, Russell Sage Foundation, New York, 1995); Philip Moss and Chris Tilly, "Space As a Signal, Space As a Barrier: How Employers Map and Use Space in Four Metropolitan Labor Markets," working paper, Russell Sage Foundation, New York, February 8–9, 1996; Philip Kasinitz, "Missing the Connection: Social Isolation and Employment on the Brooklyn Waterfront," *Social Problems* 43, no. 2 (May 1996): 501–519.

6. Stephen Steinberg, *The Ethnic Myth* (New York: Atheneum, 1981); Stephen Steinberg, *Turning Back: The Retreat of Racial Justice in American Thought and Policy* (Boston: Beacon Press, 1996).

7. Julius Wilson, *The Declining Significance of Race: Blacks and Changing American Institutions* (Chicago: University of Chicago Press, 1978).

8. Robert Merton, in developing the reference group theory, showed the common tendency for people to judge unequal relationships not in absolute terms but by "taking their own orientation status point as a reference point." See Raymond Boudon, "What Middle Range Theories Are," *Contemporary Sociology* 20, no. 4 (1991): 506–530.

9. Philip Kasinitz, a sociologist who has also examined employment practices concerning black Americans, showed how employers in Redhook, New York, distinguish among black workers on the basis of various features, including national origin. See Kasinitz, "Missing the Connection."

10. Malcom Gladwell, "Black Like Them," *New Yorker*, May 6, 1996, 79.

11. Michael W. Hughey and Arthur Vidich, "The New American Pluralism: Racial and Ethnic Sodalities and Their Sociological Implications," *International Journal of Politics, Culture, and Society* 2, no. 6 (1992): 159–180; Max Weber, *The Protestant Ethic and the Spirit of Capitalism* (New York: Charles Scribner's Sons, 1958).

12. The concept of blacks wanting "something for nothing" is not new and was a major response of successful working-class white ethnics to blacks in the civil rights marches in the 1960s. See Hughey and Vidich, *The New American Pluralism*.

13. Weber, *The Protestant Ethic*.

14. Elliot Leibow, *Tally's Corner: A Study of Negro Street Corner Men* (Boston and Toronto: Little, Brown, and Company, 1967), 59.

15. James Tucker, in a study of temporary workers, found that employees commonly respond to offensive behavior from their employers in various ways, including "theft, sabotage, or noncooperation." See James Tucker, "Everyday Forms of Employee Resistance," *Sociological Forum* 8, no. 1 (March 1993): 25–45. Jason Ditton, in another study, showed how low-wage workers have historically encountered a "double-bind" system whereby part of the worker's wages are paid in kind to account for theft. "His wages are geared down to an invisible pilferage value of his job, but his attempt to secure this invisible value could well lose him his job, and land him in court." See James Ditton, "Perks, Pilferage, and the Fiddle: The Historical Structure of Invisible Wages," *Theory and Society* 4, no. 1 (Spring 1977): 39–71. Employers in this system maintain the power to define the action as a perk or as a theft.

16. Jennifer Parker Talwar, "Contradictory Assumptions in the Minimum-Wage Workplace," *Journal of Contemporary Ethnography*, 30, no. 1 (February 2001): 92–127.

Chapter 8

1. Jonathan Kaufman, "A McDonald's Owner Becomes a Role Model for Black Teenagers," *Wall Street Journal*, 23 August 1995, sec. A, p. 1.

2. Barbara Presley Noble, "At Work: The Women Behind McDonald's," *New York Times*, 27 March 1994, sec. 3, p. 23.

3. Barnaby Feder, "Dead-End Jobs? Not for These Three," *New York Times*, 4 July 1995, sec. 1, p. 45.

4. Toby L. Parcel and Marie B. Sickmeier, "One Firm, Two Labor Markets: The Case of McDonald's in the Fast Food Industry," *The Sociological Quarterly* 29, no. 1 (1988): 42.

5. New York State Department of Labor, *Occupational Outlook, 1991–1996* (New York: Author, 1992).

6. U.S. Bureau of the Census, *1990 Census of Population, Social and Economic Characteristics, Metropolitan Areas, Release CP–2–1B* (Washington, D.C.: Author, 1990).

7. The New York State Department of Labor lists nine growth occupations that do not require postsecondary training or education. The other eight include: receptionist, cleaner and domestic (household), dining room and bartender helpers, cooks in restaurants, cooks in institutions, home health aids, maids and housekeeping cleaners, and child care workers. Earnings differences are substantial across growth occupations according to their educational requirements. Among growth occupations that require a bachelor's degree or more, the average weekly earnings are $636. For those that require some postsecondary education or significant employment training, the average weekly earnings are $442. And for those that require a high school diploma or less, the average weekly earnings are $317. See New York State Department of Labor, *Tomorrow's Jobs, Tomorrow's Workers, New York City, 1993–94* (New York: Author, 1994).

8. In 1993, for example, the overall unemployment rate in New York City was around 12 percent, but for the white population, it was only 9 percent. Among the black and Hispanic populations, the unemployment rate was around 14 percent. See New York State Department of Labor, *Tomorrow's Jobs, Tomorrow's Workers.*

9. In 1990, non-Hispanic whites were still the largest group in New York City, comprising 47 percent of the population. Yet their population declined by about 5 percent between 1980 and 1990 (about 20 percent of the white population were foreign-born). All growth has been with minority groups. In 1990, blacks comprised 25 percent of the population (about 27 percent were foreign-born). Hispanics comprised 21 percent of the population (about 35 percent were foreign-born). Asian and Pacific Islanders represented the fastest growing proportion of the population, although they comprised only about 8 percent of New York's population as a whole (about 80 percent were foreign-born). See U.S. Bureau of the Census, *Socioeconomic Characteristics of the U.S. Foreign-Born Population Detailed in Bureau Tabulations, Release CB84–179* (Washington, D.C: Author, 1990).

10. U.S. Bureau of the Census, *1990 Census of Population.*

11. Food worker is a category that includes U.S. Bureau of the Census categories of "Food counter, fountain and related occupations," "kitchen workers, food preparation," and "miscellaneous food preparation occupations." See U.S. Bureau

of Census, *1990 EEO Files: Detailed Occupation, New York City* (Washington, D.C.: U.S. Department of Commerce, 1990). There is no further breakdown of food workers that would isolate fast food workers as a single category.

12. Racial hierarchies in the labor market at large reinforce, amplify, and, in some cases, reconfigure those that exist in the food industry. Nearly two-thirds (66 percent) of those in managerial and professional specialty occupations across all New York City industries are white. This category is important because it includes not only food service supervisory and managerial positions but also every other managerial and professional occupation in New York. Therefore, in general, it generates the highest social status and wages in the occupational hierarchy. Because whites make up less than 50 percent of the New York City labor force, they are, as a whole, overrepresented in the top occupations. Significantly, this is a much larger percentage than whites in food service supervisory positions. Hispanics, however, are considerably less represented (less than 9 percent) overall in the managerial and professional specialty occupations across New York City industries than they are in food service managerial positions. Since they make up about 16 percent of New York's labor force, they are considerably underrepresented in the top occupations. Their much higher representation in food supervisory positions suggests that when Hispanics are managers, they tend to be concentrated in low-wage industries such as food service. Asians who are managers, like Hispanics, also seem to be more concentrated in low-level industries such as food service, their representation in the managerial/professional occupations across industries in New York being only about 6 percent—significantly lower than in food service. Blacks are much more represented in managerial/professional occupations as a whole in New York City than in food service in particular. About 15 percent of all managers and professionals across industries in New York City are black—indicative of the polarization of the black population at large (see U.S. Bureau of the Census, *Detailed Occupation, New York City, 1990 EEO Files* (Washington, D.C.: Author, 1990).

13. New York State Department of Labor, Occupational Employment Statistics (OES) Weight Survey, 1998.

14. David M. Gordon, *Fat and Mean: The Corporate Squeeze of Working Americans and the Myth of Managerial "Downsizing"* (New York: Free Press, 1996).

15. This view would seem to challenge the assumptions made by Parcel and Sickmeier, who studied the structures of opportunity in the fast food industry. They claim that the channels of upward mobility in the top fast food companies "begin at the store/unit level and proceed upwards to corporate headquarters." Parcel and Sickmeier distinguish between wage jobs (or "secondary jobs") at the bottom of the hierarchy and salaried positions (or "primary jobs") at the top. But they claim that the existence of job ladders, in general, is a significant and positive feature. My study, in contrast, shows that the industry cannot be examined on a uniform basis. Entry-level job seekers may not discriminate between a McDonald's restaurant owned by a large local corporation and one owned by a small-scale entrepreneur when applying for a job. But where they find a job will have a determining influence on the extent of opportunity that exists. Moreover, most job op-

portunity appears to be at the level of the restaurant in the lower-tiered (secondary) positions. See Parcel and Sickmeier, "One Firm, Two Labor Markets."

16. Howard Botwinick, *Persistent Inequalities* (Princeton: Princeton University Press, 1993), 6.

17. Ibid.; John A. Byrn, "The Flap Over Executive Pay," *Business Week,* May 6 1991, 90.

18. Cultural capital helps shape managerial opportunity in restaurants and neighborhoods that demand foreign-language or other cultural skills. Most manager respondents in my study are valued for their multilingual language skills and for their cultural knowledge of and social links with the neighborhoods in which they work. Such knowledge and ethnic affinities help build and sustain local customers.

19. Like youth, women are considered more willing than men to work for the low salaries paid at the lower management levels. Women tend to have less opportunity in the labor market at large to become managers and therefore more aggressively seize the opportunity in the fast food industry. Women are also considered more malleable, more emotional, and more enthusiastic while performing their work. Owners and managers claim that women are more meticulous about and attentive to the service aspects of the organization, including the relationship between employees and customers, the appearance of employees, and the cleanliness of the restaurant. Although some employers and female employees attribute women's more meticulous ways to a natural gender difference, other employers and employees view it as women's perceived need to prove their capability, especially around male managers.

20. Those who do not plan to pursue the fast food job ladder vary a great deal. They range from part-time employees in high school en route to college and a professional career to older adults who have no college experience and who are working full-time and sometimes have a second job. The latter are invariably people with a long history of low-wage employment who have not given up the idea that a better opportunity will eventually come along.

21. See Noble, "At Work."

22. Since the 1980 Refugee Act went into effect, the United States has granted refugee status to hundreds of thousands of people, primarily from communist or postcommunist regimes in Southeast Asia and Eastern Europe. See Alejandro Portes and Ruben G. Rumbaut, *Immigrant America* (Berkeley: University of California Press, 1996). Brusso's family's emigration was preceded and partly motivated by relatives who were already living in New York City. Most of them resided in Little Odessa, a decades-old Russian neighborhood, where Russian restaurants serving perogies and vodka, and Russian-speaking families taking after-dinner walks on the boardwalk capture some of the "home" culture. Their relatives found them a relatively inexpensive apartment in the neighborhood and assist them with basic living expenses.

23. In recent years, women have been promoted into managerial positions at faster rates than men, and in these two companies are said to occupy about 50 percent of all managerial positions. In Little Dominican Republic, the majority of fast

food managers are women. Yet women are still concentrated on the lower manage-rial rungs. In the seven restaurants I examined, only one woman occupied the posi-tion of general manager.

24. Portes and Rumbaut, *Immigrant America*.

25. Nina Bernstein, "Poverty Found to Be Rising in Families Considered Safe," *New York Times*, 20 April 2000, sec. 2, p. 1.

26. It is clear, considering how many previous jobs respondents held before their current entry-level fast food jobs, that certain ethnic groups may be more likely to "hop around" than others. The American-born, regardless of race and eth-nicity, had considerably more job experience before their current fast food posi-tions than immigrant groups. They also started working at younger ages. South Asians had the least amount of job experience (0.3 jobs on average), and started working at the oldest age (20.7 years on average). American-born respondents of Hispanic descent (second-generation Latinos) had the most amount of job experi-ence (2.7 jobs on average), and started working at the youngest age (14.7 on aver-age). These differences may be rooted in class distinctions between the ethnic groups. Starting work at a young age may reflect the relatively inferior socioeco-nomic status of particular ethnic groups, including American-born racial minori-ties. Immigrant fast food workers, in general, tend to be one up on the socioeco-nomic scale compared to their American-born counterparts. The differences may also reflect aspects of the American youth culture that stress an independent and consumerist lifestyle. There is some indication, too, that the American-born hop around more than their immigrant counterparts. Beginning work at a younger age does not necessarily account for all the differences in how many previous jobs held. While hopping around can be explained by various factors, it also has its conse-quences, including a lesser likelihood of developing occupational niches in the in-dustry and fewer chances for promotion.

Chapter 9

1. James Watson, *Golden Arches East: McDonald's in East Asia* (Stanford: Stan-ford University Press, 1998).

2. George Ritzer, *The McDonaldization of Society* (London: Pine Forge Press, 1993).

3. Alejandro Portes and Robert L. Bach, *Latin Journey: Cuban and Mexican Im-migrants in the United States* (Berkeley: University of California Press, 1985).

4. Ritzer, *The McDonaldization of Society*.

5. Robin Kelly, *Race Rebels: Culture, Politics, and the Black Working Class* (New York: The Free Press, 1996).

6. Richard Sennett, *The Corrosion of Character: The Personal Consequences of Work in the New Capitalism* (New York and London: W. W. Norton & Company, 1998).

7. Ibid.

APPENDIX A:
THE RESPONDENTS

LIST A.1   The Respondents: Language, Ethnicity, and National Origin/Ancestry Chinatown, McDonald's (n=8)

Pseudonym	Level of Job	Language	Ethnicity	National Origin/Ancestry
Charles	General Manager	Chinese (3 dialects) and English	Chinese	Taiwan
Alison	Assistant Manager	Malay, Chinese, and English	Chinese	Malaysia
Amy	Crewmember	Chinese and English	Chinese	Taiwan
Tina	Crewmember	Chinese and learning English	Chinese	Mainland China
Janet	Crewmember	Chinese and learning English	Chinese	Mainland China
Lila	Crewmember	Spanish and English	Latino	Honduras (2nd generation)
Brusso	Crewmember	Russian and learning English	Russian	Russia
Koreen	Crewmember	French and English	African	Togo, Africa

LIST A.2 The Respondents: Language, Ethnicity, and National Origin/Ancestry Chinatown,
Burger King (n=10)

Pseudonym	Level of Job	Language	Ethnicity	National Origin/Ancestry
Pedro	General Manager	Spanish and English	Latino	Colombia
Julia	Assistant Manager	Spanish and English	Latino	U.S. (Puerto Rico–2nd generation)
Catrina	Crewmember	Chinese and English	Chinese	Mainland China
Lisa	Crewmember	Chinese and English	Chinese	Mainland China
Jesus	Crewmember	Spanish and English	Latino	Puerto Rico/ Dom.Rep. (2nd gen.)
Claudia	Crewmember	Spanish and English	Latino	Venezuela
Harold	Crewmember	Spanish	Latino	Venezuela
Juan	Crewmember	Spanish and English	Latino	Dominican Republic
Roberto	Crewmember	Spanish and English	Latino	Dominican Republic
Hassan	Crewmember	Bengali and English	South Asian	Bangladesh

LIST A.3 The Respondents: Language, Ethnicity, and National Origin/Ancestry Little Dominican Republic,
First McDonald's (n=7)

Pseudonym	Level of Job	Language	Ethnicity	National Origin/Ancestry
Jose	General Manager	Spanish and English	Latino	Childhood in Dom. Rep., born in NYC
Laurie	Assistant Manager	English	West Indian	Antigua
Ria	Swing Manager	Spanish and English	Latino	U.S. (Puerto Rico –2nd generation)
David	Crewmember	Spanish and English	Latino	Puerto Rico
Brenda	Crewmember	English	West Indian	Antigua
Betty	Crewmember	English	West Indian	Antigua
Tony	Crewmember	Spanish and English	Latino	Puerto Rico (2nd generation)

LIST A.4   The Respondents: Language, Ethnicity, and National Origin/Ancestry Little Dominican
Republic, Burger King (n=5)

Pseudonym	Level of Job	Language	Ethnicity	National Origin/Ancestry
Gitu	General Manager	Marathi, Hindi, and English	South Asian	India
Marco	Crewmember	Spanish and English	Latino	Cuba
Mina	Crewmember	Spanish and English	Latino	Dominican Republic
Alex	Crewmember	Spanish and English	Latino	Dominican Republic
Elian	Crewmember	Spanish and English	Latino	Dominican Republic

LIST A.5   The Respondents: Language, Ethnicity, and National Origin/Ancestry Little Dominican
Republic, Second McDonald's (n=8)

Pseudonym	Level of Job	Language	Ethnicity	National Origin/Ancestry
Fabiola	Assistant Manager	Spanish and English	Latino	Dominican Republic
Miguel	Assistant Manager	Spanish	Latino	U.S. (Puerto Rico)
Robi	Crewmember	Spanish	Latino	Dominican Republic
Jared	Crewmember	Spanish	Latino	Dominican Republic
Thomas	Crewmember	Spanish	Latino	Dominican Republic
Wendy	Crewmember	Spanish and English	Latino	Dominican Republic
Bettina	Crewmember	Spanish and English	Latino	Childhood in Dom. Rep., born in NYC
Miriam	Crewmember	Spanish and English	Latino	Cuba

LIST A.6   The Respondents: Language, Ethnicity, and National Origin/Ancestry Downtown Brooklyn,
McDonald's (n=5)

Pseudonym	Level of Job	Language	Ethnicity	National Origin/Ancestry
Julio	Assistant Manager	Spanish and English	Latino	U.S. (Puerto Rico–2nd generation)
Debbie	Crewmember	English	White-Am.	U.S.
Peggy	Crewmember	English	West Indian	Jamaica
Tracy	Crewmember	English	West Indian	Jamaica
Ann	Crewmember	English	West Indian	Barbados

LIST A.7   The Respondents: Language, Ethnicity, and National Origin/Ancestry
Downtown Brooklyn, Burger King (n=13)

Pseudonym	Level of Job	Language	Ethnicity	National Origin/Ancestry
Loren	Assistant Manager	English	African-Am.	U.S.
Sandeep	Assistant Manager	Hindi and English	South Asian	India
Bill	Assistant Manager	English	White-Am.	U.S.
George	Assistant Manager	English	White-Am.	U.S.
Edward	Production Leader	English	West Ind./ Af. Am.	Antigua (2nd generation)
Peter	Crewmember	Spanish and English	Latino	U.S. (Puerto Rico –2nd generation)
Carlos	Crewmember	Spanish and English	Latino	U.S. (Puerto Rico –2nd generation)
Carla	Crewmember	English	West Indian	Guyana
Eliza	Crewmember	English	West Indian	Guyana
Venesia	Crewmember	English	African-Am.	U.S.
Tanya	Crewmember	English	African-Am.	U.S.
Roy	Crewmember	English	African-Am.	U.S.
Maria	Crewmember	Spanish and English	Latino	U.S. (Puerto Rico)

INDEX